Tony Blair

Tony Blair

THE MAKING OF A WORLD LEADER

Philip Stephens

VIKING

VIKING
Published by the Penguin Group
Penguin Group (USA) Inc., 375 Hudson Street,
New York, New York 10014, U.S.A.
Penguin Books Ltd, 80 Strand, London WC2R 0RL, England
Penguin Books Australia Ltd, 250 Camberwell Road, Camberwell,
Victoria 3124, Australia
Penguin Books Canada Ltd, 10 Alcorn Avenue,
Toronto, Ontario, Canada M4V 3B2
Penguin Books India (P) Ltd, 11 Community Centre, Panchsheel Park,
New Delhi – 110 017, India
Penguin Books (N.Z.) Ltd, Cnr Rosedale and Airborne Roads, Albany,
Auckland, New Zealand
Penguin Books (South Africa) (Pty) Ltd, 24 Sturdee Avenue,
Rosebank, Johannesburg 2196, South Africa

Penguin Books Ltd, Registered Offices:
80 Strand, London WC2R 0RL, England

First published in 2004 by Viking Penguin,
a member of Penguin Group (USA) Inc.

10 9 8 7 6 5 4 3 2 1

LIBRARY OF CONGRESS CATALOGING IN PUBLICATION DATA
Stephens, Philip.
 Tony Blair : the making of a world leader / Philip Stephens.
 p. cm.
 ISBN 0-670-03300-6
 1. Blair, Tony, 1953– 2. Labour Party (Great Britain)–Biography. 3. Prime ministers–
Great Britain–Biography. 4. Great Britain–Politics and government–1997– I. Title.
 DA591.B56S74 2004
 941.085'9'092–dc22
 [B] 2003066566

This book is printed on acid-free paper. ∞

Printed in the United States of America
Set in Caslon Book
Designed by Francesca Belanger

For my brother, Paul, and for the parents we still miss

ACKNOWLEDGMENTS

THE IDEA FOR THIS BOOK came during a visit to Washington in the spring of 2003. The United States and Britain were on the brink of war with Saddam Hussein's regime in Iraq and, as I met friends and contacts in Washington, I was increasingly aware of a fascination with Tony Blair. Who was this British prime minister who ready to risk his own political career to go to war alongside President George W. Bush? What had made him such a staunch ally of America in the aftermath of the terrorist attacks of September 11, 2001? How was it that a prime minister who had remained firm friends with former president Bill Clinton could strike up such a close relationship with George W. Bush? These and other questions were thrown constantly at me during meetings with administration officials and during informal social gatherings with American friends. My purpose is to provide some answers and insights in a way accessible to American readers, who, for good reason, do not follow every twist and turn in British political life.

This book draws on countless conversations with politicians and officials (opponents as well as friends of the prime minister) over many years, with Blair himself, with his closest aides, and with every relevant senior adviser in his office. These officials gave their time generously—and with the willing understanding that none of them would have influence over, or sight of, my account until publication.

Sadly, the conventions of British politics mean that I cannot thank them by name. Government officials must talk to journalists under the cloak of anonymity. Blair's cabinet colleagues were willing to speak frankly only on the same terms. But they know who they are and I am grateful to them for treating this as a grown-up exercise. Where I have cited Blair directly in the book, I have specified where the remarks are

drawn from: newspaper and television interviews, speeches, and so forth. Where I have not given such a context, the quotations are taken from my own conversations with him, including a lengthy interview in July 2003. In other instances where I have cited comments made by Blair or others in private meetings with foreign leaders, colleagues, or officials, I have done so only when I could confirm the remarks with someone who had been in the room at the time or who had direct access to the official note of the meeting. Where I use the term senior aide or senior official, I mean senior—someone in the inner circle with direct and frequent access to the principal.

I hope this book whets the appetite of Americans to read more about what is happening on the British side of the Atlantic and to that end I have included a short British bibliography. For those tempted to dig deep into the life and times of Tony Blair I would recommend John Rentoul's biography, *Tony Blair, Prime Minister.* Those interested in a beautifully written account of the passions and frictions at the top of his government should try James Naughtie's *The Rivals.*

Felicity Bryan, my agent, turned that first thought of mine in Washington into a serious project. Her infectious enthusiasm and advice were invaluable. My thanks go to Andrew Gowers, the editor of the *Financial Times,* for allowing me the time and space to write this book on a tight schedule. Graham Watts, the deputy editor of the *Financial Times* magazine, gave me real encouragement and valuable insights during the most difficult early stages of writing. Richard Lambert, the former editor of the *Financial Times,* read much of the book in draft and provided a great morale boost as well as his usual good advice. Peter Cheek, another colleague at the newspaper, was all an author could expect of a researcher—and then more. At Viking, Rick Kot was a calm and thoughtful editor who improved both the prose and the structure. Kate Griggs handled the production stages against the tightest of deadlines.

Needless to say, any flaws are mine alone.

Most of all, though, I owe a debt to Patty, Jessica, and Benedict for putting up with my absences and my grumpiness during a long, hot summer. Thank you.

CONTENTS

INTRODUCTION

ON MARCH 18, 2003, the atmosphere in the ornate wood-paneled chamber of Britain's House of Commons crackled with electricity. The green leather benches of the nation's legislative chamber were packed to overflowing. Tony Blair was preparing to take his country to war alongside George W. Bush. Confounded, exhausted, and dismayed by the diplomatic failures at the United Nations during the previous few weeks, the British prime minister had set his course. The mood of Britain, though, was against risking the lives of its soldiers to topple Iraq's Saddam Hussein. In his own left-of-center Labour Party, intense hostility to a Republican president in the White House was combined with genuine doubts about the justification for war. Even as British troops gathered on the Kuwait-Iraq border, Blair faced a mounting rebellion among his supporters. One senior member of his government, the former foreign secretary Robin Cook, had already resigned. Other ministers were preparing to quit. Scores of Labour members of Parliament (MPs) had resolved to vote against their own government. Beyond the political village of Westminster once-warm relationships with key allies in Europe lay badly broken.

Tony Blair was unmoved. Ending Saddam's defiance of the international community was, in the phrase he had used over and again, "the right thing to do." That was his decision, he told colleagues in the British cabinet, whatever the cost. Government officials made contingency plans should he be forced to resign after the votes had been counted. On that overcast March morning the prime minister was sure of a majority in Parliament because the opposition Conservative Party backed a war to topple the Baghdad regime. The risk he faced, however, was that more than half of his own supporters would rebel. In

such circumstances, his premiership would be unsustainable. Britain and the rest of the world were being introduced to a leader they had not properly met. Blair had already transformed his party's electoral fortunes and had many times proved himself an accomplished politician. This, though, was the politics of conviction.

He had everything to lose. Six years earlier, a few days before his forty-fourth birthday, Anthony Charles Lynton Blair had become the youngest British prime minister since the Napoleonic Wars of the early nineteenth century. Three years later, he was the first prime minister in more than 150 years to father a child while in 10 Downing Street. In June 2001 he had won a second landslide election victory against the Conservatives, seemingly assuring himself a place in the record books as the longest-serving Labour prime minister in history. More than that, he had remade the landscape of British politics, wrenching the party he had rechristened New Labour from the barren socialist left into the fertile center ground. While his policies and campaign techniques had been borrowed from Bill Clinton's New Democrats, Blair had always been a politician impatiently dismissive of the old ideological divides between right and left. They owed their place, he thought, to an age that had passed with the fall of the Berlin Wall. He embraced the values of progressive politics while discarding the accumulation of sacred socialist texts that had locked his party out of government for nearly two decades. Most politicians start from a set of traditional political positions; Blair started from the values he had imbibed with his Christian faith. His political heroes were the leaders of the centrist Liberal Party, which had ruled Britain during much of the nineteenth century, rather than the giants of the Labour movement that he now led. The product of a privileged private education and the son of a Conservative lawyer, he had always been at something of a distance from his own party. To the discomfort of many of his colleagues he saw himself as a national, rather than a partisan, leader, even though he had succeeded in exiling the Conservatives, the dominant political force in Britain for most of the twentieth century, to the frozen margins of politics. But, as British troops moved to the "start line" in Kuwait, all this was now imperiled.

During the weeks and months before the crucial debate, the prime minister had emerged as the most articulate and passionate advocate of decisive action to force Saddam into compliance with the United Nations resolutions passed at the end of the 1991 Gulf War. His speeches and interviews resonated well beyond Britain's shores. The strong rapport he had forged with George W. Bush in the wake of the terrorist attacks on America on September 11, 2001, had become the fulcrum of the West's response to the new threats to its security posed by so-called rogue states and the proliferation of weapons of mass destruction. But this relationship between prime minister and president was one replete with puzzles and paradoxes. Blair was a politician of the center-left, a leader who still counted former president Bill Clinton among his closest political allies and friends. The prime minister once said that Clinton was the most brilliant politician he had ever met–a judgment from which he never resiled. Bush was the Republican from Texas, the president whom most European leaders of the center-left had come to scorn and, sometimes, despise. Throughout the Iraq crisis, Blair sought Clinton's private counsel. Most recently, on the very morning of that House of Commons vote Clinton had been enlisted to help his old friend. The former president wrote an article for the *Guardian,* the newspaper of choice of Labour members of Parliament, urging them to back their leader. "Trust Tony's Judgement," the headline declared. For one extraordinary moment on that March day, it was almost as if Bush, Blair, and Clinton were standing side by side.

The prime minister was unapologetic about his relationship with Bush, judging it in his country's vital strategic interests to stay close to Washington regardless of who occupied the White House. He saw Britain's role as that of a "pivotal" power, the essential hinge of the transatlantic alliance between Europe and the United States that had kept the peace since 1945. He shared many of the president's fears–more so than most other European leaders–about the new security threats of the twenty-first century. The destruction of New York's twin towers in the terrorist attacks of September 11, 2001, had exposed a perilous threat that had to be met with military resolve. But the menace could be effec-

tively countered only if the United States and Europe stood together. The attack on New York, the prime minister would often say, had "changed the psychology of America," though "it should have changed the psychology of the world." While the end of the cold war had seemed for a time to rob the transatlantic alliance of its raison d'être, Blair believed that the terrorism of Al Qaeda, the defiance of Saddam, and the growing number of failed and failing states around the world were reasons to rebuild it. Befriending a Republican president was a matter of temperament as well as realpolitik. For all that he had worked with Bill Clinton to create a Third Way movement of the center-left, Blair has never been a tribal politician. His relationships in Europe saw him closer to Spain's center-right prime minister José María Aznar than to the French socialist Lionel Jospin.

Yet Tony Blair's war against Iraq differed in many respects from the one fought by George W. Bush. Beyond the common purpose of the expulsion of Saddam Hussein, Washington and London seemed to have divergent designs for the world. The driving motivation within the U.S. administration seemed to be the removal of a defiant enemy—a demonstration to the world that America would deploy all of its military might to defend itself. America had to assert its primacy, to fulfill its role as the world's sole superpower. Richard Cheney, the vice president, and Donald Rumsfeld at the Pentagon were briskly dismissive of talk in Downing Street of a new multilateral order hinged on a partnership between the United States and Europe. Blair wanted to build just such a new international system. For all his instinctive Atlanticism, he is a multilateralist—convinced that the West's security depends on an effective international alliance. In his analysis, September 11, 2001, was a tragic demonstration of the inescapable interdependence of the modern world. Even a nation as uniquely powerful as the United States could not alone secure itself against the dangers beyond its shores. Blair believes, too, in "nation-building," the responsibility of the West to make and safeguard peace as well as, when necessary, to wage war. In this he has something in common with American neoconservatives like Paul Wolfowitz, but nothing at all with assertive nationalists like Cheney and Rumsfeld. The price of his support for President Bush in

the war against Saddam Hussein was that the administration first give the United Nations a last chance to secure Iraqi compliance. The second pledge he sought of the president on every occasion they met was that the United States give impetus to peace talks between Israel and the Palestinians. Terrorism, he told Bush more times than he could remember, would only be tamed when a durable peace agreement had been secured in the Middle East.

There are echoes of an earlier age in Tony Blair's premiership. His approach to foreign policy has its roots in the interventionism of the nineteenth-century Liberal British prime minister William Gladstone. Like his distinguished predecessor, he is impatient of the strategic doctrines that say governments should turn their backs on tyranny and injustice in the world unless their narrow national interests are in imminent danger. His politics—and a deep Christian faith—tell him that civilized nations have the right and duty to confront suffering beyond their boundaries; in the medium to long term, such intervention is a matter of enlightened self-interest. Even before the events of September 11, Blair had emerged as the most outspoken advocate of military action to end Slobodan Milosevic's tyranny in Kosovo, and had sent British troops to end the civil war raging in the West African state of Sierra Leone. In the spring of 1999, during the Kosovo war, he enunciated a new "doctrine of international community." Tyrants, he declared, could no longer be permitted to shield behind the United Nations charter in pursuit of the oppression of their own peoples. The NATO military campaign against Serbia was "a just war based not in territorial ambitions but on values." But it was also a matter of self-interest: "If we let an evil dictator range unchallenged, we will have to spill infinitely more blood and treasure to stop him later."

For all his idealism, Tony Blair bears the blemishes of his profession. No one would ever accuse him of lacking personal ambition. And, though he prefers to make friends rather than enemies in politics, he has never lacked the ruthlessness required of politicians to reach the top. A friend and admirer in Blair's own cabinet states quite simply, "He is the most ruthless leader I know. He is very unsentimental about doing tough things." The high moral tone of a political message infused

with Christian belief has often jostled with the low politics he has employed to win and retain power. The unshakable conviction that has marked his foreign policy has often stood in contrast with a curious timidity and hesitancy in his domestic agenda. As an opposition leader, Blair remade the Labour Party in his own image, destroying the assumptions of British postwar politics. He placed himself between the Conservatives' Margaret Thatcher and the far-left leaders of his own party. The old left, he often said, had stressed social rights to the exclusion of individual responsibilities, while Thatcherism emphasized individual economic rights to the exclusion of social responsibility. New Labour joined rights and responsibilities. Yet sometimes it seemed that the guiding purpose of Blair's domestic politics was simply to win a second term. Early on he was held in thrall by the focus-group and opinion-polling obsessions imported from Bill Clinton's White House. His political skills—he is the most fluent and persuasive communicator in British politics—are not matched by a natural mastery of the cumbersome machinery of government. Yet his gifts as one of politics' great persuaders rest upon a foundation of staunch self-belief. In Northern Ireland, where six years of patient peacemaking ended a bloody terrorist war against the British state, he deployed a genius for convincing unreasonable people to do reasonable things to brilliant effect. At other times, he seemed to think that stirring rhetoric was sufficient to make the world a better place. More than once he has learned that vision is a poor substitute for the hard choices demanded of those in power.

For all such flaws, the aftermath of September 11 and of the conflict in Iraq marked out Tony Blair as a different sort of leader. The gifted thespian had met the conviction politician. In the months after the attacks on America he traveled many tens of thousands of miles and met dozens of world leaders as the most eloquent spokesman for a new coalition behind America's fight against terrorism. Right or wrong on the best way to deal with Saddam Hussein, his approach was rooted in principle and carried through with courage. This was a personal as much as a political watershed. The war told Britain and the wider world where the prime minister came from as a politician and where

he intended to go. There were many reasons–the realpolitik of the Anglo-American relationship high on the list–why he might have decided to go to war against Iraq. And, doubtless, matters of strategic interest played a central part. But the moral certainty that prompted Blair to risk everything on the war came from the conviction that the world would be a better place once it was rid of Saddam Hussein. If this Manichaean outlook unsettles even some of his close supporters, a willingness to gamble all distinguishes him as a man who is in politics to change things. He was sanguine about the idea that the venture might cost him his career, because if he could not do the things he believed to be right in his position, he saw little purpose in staying. The heavy irony of the furor after the Iraq war over whether Saddam's regime really did have weapons of mass destruction is that Blair would have liked from the start to frame the war in a different context. For him, removing a dangerous and murderous tyrant was as compelling a moral cause as a hunt for weapons of mass destruction. Blair's Christian faith is open-minded, tolerant of human frailties, and respectful of Jewish and Muslim teaching. But Christianity–and the concept that he draws from it of the world as a place of interdependent individuals and communities–informs and infuses all his political thinking.

Tony Blair's response to the attacks on America on September 11, 2001, turned a politician who was strong at home and well known in Europe into a leading figure on the world stage. The support he offered to George W. Bush–first to fight terrorism and then to remove Iraq's Saddam Hussein–gave him a public profile in the United States unmatched by most postwar British prime ministers. Only Margaret Thatcher could claim the same sort of recognition among Americans and, arguably, Blair did more even than the "Iron Lady" to establish Britain as Washington's staunchest ally. He did so, however, at substantial cost to his popularity and reputation at home.

The prime minister won the vote for war on March 18. While some 139, or about a third, of his own MPs in the House of Commons rebelled, it was enough that Blair had carried the support of more than half of his party. Ten days later, when the British and American leaders

met in Washington, George W. Bush offered his now-famous tribute: "America has learned a lot about Tony Blair over the last weeks," the president said. "We've learned that he's a man of his word. We've learned that he's a man of courage, that he's a man of vision. And we're proud to have him as a friend." But for both men, the peace would bring many more problems than the war.

A few months later, in early August, Blair passed another political milestone when his government became the longest continuously serving administration in Labour's history. Yet while Britain now had a prime minister who had changed the political weather in Britain and emerged as a powerful leader on the international stage, the nation was hardly in a grateful mood. The war had ended in Iraq but left a bloody and chaotic peace. Failure to find Saddam's weapons of mass destruction in the months after the war badly damaged trust in Blair's leadership. So, too, did a loud public controversy over whether the British government had deliberately exaggerated the extent of the threat posed by the Iraqi leader. In his determination to fight at America's side Blair had put too much emphasis on the immediate danger. During the summer of 2003, a public inquiry into the suicide of a distinguished British weapons scientist revealed the flaws in the intelligence reports that had been presented as cause for war–and shone a harsh light on the way that Blair's office had sought to play up the potential threat. Many questioned whether Blair had put his determination to preserve a "special relationship" with Washington above all other judgments. Perhaps, as Winston Churchill discovered when he was voted out of office at the end of World War II, it is the fate of British leaders to be admired abroad and mistrusted at home. In any event, when he reflected on all this in an interview at the end of July 2003, the voice of the nineteenth-century moral missionary in Tony Blair was as clear as it had ever been that toppling Saddam had been "the right thing to do."

I first met Tony Blair during the 1980s, when he was a junior Treasury spokesman for the Labour Party and I was an economics reporter for the *Financial Times*. Subsequently, I followed his career as the newspaper's political editor, as a columnist, and as UK editor. I have spoken to

and interviewed him on dozens of occasions, watching and charting the rise of the young, determined politician as he first became leader of his party, then Britain's prime minister, and ultimately a politician determined to make an impact on the world well beyond Britain's shores. Many of these encounters became interviews published in the *Financial Times;* others provided the basis for columns in the newspaper. I have drawn on all of them, as well as many more conversations with his friends, his political allies and aides, and his opponents, in writing this biography. In late July 2003, Blair also agreed to give a lengthy on-the-record interview specifically for this book, in which he spoke candidly about the early influences on his political life, as well as of his thoughts on presidents Clinton and Bush and on the war against Iraq.

Tony Blair is a remarkable politician. His achievements, at home in Britain and abroad, have belied his youth and inexperience. He is a leader willing to take risks in pursuit of conviction. But this is a biography, not a hagiography. Blair's admirers have long been confounded by the ruthless political gamesmanship that sits alongside the conviction; his critics are disarmed by the principles that lie behind the constant quest for popular acclaim. My intention is to provide a portrait that allows readers to make their own judgments.

Tony Blair

1. STEEPLES AND SPIRES

TONY BLAIR GREW UP on a journey through the pages of British history. The nation's future prime minister lived his early life among the church steeples, ancient clock towers, and medieval quadrangles that are the childhood playgrounds of England's affluent middle classes. The Chorister School, attached to the ancient cathedral in the English city of Durham, was his stepping-stone to Fettes College, Scotland's most renowned public (what Americans know as "private") school. From there the road led to St. John's, one of the richest colleges amid the dreaming spires of the University of Oxford; and then, as a prelude for a young man seeking a career in the law, to the Inns of Court, the London home to the elaborate wigs and flowing gowns of the English legal establishment. When Blair finally arrived as a member of Parliament at the Palace of Westminster in 1983, the Gothic splendor of the nation's seat of democracy seemed all of a piece with the cloisters of his youth.

Somewhere along the way, though, his path had veered. The august institutions of his early life were the conventional route to a career on the right, or Conservative, wing of British politics. No one would have been surprised if Blair had risen quickly through the ranks of the Conservative Party. After all, his own father, Leo, before he had fallen victim to ill health, had harbored serious hopes himself of becoming a Tory MP. But the son chose the politics of the left, membership in a Labour Party that, even as he joined it, seemed to be facing inexorable decline. The roots of the young Tony Blair's political outlook, his moral conviction and the internationalism that would cast him as a formidable actor on the world stage, were thus located beyond the ornamented architecture of his youth: in Christian faith, in experience

forged by family tragedy, in a set of values borrowed from another age, in unshakable self-belief, and, as ever in politics, in personal ambition. Many times in his later political career, Blair would remind his audiences that he was a Labour politician by *choice*. Others had been born to the party of the left, their beliefs nurtured by family tradition, by childhood deprivation, or by tribal class loyalties. Tony Blair was different. Even as its leader and as prime minister, he maintained a degree of detachment from his party.

Anthony Charles Lynton Blair was born in the Scottish capital of Edinburgh on May 6, 1953. His father, Leo, was a university lecturer in law, a career that took the family during the children's earliest years to Adelaide, Australia. By the time the future prime minister had reached the age of five, they had returned to England, where Leo combined a blossoming career as a lawyer with his teaching. Their base was the northeastern city of Durham, which boasted contemporary prosperity and an illustrious past. Home to a prominent university, it was also a place where Leo could build a flourishing practice as a senior courtroom lawyer–in the British term, a barrister–on England's northern judicial circuit. Young Tony, the second of three children, enjoyed a world of comfortable privilege. His father was scarcely rich, but he was prosperous enough to opt out of the state-funded schools system and himself pay for the children's education. Leo was a man who had made his own luck in life. He was ambitious for himself, and equally so for his two sons and daughter.

Affluence had not come easily. Born to parents who led the peripatetic life of music hall performers, Leo Blair had been all but abandoned as a child to a foster family in Glasgow, the city that was then at the industrial heart of Scotland. He did keep one link, though, to his parents: his son Tony's middle names, Lynton and Charles, were borrowed from Leo's natural father–one was the music hall performer's given name, the other his stage name. Leo's escape route from the grim tenement blocks of his childhood was service in the army during World War II. Before the war he had been forced to leave school at the age of fourteen to take a job as a clerk, but he rose quickly through the junior ranks of the military to become an officer. Once the war was

over he returned to full-time education and a career, eventually, in the law. Like many in a generation that had had to struggle, he determined that his children would have better. His politics had also changed. As a teenager from a deprived background Leo had flirted with the politics of the extreme left; as an army officer about to take up a career in the law, he decided to join the Conservatives.

Tony's mother, Hazel, was of a different character. Where Leo was ambitious and gregarious, she was gentle and quiet. Born in Ireland–in her famous son's description, "in the flat above her grandmother's hardware shop on the main street of Ballyshannon in Donegal"–she had moved to Glasgow when her father had died, and there had met and married Leo. The family kept its ties with Ireland. When Tony Blair became the first British prime minister to address the Irish parliament, he recalled fondly that as a schoolboy he had spent almost every summer vacation in Donegal: "It was there in the seas off the Irish coast that I learned to swim, there that my father took me to my first pub, a remote little house in the country, for a Guinness." Lacking the career ambitions of her husband, Hazel looked after the house and raised the family. She was "almost painfully shy," her son said many years later. "She was entirely without malice. I don't think I ever heard her say a bad word about anyone." She steered the family through not just her husband's recovery from a sudden stroke but also the illness of her daughter, Sarah, the youngest of the three children. At the age of eight Sarah had developed Still's disease, a form of rheumatoid arthritis. Hazel moved on from nursing her husband to caring for her daughter. Sarah recovered, but only after intensive treatment that required long spells in the hospital and unpleasant side effects from the prescribed drug treatment.

Durham Chorister School, which Tony attended from the age of eight (he followed in the footsteps of his elder brother, William), had been founded several centuries earlier to educate the boys who sang in the city's ancient cathedral choir. In the 1950s the traditions of the church school still lived on, but it had a broader intake, serving as one of the quintessentially English preparatory or "prep" schools, to which the middle classes sent their children to begin a formal education.

Later the prime minister would recall of these early experiences an age and an education in which the premium was on good manners, values that were reinforced by his parents. What mattered, Blair remembered in newspaper interviews, was "respect for others, courtesy, giving up your seat for the elderly, saying please and then thank you." If he was told off at school, he recalled, his mother would apologize on his behalf to the teacher. Tony Blair carried Hazel's admonitions into political life. The young politician made his way in the Labour Party as a "modernizer," a leader eager to discard the past. But his personal manners, almost Victorian in their studied politeness, harked back to gentler times. Whatever his faults, Blair is an unfailingly courteous politician, one rarely heard to raise his voice in anger, one who always dispatches a note of thanks in response to a kindness or courtesy.

His time at Fettes College, to which he traveled at the age of thirteen, was an unhappy interlude. His father's choice of Scotland's foremost public school in part spoke to his own roots in Scotland. But it was primarily a statement of social intent. In the mind of a father who had struggled to succeed, Tony and his siblings were destined for the upper ranks of British society. Perched on the edge of Edinburgh and built in a chaos of architectural styles that somehow manage to combine the Scottish baronial with the French Gothic, Fettes was established in 1870 as a boarding school for Scotland's rich merchant classes. The school's founding ambition was to produce the educated young men who would go out into the world in pursuit of the nation's commercial fortunes and in service of the British Empire. It was organized from the start on the English public school principle that said rigorous discipline and austerity would build what the English call "character" in the children of the wealthy. This was the world, harsh and often calculatedly cruel, immortalized by Thomas Hughes in the classic 1857 novel *Tom Brown's Schooldays.*

Nearly a century on, the vast empire the school once served had dissolved. But the atmosphere at Fettes was still austere, the discipline rigorous and often illogical. Ian MacIntosh, the headmaster, would have been happier in an earlier century. A staunch traditionalist and disciplinarian, his ambition at Fettes was to preserve the past. But the

times were against him, for the 1960s were a period of social upheaval. The age of deference was passing, to be replaced by rock music, long hair, and satirical irreverence. MacIntosh refused to acknowledge the thirst for modernity, and to those who complained he would reply, "I'd like to hear everything you say—before I say, 'No.'" When the boys grew their hair longer, he ordered it cut. The young Tony Blair was one of the victims. The school's official history records that Blair found himself marched to the barber's shop by the headmaster: "He took him straight in and stood there, unrelenting, as the cherished mop was trimmed." Blair would remember his years there as a difficult time. Much later, when he was asked as prime minister to write the foreword to the school history, he felt obliged to agree. But there was no warmth of memory in the published words.

The young Blair rebelled against Fettes's petty regulations and archaic ordinances. The bulging book of rules extended even to the number of blazer buttons the boys (the school finally decided to admit girls only in his final year there) were required to keep closed at all times. Seniority gave prefects the right to flog younger boys with a cane, the beatings sometimes taking the form of public rituals to humiliate as well as hurt the victims. The hierarchy required younger boys to polish the seniors' boots, clean their sports kits, and run errands for them. The shared dormitories—MacIntosh thought private rooms even for senior boys would soon have become "dens of iniquity"—were spartan, the showers cold. Blair found the environment suffocating. More than once he was caught escaping over the school walls to evade the ban on excursions into Edinburgh's city center. He left at the age of eighteen with a clutch of unhappy memories and a reputation among the school's masters as a rebel, albeit one whose misdemeanors were rarely grave. Yet Fettes had left its mark. Later, friends and acquaintances would comment that Blair showed in later life the very respect for authority against which he had rebelled at school.

Though he could scarcely have known it at the time, Tony Blair took something else from this stifling world behind high walls. As he began to prosper in politics it was soon obvious that he was a remarkable actor. He stood out as a natural communicator, a young man with

an instinctive ability to empathize with audiences, to strike just the right pose and cadence at just the right moment. Blair gave no hint at Fettes of the political career to come, for the ambition had yet to form. "No, you could not tell that he was going to be prime minister, nor even a politician. There was no sense of divine purpose about him," one of his oldest and closest friends told me. But equally, it was obvious from an early age that Blair was entranced by the footlights. "You have to remember that he's an actor, no, a performer, he's exuberant. . . . He still gets nervous beforehand but he loves it," this friend added, commenting on Blair's prime ministerial performances.

One senior master at Fettes could claim some of the credit for Blair's later seemingly effortless command of the national mood. Eric Anderson was among the few authority figures at the school with whom the rebellious schoolboy established a rapport. Later he would say privately that the young Blair was "difficult." Anderson was often exasperated by his student's habit of questioning every rule–"Why" was his favorite word–yet he quite admired Blair's ability to charm himself out of awkward binds. Anderson, who went on to become headmaster of Eton, England's most famous public school, encouraged the future prime minister to channel some of this precocious energy into school drama. Early on, Blair was cast as Mark Anthony in Shakespeare's *Julius Caesar*. When his pupil became leader of the Labour Party, Anderson recounted, "He did the 'Friends, Romans, countrymen' speech brilliantly, and I wonder if that gave him a taste for politics." A more challenging role followed as Captain Stanhope in *Journey's End*, a play by R. C. Sherriff that was popular at the time because of its depiction of the futility of war. Blair's portrayal of the army officer tormented by the bloody, hopeless battles between British and German soldiers across the trenches of World War I was widely acclaimed by his peers at Fettes and attracted a glowing review in the school magazine. Blair remembered this particular stage role well when more than three decades later he was leading Britain into war against Iraq. There were more parts in plays and reviews at Fettes and later at Oxford. David Kennedy, another of his teachers, was less kind than Anderson when he spoke to one of Blair's early biographers: "He

[Blair] has always been conscious of how he appears to other people. The façade is always there. He is very intelligent and calculating. Don't forget that he was a superb actor."

The politician never lost his care with words, phrases, and presentation. Though as prime minister he could call on battalions of aides to draft his speeches, he preferred to craft them himself. In another nod to an earlier age, he composed them in longhand with a fountain pen rather than tap the keys of a personal computer. The meticulous care Blair takes with his personal appearance is another, albeit unconscious, legacy of his school days. Jeans and a polo shirt are fine when the prime minister is relaxing with his family, but once in the public eye, his suits, shirts, and ties are chosen with great care, his shoes always brightly polished. In the slightly barbed observation of one close adviser, "He's a politician who can never pass a mirror without looking into it." Vanity no doubt plays its part, and the performer still has a starring role in Blair's political persona. But the attention to detail also reflects that very English childhood.

Blair's theatrical gifts would be shown in their most brilliant light many years later in the aftermath of the death of Diana, the Princess of Wales. He had been prime minister for only a few months when the former wife of the Prince of Wales and heir to the throne died in a terrible car accident in Paris. Filmed against the backdrop of the local church in his Sedgefield constituency on that extraordinary Sunday morning in August 1997, Blair's televised response to the nation was a performance worthy of the most celebrated of thespians. "I feel like everyone else in this country today. I am utterly devastated," the prime minister began. Diana had been liked and loved by the whole nation. She was, Blair said in one brilliantly evocative phrase, "the People's Princess," and "that is how she will stay, how she will remain in our hearts and memories forever." The words were perfectly delivered, the voice breaking at precisely the right moment, the grief etched on the prime minister's face. Those who watched the appearance were sure they could see a tear in the corner of his eye. To the nation it seemed that this lament for "the People's Princess" was as real as her sudden death had been in-

credible. The initial reaction of the Queen and Prince Charles to the death of the estranged princess had been cold and distant, and it was left to the prime minister to speak for the nation at a time of tragedy. At Diana's funeral in Westminster Abbey, watched by hundreds of millions of people across the world, Blair delivered the famous passage from Corinthians—"When I was a child, I spoke like a child"—with the same emotional intensity. Within weeks his personal rating had soared off the opinion pollsters' scales. These were the most brilliantly accomplished of the many performances that marked out Blair's political ascent. They signaled a style of politics unfamiliar in Britain, but one that fitted his personality and his political ambition in equal measure. Eric Anderson could be proud of his handiwork.

Inevitably, such performances raised questions about Blair's political leadership. Where did the actor end and the real Tony Blair begin? For political opponents, the love of the stage was proof of a "phony" Tony. It's all an act, they would charge, and a deeply cynical one at that. Friends, too, sometimes wondered whether the prime minister was a touch too eager to apply the greasepaint. But by the time he reached 10 Downing Street the politician and the performer could no longer be separated. Those who knew Blair well insisted with convincing certainty that he had been genuinely upset by the death of Diana. He had met her privately on a number of occasions and, like many others, had been won over by her tragic charm. But yes, he also understood instinctively that her death offered an opportunity to cast himself as more than a mere politician, more even than a prime minister. When Alistair Campbell, his communications director, suggested the phrase "People's Princess," Blair instantly understood its unifying force. As prime minister, he practiced the politics of inclusion. The death of Diana offered a moment to bring the entire nation into the New Labour tent. If that required a few dramatic flourishes for the television cameras, so be it.

Soon after his election as Labour leader, Tony Blair was asked the question now put to every politician of the baby boom generation. Had he ever smoked dope? His reply blended wit with innocence. "No, but

if I had, I would have inhaled." Here was a gentle tease at the expense of Bill Clinton, who had been a Rhodes Scholar at Oxford a few years before Blair arrived at the university. (When pressed about his youthful acquaintance with cannabis, Clinton had said, rather lamely, that, yes, he had taken a puff or two while sitting around with fellow students, but he had never actually inhaled.) Blair's response seemed spontaneously clever; people laughed, and the question went away. In fact, this small, unimportant episode betrayed the strenuous efforts that Blair took to guard his image and reputation. As soon as he had become the leader of his party in 1994, his political aides had hit the telephones. They knew the media would be digging into his past. Anyone and everyone who had befriended Blair in his earlier life was contacted by his office. Were they aware of any skeletons in the closets of his past? Were they prepared to be discreet? Oh, and by the way, they should know that when the cannabis question was asked of the new Labour leader he would respond with a quip at Clinton's expense. In truth, although there were no great scandals to be uncovered, Blair's past would henceforth be choreographed as carefully as his political future.

When Blair arrived at St. John's at Oxford in 1972, the university was scarcely a hotbed of student revolution. The most it could muster in the way of activism was a few noisy demonstrations against the policies of the then Conservative government and a short occupation of the university's examination buildings in protest at the school's medieval statutes. But cannabis was cheap and ubiquitous. Most of Blair's crowd smoked it–by their own accounts, often in his presence. So had Tony really said no every time a joint was passed around during those long nights of rock music and earnest conversation about the dismal state of society? For someone of Blair's class and generation it would almost be stranger if he had *not* experimented. After all, the head of Britain's criminal prosecution service, who was an Oxford contemporary, has a conviction for cannabis possession. If youthful encounters with the drug were a bar to high office, the present generation of politicians would be eerily small. More interesting, perhaps, than whether Blair had actually experimented with cannabis was the concern that not even the smallest transgression should be allowed to sully his record.

————————

He was a diligent student at Oxford. His three-year degree course saw him following in his father's and his elder brother's footsteps in law. The young Blair found plenty of time for rock music and girlfriends, but he also worked hard to secure a good, if not greatly distinguished, degree. In other words, his was the normal student life in the Britain of the 1970s. If he pushed against the boundaries of college discipline, as at Fettes, the rebelliousness had limits. Friends recall that he spent more than the requisite number of hours pouring over the detail of arcane legal precedents in the college library. The most risqué story told by a contemporary concerns an evening spent playing "strip poker"– with Blair and a female friend duly paying the required forfeit in full when the cards went against them. True to his love of the stage, he was lead singer for a rock band. His role model was the Rolling Stones' Mick Jagger–who else in the early 1970s? He also played at playing guitar. Those who saw Ugly Rumours (the band's name was taken from the cover of a Grateful Dead album) at student concerts recall the music as energetic but pretty dire. Blair dressed in the student uniform of the age–shoulder-length hair, multicolored T-shirts, cotton trousers tight at the waist and flared at the ankles. Folklore has it he added platform shoes to the ensemble. The lead singer's gyrations, friends remember, served him well as far as meeting girls was concerned, but Ugly Rumours struggled to find paying audiences. "It's true that they did not play very often . . . but they practiced a lot," jokes one friend. Like the quip about cannabis, the band became part of the official narrative of the Labour leader's early life. A rock-star youth fitted the image of a rising young politician. And as prime minister, Blair did start paying serious attention to playing the guitar, which he found helped relieve the stress.

One friend recalls that at school and university Blair was indeed a natural leader–in organizing social excursions: "He was always the one saying let's go to this party or that concert . . . the rest of us followed along." But if he enjoyed the rock-star image and honing his acting talents in college revues, Blair eschewed the traditional playgrounds of student politics. He took no interest in the Oxford Union, the debating

society that through the generations has nurtured and polished the oratorical skills of scores of Britain's most distinguished politicians. He did participate in one or two student demonstrations, but belonged to neither the Conservative nor Labour party clubs. "The fact that he became leader of the Labour Party surprised and puzzled lots of people," recalled one of his contemporaries at St. John's. "It didn't surprise us that he turned into an earnest young man, nor probably that he chose politics as his way of making a difference. But it was a surprise that he reached the top." Other contemporaries thought he would continue to follow in the footsteps of his father and elder brother and turn out to be a successful lawyer. The stage was good practice, after all, for the courtroom. Perhaps, at a stretch, he would become an impresario, or something else in the entertainment business—he had spent much of the "gap" year between leaving school and starting university as a would-be promoter of up-and-coming rock bands in London. No one thought they had made friends with a future prime minister.

In later life, members of Blair's university set would join the worlds of business, banking, public service, and journalism, as well as politics. Several, including the future Australian politician Geoff Gallop and another Australian, a priest by the name of Peter Thomson, remained friends with the future prime minister. One in particular, though, stood out. Anji Hunter, two years younger than Blair, had first met him when he was at Fettes and she at a nearby boarding school for girls. This was not an early romance—or so at least both parties have always insisted. But Hunter arrived in Oxford to finish her schooling while he was at St. John's. Their friendship thrived and was to endure well beyond their student days. During the late 1980s Hunter served as the manager of Blair's Westminster office and was soon one of his indispensable aides. After his election victory in 1997 she was appointed special assistant to the prime minister—friend, confidante, and political fixer rolled into one.

Looking back, there were one or two clues as to the direction of Blair's own future. The rock and roll and the long spells in the library grappling with case law still left time during Oxford evenings for deep philosophical discussions about the nature of man, the future of society, and the dismal condition of politics in its broad sense. The world

of the early 1970s was a turbulent place, and the mood of young university students correspondingly restless. The Vietnam War was just drawing to its close, the cold war ever present; the OPEC oil price rises had shocked the West out of its economic complacency; the world's poor seemed to be getting poorer. Closer to home, Edward Heath's Conservative government was embroiled in a titanic struggle with the trade unions, and in Northern Ireland the British army was fighting in the streets against Irish Republicans. This was more than enough to worry and intrigue a group of intelligent young people interested in the nature of the society they would join. In the shifting circle of four or five, sometimes six or seven, undergraduates of which Blair was part, the political and philosophical works of Marx, Engels, and Gramsci were the subject of earnest discussion. The group included a young Ugandan, Olaro Otunno, who went on to become his country's foreign minister, as well as Geoff Gallop.

Philosophy, politics, and religion were all part of the discourse. Friday afternoons at St. John's were given over to public debate among the college's students. At one such event the young Blair offered a rather dry analysis of Marx's philosophical manuscripts. More important, though, his mind was open to fresh ideas. Speaking in the summer of 2003, he recalled that, in spite of all those spires and cloisters, he never felt any great weight of tradition. Because his family had moved around when he was young, and his father was a foster child, "I couldn't trace my family back three centuries. My parents had worked their way up and they came from different backgrounds. I have always therefore accepted people pretty much as they are rather than [in relation to] where they have come from." That did not mean he lacked roots, but rather that "they were very much in the ideas you formed rather than in a particular sort of traditional upbringing."

The memories etched most deeply on the mind of the young Tony Blair were not those of brushes with authority at school, wrestling with Marx's dialectic, or playing in a rock band. For all the material comforts of his childhood, his formative moments were those of family misfortune and spiritual awakening. The first shock to the comfortable as-

sumptions of youth came at the age of eleven when he was woken one morning by his mother to be told his father had suffered a sudden stroke. For a short time it seemed that Leo, still only forty and in the prime of a successful career, might not survive. Much later Blair recalled the event as "the day my childhood ended." His father pulled through, but he had lost his speech and much of his movement, leaving him effectively bedridden for months. Hazel nursed him back to health, but it was an agonizingly slow process, and several years passed before Leo recovered sufficiently to return to work. The family remained financially secure, but without the room to spare of earlier years. Gradually, Leo was able to rebuild his legal career, but the burgeoning ambitions for a life in Conservative politics—he had by now become the chairman of the party's local association and was looking for a seat in Parliament—had to be abandoned. More than two decades afterward, Tony spoke movingly about this period during a speech to the Labour Party's annual conference. His father's illness, he said, "taught me the value of the family, because my mother worked for three years to help him walk and talk again." He also learned the worth of community. The fair-weather friends disappeared, "but the real friends, the true friends, they stayed with us . . . they stuck with us for no other reason than that it was the right thing to do." "I don't pretend to you," Blair told a now-hushed audience, "that I had a deprived childhood. I didn't. But I learned a sense of values in my childhood."

As he finished his studies at Oxford, the twenty-two-year-old learned that now his mother was desperately ill, having been diagnosed a few years earlier with cancer of the thyroid. Surgery had removed the growth, and for a time there were hopes of a remission. But the disease had taken hold. Returning home from Oxford after his final examinations in the summer of 1975, Blair found that the worst had been kept from him for fear it might disrupt his studies. His mother had only a short time left. During her last days in the hospital, Hazel saw each of her three children in turn and, as Tony put it, "went through things with us." Then, at the age of only fifty-two, she was gone. The loss of a mother is the most painful moment in the life of a son. After the illnesses of his father and sister, the effect on the young

Tony Blair was devastating. Some thirty years later, when Tony was in 10 Downing Street, his brother, William, recalled their mother's death. "The effect of our father's stroke on Tony has often been analyzed," he said in a newspaper interview. "Many people say the ambition of the father was transferred to the son. But it was more complicated than that. . . . I think people have tended to underestimate the role my mother played in forming Tony's view of life."

As the prime minister himself explained further in July 2003, his father's illness had been a tremendous blow "because the family's security disappeared overnight. . . . And when I look back, I think that was very important." Then, just as he crossed the threshold into adulthood, came his mother's death. "I remember when my father told me that my mother was dying, and she was going to die. I remember the shock of it absolutely. You thought that these things just didn't happen." As with his father's illness, he said, it was as if the family had been robbed of its security. He found it a deeply sobering as well as a sad time. There had been moments, he said, when he could have gone off and "done something wild. . . . I definitely had that part in me to be like that." His father's stroke had pulled him back from such adventures. Now, after the death of his mother, he approached everything "with a lot more focus and determination, which I suppose is natural."

2. FAITH AND FAMILY

PERHAPS IT WAS A COINCIDENCE, perhaps something more, but even as his mother struggled with her illness, Tony Blair took his first steps on the spiritual journey that would shape his life. He had begun taking religious instruction at St. John's, and before he left Oxford he was confirmed in the Anglican Church by the chaplain of the college. As he explained, "At university what happened was that I met a group of people, one of whom happened to be a vicar. . . . The others were more involved in politics and all of them were actually interested in religion, even if not religious themselves. It was really an awakening of ideas." He saw the bridge in these discussions between Christianity and politics: "I remember at university . . . for the first time realizing the part that social conditions played in shaping people." The loss of his mother gave Blair the determination to succeed; Christianity was becoming a motive force in his life. In these huge emotional upheavals some of those close to him would see the fusion of moral conviction and burning ambition that put the young man on the path to the premiership.

Blair's subsequent political career was built on the foundations of his religious faith and family. "He's the only prime minister I can recall who both believes in God and loves his family," is the observation of a close acquaintance. A long-standing personal friend from beyond the realm of politics observes that, during the many years of their friendship, three things have mattered to Blair: family, religion, and politics. Such judgments capture something vital about the style of Blair's political leadership and also mark him out from most of his peers in the crowded casino of modern British politics. For all the ancient churches and cathedrals that adorn the nation's towns and villages, Britain is a self-consciously secular society. In its political life, to be religious gen-

erally is to be suspect; to be visibly devoted to one's family, perhaps doubly so.

Students of politics have had to go back a long way to find an occupant of 10 Downing Street whose outlook was so obviously grounded in spiritual conviction. William Gladstone, who had held the office more than a century earlier as leader of the then Liberal Party, had been the last prime minister to put moral conscience visibly at the center of his politics. Gladstone, too, had kept a Bible by his bedside. The centrist Liberal Party had fallen from the center stage of British politics in the early decades of the twentieth century, a victim of the rise of the more left-leaning Labour. But Blair preferred to place himself in the company of these Liberals rather than in the pantheon of previous Labour leaders. He looked for reflections of his own career in Gladstone's premiership. The interventionism that was to inform British foreign policy at the start of the twenty-first century carried audible echoes of Gladstone's ethical internationalism during the 1880s. Unlike his distinguished predecessor from that Victorian age, Blair did not walk the streets of London accosting prostitutes in the hope of rescuing their souls. But friends did see an eagerness on his part to draw the parallel with his predecessor. "There is that definite nineteenth-century side to him," one says. "It's a part of him which sees a marriage between political belief, moral conscience, and public service."

Blair's Christianity was not a product of his childhood. While his wife, Cherie, hailed from a solidly Catholic family, and attended a convent school where prayer was built into every part of the teaching day, religion made far less conspicuous intrusions into Tony's early life. Hazel would sometimes take the children to church on Sunday mornings, and there were hymns and services at school. But these were incidental rather than central to his youth. Leo was agnostic, an outlook that was to harden into atheism after the death of his wife. Tony Blair entered into serious engagement with religion only when he reached Oxford.

To the young undergraduates who would gather in the evenings to debate the condition of the world, Peter Thomson was a particular in-

spiration. As a mature student of theology the Australian prelate was
already in his mid-thirties. But he was unstuffy and young in spirit. One
of Blair's contemporaries recalls that he defied the image of the dour
priest: "He was a rather charismatic figure. His mind was one of a per-
manent state of inquiry but he also had a great sense of fun." The future
prime minister and his friends would share Thomson's plentiful supply
of wine and cigarettes. He played superb tennis; Blair struggled to
match him. And he had a rumbustious sense of humor. His brand of
Christianity was at odds with the incense-burning High Anglicanism
of St. John's—one student recalls him delivering a particularly fiery ser-
mon in the college chapel after which Thomson was rarely seen again
in the pulpit. But to the young people preoccupied with the condition
of a world they would soon join as adults, his philosophical musings
seemed relevant—and refreshing. James Naughtie, the Scottish broad-
caster and writer, tells a nice story of the reverent Thomson's irrever-
ent sense of humor. By chance, the Australian priest had come to know
the Prince of Wales when the heir to the British throne was sent to
Australia to complete his schooling during the 1960s. Invited more
than twenty years later to attend a lunch with royal aides at Bucking-
ham Palace, Thomson was asked to pronounce on Charles's progress.
The future king was a "good bloke," the priest offered. But wasn't it a
pity that, at his public appearances, the next King of England always
looked "as if he had a carrot stuck up his arse." A long, regal silence fol-
lowed.

Thomson's view of Christianity was not drawn from the arcane ab-
stractions of learned theologians. Rather, he saw a faith demanding ac-
tion to improve the human condition as well as a spiritual relationship
with God. While there were elements here of the "liberation theology"
of the Jesuit missionaries who were then challenging authoritarian
regimes in Latin America, Thomson's source of inspiration was not
Karl Marx. Instead he looked to the connections between politics, phi-
losophy, and theology made by John Macmurray, a Scottish university
lecturer. Macmurray had taught at London and Edinburgh universities
during the 1930s and 1940s and, though not among the most cele-
brated of British philosophers, had written several books. His central

idea was the concept of "community"—the belief that individual self-realization depends on partnership with and trust of others. Macmurray challenged the then fashionable view that societies are entirely defined by the individuals within them. The relationship, he argued, was the other way around—individuals were shaped by their relationships with others in the communities in which they grew up. The family was central to this model, laying the foundation for the wider networks on which strong societies depended. Macmurray left a particularly strong impression on Tony Blair. The belief that individuals prosper in strong, mutually supportive communities later became the very core of Blair's political message, sitting easily alongside the Christian exhortation to "love thy neighbor as thyself." "If you really want to understand what I'm all about," Blair told an interviewer in 1994, "you have to take a look at a guy called John Macmurray. It's all there."

In the summer of 2003, Blair further explained how those late-night discussions at Oxford had proposed an answer to the eternal dilemma of the left in politics—how to ensure that active government is the friend rather than the enemy of individual fulfillment. "[Macmurray's work] was a powerful influence on me because it seemed to make sense of the need to involve the individual in society without the individual being subsumed in society. This is really, I think, the struggle the political left has been engaged in—how you retain the sense of solidarity without that becoming the collectivization of society, And so that concept struck me at the time as the right concept politically, as well as theologically." This was the very dilemma with which the Liberal prime ministers he so admired had wrestled—how to set the individual free to realize his potential while extending opportunity to the weak and the disadvantaged. The answer had been found by David Lloyd George, the founder of the welfare state in the first decade of the twentieth century. If the Gladstonian impulse was ever present in his foreign policy, Blair's domestic agenda owed a debt to Lloyd George.

Spurred by his dialogue with Thomson and his own awakening faith, Blair sought formal instruction from the chaplain at St. John's so that he could be confirmed as a full member of the Anglican Church. His contemporaries say that all this was done without fuss or fanfare,

as were Blair's Sunday morning attendances at the college chapel. Some were barely aware that Christianity had made such an impression on him, for evenings with Thomson were spent in philosophical discussion rather than in prayer. Nearly three decades on, one of his close aides in 10 Downing Street put it thus: "Christianity is not part of his day-to-day discourse. In that sense he is different from George W. Bush. But his faith is always there as the framework for his political thinking."

After Oxford, Thomson returned to Australia to a career that variously combined a religious ministry with teaching and cattle ranching. But the prelate and the soon-to-be politician remained firm friends. A few months before the general election victory that took Blair into 10 Downing Street in 1997, he and his family crossed the world to vacation on Thomson's ranch in the Australian outback. The following year Thomson returned to Britain, taking up for a time a Christian ministry near the Blair family home in North London to celebrate his student's political success.

Blair set out his thoughts on the synthesis of faith and politics in a short essay written in 1993, the year before he became the leader of the Labour Party. The article began with an assertion of his ecumenism, and of the parity of esteem that Christians should afford to other religions such as Islam and Judaism. From the beginning Blair disavowed the idea that the Christian faith conferred any degree of moral superiority on its followers. The history of the church, he said, was hardly free of blemishes. Nor was it for politicians try to "solve political problems by simplistic theological solutions." But, at its best, Christianity had inspired people for almost two thousand years to work for a more just and humane world. Drawing on his mentor, Macmurray, Blair stated that the Christian faith was about "the union between individual and community." It enshrined the belief that "we are not stranded in helpless isolation, but owe a duty both to others and to ourselves." Christ's teaching was that individuals flourished through communion with others: "The act of Holy Communion is symbolic of this message. It acknowledges that we do not grow up in total independence, but in-

terdependently." The values of the Labour Party, he concluded, rested on a belief in the importance of society and of solidarity with others. These were "closely intertwined with those of Christianity."

Some of these reflections drew on the teachings of Christian Socialism, which had long been an important strand in Labour's philosophy. Indeed, the book in which Blair's article was published had been the idea of John Smith, the then party leader and a long-standing Christian. Yet Blair's willingness to put his faith so close to the front of his politics was unusual, and for some of his colleagues it would always be unsettling. The line between righteousness and sanctimony is perilously thin, and Blair sometimes seemed to step across it. By championing the idea of moral absolutes, he also challenged the prevailing orthodoxy of the left. Thirty years earlier the social revolution of the 1960s had elbowed aside universal ethical judgments in favor of individual choice, a libertarianism that had carried through the 1970s and 1980s. Blair judged that the tide of moral relativism had flowed too fast and too far, and society now needed to rediscover its bearings.

For Tony Blair, religion coalesces with family. Mass on Sunday is a family affair. Visitors to the Blair apartment above the office in Downing Street have to tread carefully between the train sets, building blocks, and general infant chaos left by his youngest son. Leo, born in the summer of 2000, was a late addition to the family, a "happy accident" of middle age, as a proud but visibly shocked father put it at the time. The last prime minister to raise a young family in 10 Downing Street had been the leader of the then Liberal Party, Herbert Asquith, in the opening years of the twentieth century. The last to father a child while still in office had predated even Gladstone—the other claim to a place in the history books for Lord John Russell was reform of the nineteenth-century poor laws. A century and a half after Russell, the grounds of Chequers, the grand Tudor mansion outside London reserved for the use of the prime minister, were marked out with a soccer pitch. Regular weekend games pitted the prime minister and his two teenage sons against Downing Street staff and personal security officers. (As in politics, so, apparently in soccer—even when playing with

his family Blair prefers to run for goal rather than pass the ball.) The prime minister describes his family as the rock on which his career has been built. From the beginning of his political life, he has made time for his children. Now and then, less scrupulously, he has also pushed them into the public eye to promote his image as the thoroughly modern politician.

The prevailing winds had been blowing against social orthodoxy. Labour had become a torchbearer for those who chose forms of relationships other than marriage. Esteem for gays, single mothers, and those in less formal partnerships need not have put the party in opposition to marriage. But in the Britain of the 1980s it seemed to have done just that. Margaret Thatcher's Conservatives had fixed themselves in the public mind as the party that would stand up for the values of family life, while a vote for Labour seemed to be a vote for an alternative lifestyle. This was one of those dividing lines in British politics that Blair knew had to be erased if Labour was to rebuild its electoral support. "I have no doubt," he said in a speech a few months after the horrific murder of a two-year-old boy in 1993, "that the breakdown of law and order is intimately linked to the breakup of a strong sense of community. And the breakup of community in turn is, to a crucial degree, consequent on the breakdown of family life." The family, he continued, was the first place that people learned the rules of social behavior: "It is largely from family discipline that social discipline and a sense of responsibility is learned." Personal preference joined neatly here with political purpose. Many times during his career, Blair's principles would sit in happy alignment with his political ambitions—to pursue the former was to advance the latter. There was a measure of coincidence, as well as one of expediency. In any event, respect for the traditional model of the family chimed perfectly with the values of the citizens of Middle Britain, who on issues like the family, social disorder, and crime were conservative with a small "c."

Blair's Christian faith is hard-edged—optimistic about the condition of the human soul but demanding duty to others as well as devotion to God. The idea of sin, he once said, had gone out of fashion. "Yet the concept is simple and important. In theological terms, it is alienation

from God. In everyday terms, it is acknowledgment of right and wrong. It is the rejection of the purely libertarian ethos. This is an area that will become of increasing importance in politics." Soon after his election as Labour leader in July 1994, he began to rewrite his party's values. Labour's social policy, he said, would henceforth be based on "common sense" rather than ideology. He attacked the Conservatives for "stigmatizing" single parents, but he went on to declare that adults should not choose to have children outside stable relationships. A Labour government would treat the family as "the essential, stable social unit." For their part, parents would have to recognize responsibilities as well as rights in the upbringing of their children. To many of the voters of Middle Britain, this might have seemed a statement of the unremarkable. But no other Labour leader could or would have put it quite so bluntly.

Blair drew on his Christianity to confront another issue that had troubled Labour leaders. For many on the left of British politics, the goal of equality was the touchstone of political faith. Even if their heads told them that society would never actually reach this utopian state, their hearts said Labour must always travel toward it. But the ideal put principle and pragmatism in permanent conflict, and compromise inevitably became synonymous with betrayal. The party's history carried deep scars from a protracted ideological struggle about how precisely equality should be defined. Did it mean that everyone must be equal in all respects? Was the aim equality of income, or wealth? Or was equality of opportunity enough? Even those Labour leaders who paid lip service to the principle recognized the impossibility of achieving it in a modern democracy. But they also knew that to abandon this was to lose their support from the left.

As the left strengthened its hold on the party during the 1970s, all kinds of lunacies were justified in the name of the long march to the promised land of a truly equal society. By way of insight into the frustrations this caused politicians like Blair during the early 1980s, a friend of the prime minister from those times recounts the story of one such absurdity. A Labour-controlled district council, he recalled, had decided to build a new municipal apartment block on a site overlooking

a leafy park in East London. The apartments would be rented at subsidized rates to people on low incomes. Reviewing the plans, the local politicians could see that only half of the apartments would enjoy the glorious view over the park, while the rest would look out over a grim industrial landscape–an obvious affront to equality. So the plans were redrawn and the block turned 90 degrees to stand perpendicular to the park. Although every apartment was now denied sight of the lush grass and trees, the council could proudly declare that every tenant was equal in his misery.

For Tony Blair the quest for the impossible had become the enemy of progress, not just in decisions about apartment blocks but through the entire range of provisions for mainstream public services, such as health and education. He offered a different perspective on equality. The ideal, he said, was central to Christianity, for as the Gospels showed, everyone was equal in the sight of God. But "this does not mean we are uniform in position or character but rather that, despite our differences, we are entitled to be treated equally, without regard to wealth, race, gender, or standing in society. We should all have the opportunity to make the most of ourselves." Here was a redefinition of Labour's historic goal that sat far more comfortably with the voters of Middle Britain. Blair the devout Christian was also Blair the adroit politician, even though his political opponents would find in this another example of the way he cloaked expediency in the guise of ethics.

Blair has never denied, though, the compromises politicians make with their consciences–the endless pull between principle and pragmatism. In the spring of 1996 the Labour leader offered an intriguing insight into his thinking when he wrote in a newspaper article about the message Christians might take from the celebration of Easter. The story he told was of Saint Matthew's description of Jesus being brought before Pontius Pilate for judgment. The familiar characterization of Pilate is as someone who put self before justice–his washing of his hands being testimony to an indifference to the fate of others. But the story, Blair suggested, was a more complicated one. Pilate was fascinating because he was so obviously human and imperfect, torn between belief and political reality. He was intriguing to the extent that he tried to do

the good thing rather than the bad: "One can imagine him agonizing, seeing that Jesus had done nothing wrong, and wishing to release him. Just as easily, however, one can envisage Pilate's advisers telling him of the risks, warning him not to cause a riot or inflame Jewish opinion." That made the story, the future prime minister concluded, "a timeless parable of political life."

On other occasions his faith stirred unwanted controversy. Though confirmed as an Anglican, he would regularly attend Catholic mass with Cherie, who had insisted the children be brought up in the Church of Rome. Blair's habit of taking the sacrament of communion with his family, however, caused consternation among the Catholic hierarchy, and questions were raised by his local priest after the conservative papacy of John Paul II toughened the rules on the participation of non-Catholics in the church's rites. Eventually Cardinal Basil Hume, then head of the Catholic Church in England, wrote to the prime minister asking him, as an Anglican, to forgo the sacrament when he chose to attend Catholic mass. Blair replied courteously that he would, of course, comply with this seemingly narrow-minded edict. But he could not resist a small protest at the ruling, asking the cardinal, "I wonder what Jesus would make of it?"

Many years later, on the eve of the war against Iraq in the spring of 2003, Blair accepted an invitation from Pope John Paul II to stay overnight with his family at the Vatican. It was a rare meeting between a British prime minister and the Catholic pontiff; Winston Churchill had been the last to be granted such an extended papal audience. Blair's visit was the more extraordinary because only a week earlier the pope had attacked the American and British plan to remove Saddam Hussein as a "crime against humanity." The pontiff had also been shown on television clasping the hand of Tariq Aziz, the Catholic deputy prime minister of Saddam's regime and one of its most infamous apologists. On his return to London, Blair said nothing publicly of his private conversations at the Holy See. He was silent, too, on the subject of whether the pope had offered him communion at the private mass he had celebrated for the family in the Vatican—though one of the prime minister's friends said he was sure that on this occasion John

Paul had indeed ignored his own edict. Blair's aides were uncomfortable about the meeting, one senior staffer brushing it off as "Cherie's trip." All questions as to whether pope and prime minister had discussed the looming conflict in the Gulf were met with a brusque "No comment." Yet it is hard to believe that Blair had not indeed taken the opportunity to make the case for war, for in the prime minister's mind, ending the tyranny in Iraq was a moral cause fully in accord with the teachings on just wars of Saint Augustine and Thomas Aquinas.

Blair has always looked for spiritual enlightenment beyond, as well as within, the walls of Christianity. No one religion, he believes, has a unique claim on the human conscience. Michael (later Lord) Levy, a long-standing family friend who went on to become Labour's chief fund-raiser and the prime minister's personal emissary in the Middle East peace process, recalls Blair's early interest in Judaism. "He was always fascinated by the Jewish faith. He would come over to our house sometimes for Sabbath dinner on Friday evenings. He enjoyed the rituals. But he was intrigued, too, by Islam." Even before the terrorist attacks on America on September 11, 2001, raised fears of a new clash of civilizations between the Christian and Islamic worlds, Blair had started to study the Koran. He wanted to understand what made this holy text so compelling to so many hundreds of millions of people around the world. The Koran, he said in the spring of 2000, identified "love and fellowship" as "the guiding spirits of humanity." It came as no surprise, then, when in the wake of September 11, Blair put himself at the forefront of those who insisted that the war against Osama bin Laden's terrorist network was not an assault on Islam. Rather, the terrorists who had killed so many innocents in America had defiled the peaceful intent of the Koran. The prime minister's record as the most determined Western leader in defending the Muslims of Kosovo against Serbia's Slobodan Milosevic gave him much credibility in that respect. The common roots of Islam, Judaism, and Christianity became a constant theme of his speeches and interviews. "Jews, Muslims and Christians," he often said, were "all children of Abraham." Barry Cox, a close friend, says the theme has long been part of his private conversa-

tion: "He will say to you that if you look beyond the rituals, almost all religions share the same fundamental values."

All this sits oddly in Britain's political discourse, where there is no custom of leaders whose politics are informed by religion. The irony, of course, is that Britain's unwritten constitution affords the Anglican Church a highly privileged place in the affairs of the state. Ever since King Henry VIII broke with the papacy during the sixteenth century, the monarch has carried the title of "defender of the faith." The present Queen Elizabeth II is thus the church's titular head. Anglican bishops have their own seats in the House of Lords, Parliament's second chamber. For all that, politicians have long shunned public entanglement with matters spiritual. Harold Macmillan, a Conservative prime minister during the early 1960s, spoke for an enduring consensus when he said that politicians should leave questions of personal morality to the nation's bishops and priests. So the pulpit and the political podium have by and large been kept at a distance, and votes on ethical issues such as the death penalty, divorce, gay rights, abortion, and the age of consent have usually been on a bipartisan basis. When political parties have sought to include such issues of conscience in their official election platforms–as has the Conservative opposition party in recent years–the result has usually been internal strife.

During the approach to war with Iraq, Blair was discomfited several times by an implication that his judgment may have been colored by his religious faith. He was asked twice in television interviews whether he had prayed with President Bush during their meetings in the White House and Camp David. Was removing Saddam, in other words, a shared moral mission? The prime minister's answer on both occasions was "No." His visible unease, though, was striking. Such sensitivities surfaced again soon after the war, when an American journalist interviewing Blair pressed him on whether his decisions had been shaped by religious beliefs. Alistair Campbell, Blair's senior media adviser, intervened and replied, "We don't do God. I'm sorry. We don't do God." Campbell, an avowed atheist, was gently cautioning the prime minis-

ter, for there was the obvious risk of alienating Britain's sizable Muslim population. But beyond that, British political leaders would be unwise to claim they have God on their side. Blair was reminded of this when drafting his television address to the nation to announce the start of the war in March 2003. The prime minister wanted to end his short speech with a simple "God bless you." His aides rebelled—the tone, they said, was self-righteous, sanctimonious. Blair eventually wisely signed off with a bland "Thank you." The occasions that saw him confuse the roles of politician and prelate almost always jarred. When he launched his election campaign for a second term in office in the summer of 2001, the prime minister was pictured surrounded by children at a London school, hands clasped, singing from a hymn book. Behind him was a stained-glass window. But the British do not want sermons from their politicians, and the satirists' most wounding image of Blair is that of a sanctimonious preacher. (The pompous, self-serving "Vicar of St. Albion" is a favorite character in the satirical magazine *Private Eye*.)

In truth, Tony Blair is at once defensive and unapologetic about his Christian faith. He understands the dangers of seeming to claim a monopoly on moral wisdom. He has been careful to ensure that his own ethical canons do not intrude on the personal choices of others. For all his belief in moral absolutes and his unabashed authoritarianism on crime, he does not see it as the role of the state to impose ethical choices on the individual. His voting record on issues such as the age of consent, gay rights, and abortion has been liberal. Yet his Christianity infuses both the style and substance of his politics, and, despite the popular suspicion of self-righteous politicians, it has been central to his success. "It underpins his reasoning for being in politics," his friend Barry Cox says. "There is a nineteenth-century side to him which sees a marriage between belief and public service." For all that England's churches have long stood half-empty on Sunday mornings, Blair's espousal of such values was vital in building the electoral coalition that swept him into 10 Downing Street.

Blair's emphasis on values, as against policies, confuses political allies and opponents alike. He has often been described as a politician

lacking ideology, a reproach that lost much of force after his reelection in the summer of 2001. During his second term, the prime minister became an altogether more confident, tougher politician, as shown by his refusal to compromise over Iraq. But, in any event, the charge misses the fundamental point about Blair's political compass: he has consistently and consciously rejected the familiar manifestations of political ideology. Most politicians define themselves relative to an accumulated collection of ideas and policies drawn along the traditional axis of left and right. The things that matter for them are the precise limits or otherwise on the market economy, the size of the state, tax rates, welfare benefits, where the line is drawn in social policy between the public and private spheres of society. Blair starts with a clean sheet of paper. His question is not whether public provision is good and private bad, or indeed vice versa. Far more important are the values that inform political choices—in his case the spread of opportunity and the creation of a more cohesive community. "It is not that I don't have an ideology," he said in July 2003. "I have a very powerful set of beliefs, but they are not stereotypical in terms of the left-right divide. But then whose are nowadays—except those people who are usually in opposition?" That last phrase is revealing. While the moral seriousness is an undoubted strength, the high principles also sit alongside an acute perception of the politics of power.

Cherie Booth came from a different place. Tony Blair's childhood, if marked by family misfortune, was relatively secure. His wife made it the hard way. Like her husband, she trained as a lawyer, but her journey to the top of the legal profession was much tougher. Brought up by her mother and grandparents in a low-income district of Liverpool in northern England, Cherie knew from early on the meaning of struggle. Her actor father deserted his wife and children when she was nine. Tony Booth, who would later become something of a television personality, preferred fleeting fame, alcohol, and a string of other women to the role of father to Cherie and her sister. He returned as an interested parent only much later, when Blair's political ascent put the couple in the public spotlight. By then Cherie had a clutch of half sisters.

There were no fee-paying schools during her childhood, just the scholarships that came with hard work and ambition. At school Cherie was advanced into classes a year ahead of her age group. She secured a degree summa cum laude from the London School of Economics and went on to comfortably outshine her husband in their legal examinations. Later, as a Queen's Counsel, she would join the exclusive club of the nation's top lawyers and take her first step toward the judges' bench. The woman who emerged from all this was fiercely intelligent, unbiddable, and curiously insecure.

When Tony and Cherie first started going out in the late 1970s, friends in their close circle judged that she would be the one who made her way in politics. A year younger than Tony, she had signed up as a socialist at the age of sixteen; Blair, who had eschewed the Conservative leanings of his father, did not join the Labour Party until 1975. Cherie's socialism was part of the family inheritance, as central to her life as her mother's Catholicism. Husband and wife attended political meetings together in the early 1980s. A long-standing friend recalls that Cherie's grasp of politics and her emotional attachment to the left were patently stronger than her husband's. If during these early years friends were always a little unsure whether, in his heart, Tony really wanted a political career, no one doubted Cherie's serious intent. Luck, however, played its hand to her husband's advantage. While he secured the candidacy for the safe Labour district of Sedgefield in the 1983 general election, the best Cherie could find was an unwinnable Conservative constituency.

Blair had left Oxford in the summer of 1975, traveling to London to begin his apprenticeship as a lawyer. He sought, with the help of old school connections, a place in the legal practice of Alexander Irvine, a well-established barrister specializing in employment law. (In the British system, barristers are the advocates who appear in higher courts and, though independent, work together in different "chambers.") Irvine had initially been reluctant to employ the young graduate from St. John's. He had already hired one young "pupil" for that year, Cherie Booth, who in his judgment had a better university degree and a sharper mind. Blair's enthusiasm, though, won him over. The young

would-be lawyer had already learned how to deploy the charm that would be central to his political success. So Irvine found places in his firm for both pupils, unwittingly assuming the role of matchmaker as well as employer. Blair was later lavish in his praise of his mentor, stating, "He taught me how to think." After the 1997 election, Irvine was amply rewarded by his former pupil with a seat in the House of Lords and, until 2003, the post of lord chancellor, the head of the nation's judicial system.

For Tony and Cherie, romance led to marriage in 1980 in the chapel of St. John's. Both now looking to politics as a career, they struck a family bargain: whoever got to Parliament first would have the support of the other. Charm and luck, along with judicious use of friends and contacts, helped Tony win the bet. By the time he applied for the Labour candidacy at Sedgefield, just weeks before the 1983 general election, the selection contest had formally closed. But Irvine's law practice had strong links with Labour-supporting trade unions—much of its work involved representing the unions in employment disputes—and strings were pulled among union chiefs to keep the shortlist open. Blair then used every ounce of his energy and persuasiveness to win over local party activists. John Burton, a branch secretary in the constituency who would become Blair's agent and a lifelong friend, had harbored parliamentary ambitions of his own. But as he told one of Blair's early biographers, "As soon as I met Tony . . . I knew that he was the chap to take the party forward and not myself. That he was better able to take the party forward and change the party than I would be." So it was left to Cherie to run the family—and, as a successful lawyer, to bring in an income more substantial than that paid to members of Britain's parliament. The couple's first son, Euan, was born in January 1984. Nicholas arrived at the end of the following year, and Kathryn in 1988. Euan was already fifteen when, as much to the Blairs' surprise as to that of the outside world, Cherie announced that she was pregnant again, with Leo.

The similarities between Bill Clinton and Tony Blair are inescapable—two successful politicians of the center-left, both with intelligent, educated, and ambitious wives who put aside their own political ambitions

for their husbands. In each case, too, the wife seems to be to the left of the husband. Cherie, who chose as a rising lawyer to specialize in human rights cases, has long been seen by some of his aides as the prime minister's conscience. She is unabashed about accepting legal cases that challenge legislation passed by the government her husband leads. She has also taken sharp issue with Blair's insistence that more criminal offenders should be jailed. Staffers recall the day Cherie paid a visit to a prison as part of the training for the judiciary. She returned to 10 Downing Street to harangue her husband on the appalling conditions in which people were incarcerated—and to suggest that he find better ways to halt the rising crime rate than simply filling the already overcrowded prisons. During the Clinton presidency, the wives joined their husbands as intellectual equals for the frequent seminars and dinners at the White House or at Chequers, the prime minister's country house. Hillary and Cherie, one Downing Street aide remarked, were as much a part of the debates as Bill and Tony—insofar, that is, as the president's energy and enthusiasm left room for anyone else to contribute.

In the words of a close family friend, "Cherie is more tribal in her politics than Tony," much like Hillary. Blair's brand of inclusive politics and a temperament that abhors personal conflict ("he hates arguments," is the repeated refrain of his staff) have led him to build friendships across the political spectrum. Even Silvio Berlusconi, the Italian prime minister whose coalition government includes a party that harks back to the Fascists, is a frequent guest at 10 Downing Street. Cherie takes a less forgiving view of those on the other side of the political fence. When George W. Bush won the White House in 2000, Blair was characteristically pragmatic: Bush might be a Texan Republican, but it was the duty of a British prime minister to get along with him. Cherie and some of those around her were far less sanguine about the Supreme Court decision that handed Bush the keys to the White House. Al Gore had been "robbed" of the presidency, she believed, and she was hostile to the idea of her husband "cozying up" to the new American president.

Cherie has never disguised the fact that she holds strong views. Within the privacy of the couple's Downing Street apartment, she is

forceful in expressing them—sometimes supportive, but just as often challenging her husband's policies. Friends who dine with the prime ministerial couple are sometimes taken aback by the sharpness of her critiques. But Cherie's fundamental loyalty to her husband is unquestioned. During the first few years of his term, she stayed largely in the background, preferring charity work to active engagement in politics. She would occasionally chair prime ministerial seminars in Downing Street, but on issues safely removed from the front line of political controversy. But she was also fiercely protective of Tony. One manifestation of this was an increasingly icy relationship with Gordon Brown, the chancellor of the exchequer and the family's Downing Street neighbor. After the 1997 election victory Brown was ever impatient to succeed Blair in the top job. Cherie was equally determined that her husband would never be pressured into stepping aside prematurely. Brown, she was often heard to say, would have to wait. And wait. Another glimpse of the wife battling for her husband came in the early months of 2003, when Blair's leadership was threatened by the looming conflict with Iraq. Cherie was prominent among those convincing wavering members of Parliament to come back into the Blair fold.

Yet the parallels between the Blairs and the Clintons can be stretched too far. The U.S. president is head of state, and his spouse bears the official title of first lady. In Britain, the Queen fulfills both functions. The prime minister is merely head of government—there is no official recognition of his or her partner. The spouse's role traditionally has been ornamental—to appear at the prime minister's side at official dinners and to travel to interminable summit meetings overseas. Downing Street has nothing approximating the first lady's office in the White House. Denis Thatcher, husband to Margaret, was often held up as the model consort—frequently seen, as he put it, but almost never heard.

Cherie Blair would learn that playing this role was harder than it seemed. On the morning of May 2, 1997, she opened the door to the family's North London home, having snatched a few hours' sleep after her husband's stunning election victory. Now, bleary-eyed as she ac-

cepted flowers from a well-wisher, she was momentarily blinded by a hundred flashbulbs. Still dressed in her nightgown, her hair awry, Cherie had discovered what it was to be wife of a prime minister. Henceforth she would live three quite different lives: as lawyer, as wife and mother, and as prime ministerial consort, all of them in the public gaze. When the family crossed the threshold of 10 Downing Street, she fully intended to pursue her legal career. A paid nanny, and her mother, Gale, would help with the children. She also decided–though this was a resolution sometimes honored in the breach–to stay out of the glare of all those flashbulbs.

The combination of roles, however, often seemed an unhappy one. Once Blair's political honeymoon had come to an end, the Conservative-leaning tabloid press saw criticism of Cherie as a way to undermine her husband. Blair had assiduously courted his natural opponents in the press, and for a time the tactic worked. But deeper political allegiances soon enough reasserted themselves among the most stridently Conservative newspapers, and Cherie became a frequent target of their invective. Occasionally she was the author of her own misfortunes, most often on the subject of money. Those who knew Cherie well said her childhood had thrown up a bundle of contradictions. The staff in 10 Downing Street was divided between those who saw an earthy, unaffected woman never happier than when bursting into one of her favorite Beatles songs, and others who witnessed an increasingly imperious consort, dumping old friends, overimpressed by the glamour and glitz and determined, in the phrase of one, that "she'll never again have to check in her own luggage at the airport." There were behind-the-scenes arguments about money and about Cherie's eagerness to accept the hospitality of wealthy benefactors. In spite of her own substantial income, her husband's official salary, and his huge earning potential in life beyond politics, Cherie fretted about the family's financial position. "It's been a long journey from Crosby [Liverpool]," she once said. "And I am always conscious of that." Perhaps unwisely, Blair, too, had acknowledged his wife's insecurities. "Her childhood means Cherie doesn't take money for granted. Like lots of people who come from

virtually nothing, I think there is a lurking anxiety it might all disappear one day," he had said in interview before they reached Downing Street.

Once there, parsimony clashed with the urge for glamour. Cherie had always been careless of her appearance, with a preference for jeans and baggy pullovers instead of cocktail dresses. As prime ministerial consort she was soon sparing little expense on her wardrobe. A personal trainer and self-styled "lifestyle consultant" were hired; Cherie insisted that her personal hairdresser accompany her on official trips overseas. Even as she worried about how the family would pay the bills, she developed a taste for expensive designer clothes. The result was a series of disputes with government officials about which expenses would be paid from the public purse. She was heard to complain that she had to spend £20,000 ($33,000) a year from her personal income to pay for outfits for overseas engagements. (In Britain, the rules on such matters are strict—sometimes absurdly so. Visitors to 10 Downing Street tempted to take an apple or orange from the prime minister's fruit bowl would probably think twice if they knew that Tony Blair had to pick up the bill.) More than once Cherie clashed with officialdom over what could legitimately be charged to the taxpayer. She was furious when told that the family would do better to pay for its own vacations rather than accept the hospitality of friends. She believed the couple had sacrificed significant wealth in the cause of public service. The sale of their North London house after the 1997 election—Blair was told that security considerations demanded that the family move into Downing Street—was a particularly sore point. A subsequent house price boom saw the couple forgo a substantial financial windfall. Money, friends said, was also the most frequent source of dispute with her husband.

For all her initial resolve to stay in the background, Cherie soon found she enjoyed the limelight. The working-class girl from Liverpool was now a regular guest at the homes of the rich and famous. In the summer of 2000 a drunken spree with his teenage friends saw the Blairs' son Euan arrested by police after he was found lying facedown in a London square. Though these things commonly happen to teenagers, the

family's embarrassment was compounded by the fact that Euan had been left to fend for himself while Cherie had borrowed the Portuguese vacation home of Cliff Richard, a former British pop star. This complex of tensions between background and money, fame and privacy, came to a head in the autumn of 2002. For two weeks the family's personal affairs were splashed over the front pages of the newspapers, a furor that ended with a humiliating public apology from Cherie to the prime minister's staff and the media. The controversy exposed a curious friendship: Cherie had met Carole Caplin many years earlier when her husband's career was pushing them into the public gaze, and Caplin had offered advice on Cherie's appearance, suggesting an exercise regime, different diets, and alternative therapies, and helping Cherie to choose her clothes. The two became close. "Cherie was a cheerful working mother of three. She was slightly overweight, wore jeans and T-shirts, and had 'the dress' for special occasions," one friend says. "When Tony became leader she was panned in the media. Carole started dressing her properly, and the press applauded. No wonder Cherie became dependent on her." "Dependent" was an apt description. Caplin was soon being paid handsomely as Cherie's "lifestyle adviser." Officials raised concerns about Caplin's unconventional background as a topless model, her circle of friends, and her obvious thirst for publicity. Cherie ignored them, telling her husband's aides that she would choose her own friends.

The relationship burst into the press when it was disclosed that Cherie had accepted financial advice from Carole's lover, Peter Foster, who turned out to be a convicted con man and fraudster. The labyrinthine details of the transactions, which involved the wholly legitimate purchase of two apartments—one for the couple's eldest son, Euan, the other as an investment—were scarcely relevant. What hurt was that Cherie had been less than candid about Foster's role when she instructed her husband's officials to deny that Foster had acted as her financial adviser. To compound things, it sooned emerged that Foster was facing deportation proceedings in the British courts and that Cherie had inquired as to which judge would likely hear the case. Although there was much political malice and sensational innuendo in

the media furor, Cherie had made a serious misjudgment in seeking to obfuscate. Her press secretary, Fiona Millar–partner of the prime minister's communications director, Alistair Campbell–made little secret of her dismay at Cherie's behavior. Campbell suggested that the prime minister could be protected from such squalls only by his wife's withdrawal from public life. At Cherie's insistence, Tony refused. The storm eventually abated when Cherie made a televised statement apologizing for the confusion. But the incident had carried a cost for the prime minister as well as his wife. The couple had discovered the perils that lie at the intersection between the public and the personal in modern politics. The blurring of the line between the two had hitherto worked to Tony Blair's advantage. Early on, his marriage and family were a huge political advantage, one that he exploited. His children, he would often say, "drive you mad but keep you sane." All this reinforced his image as just the sort of levelheaded, "normal" person who would make a good prime minister. His faith seemed to carry the same message: he was a Labour leader apart from his own party, one in tune with the moral mood of Middle Britain. But not everything in the Blair household was quite so perfect. And, once invited into the private lives and thoughts of the family, the media would not willingly leave.

3. THE OUTSIDER

THE YOUNG LAWYER who arrived at Westminster in June 1983 did so with mixed emotions. His election as Labour MP for the northern English constituency, or seat, of Sedgefield had been a personal triumph. Just past celebrating his thirtieth birthday, he was Labour's youngest MP. The political demography of Sedgefield, a new electoral district created as a result of boundary changes, assured him of a place for life in the House of Commons. Older colleagues on the green leather benches at Westminster had spent many years, sometimes decades, in the quest for such a "safe" seat. Blair, by contrast, had been charmed. He had joined the Labour Party only seven years previously when he had come to London to begin a career in the law. In 1982 he had stood for election in another district after the death of the Conservative MP for Beaconsfield in southern England. He had lost, badly. But prosperous Beaconsfield had been the freehold property of the Tory party for as long as anyone could remember. Blair had entered that particular contest only to gain experience and show enthusiasm for the fight. The candidacy for Sedgefield, a stone's throw from his former home in Durham, had been an unexpectedly generous reward. To the many threads that one can draw through Tony Blair's life in politics–conviction, self-belief, ambition among them–one must also include luck. Perhaps politicians make their own good fortune. But either way, Providence has been one of Blair's reliable friends.

Personal satisfaction, however, mingled with the dismal realization that his arrival in Parliament had come at the moment of one of his party's most devastating defeats. Four years earlier, in 1979, Margaret Thatcher had ousted the Labour government of James Callaghan by winning a majority of 43 seats in the House of Commons. In the 1983

election the Conservatives' parliamentary majority soared to 144. Labour had only itself to blame for its crushing defeat, standing on a manifesto or platform that Gerald Kaufman, one of its own MPs, would famously, and aptly, describe as "the longest suicide note in history." Blair's chosen party was fracturing. In 1980 a group of the party's most senior MPs, dismayed by Labour's lurch to the socialist left, had broken away to form the centrist Social Democratic Party (SDP). Among them were distinguished former ministers such as Roy Jenkins, Shirley Williams, and David Owen. Now, in loose alliance with the small Liberal Party, the SDP had polled almost as many votes in the 1983 general election as Labour. The hope of the renegades—and for a time it seemed an entirely reasonable one—was to displace Labour as the principal party of opposition at the following general election.

The "suicide note" manifesto had shown that the political leaders of the left in Britain had learned nothing from the 1979 defeat—quite the reverse. Then, the Labour government had been turned out of office amid the industrial and public service chaos caused by overmighty trade (labor) unions, constant strikes, and internecine war over economic policy. The so-called winter of discontent that had brought down the Labour government of James Callaghan had seen rubbish pile up in the streets, the transport network paralyzed, and, shockingly, the dead go unburied because of a wave of walkouts by the unions. Thatcher had promised to tame the unions, curb inflation, reduce taxes, and cut back the size of the state. Striking the note that would resonate throughout her premiership, she pledged to break the shackles of government. Her analysis was that the people of Britain had had enough of big government and union disputes. Labour's traditional supporters among the less affluent were as frustrated as the middle classes by the party's apparent disdain for self-advancement. The brilliant emblem of Thatcher's strategy was a promise that working people would be allowed to buy, at a substantial discount, the houses and apartments they rented from municipal authorities. Britain would become a nation of homeowners, she declared. The tide of history, the defeated Callaghan acknowledged, had turned against big government in favor of the politics of individual aspiration.

In 1983 the newly elected Labour MP for Sedgefield saw the strength of her appeal. After all, his own father had joined the Conservatives as a mark of his achievement in escaping the poverty of his past. Now Leo Blair was an unabashed admirer of Margaret Thatcher, continuing to vote for her even as his son opposed her government in Parliament. Like the rest of his party, Tony Blair had signed up to the 1983 manifesto, but his doubts were already clear. The original purpose of the Labour Party had been to protect workers from exploitation by the capitalist barons who ran the economy at the turn of the twentieth century. Winning power, the trade unions that had founded the party decided, was the means to that end. But by the late 1970s this original goal had all but been lost. Blair, even at the very beginning of his political career, grasped the fact that an addiction to public ownership and to high government spending and taxes often stood in opposition to, rather than in support of, the aspirations of Labour's natural supporters. "I learned a lot from my father about why people didn't vote Labour," the prime minister said in the late summer of 2003. "My father was a foster child in a poor family, a working-class boy who became a Conservative. And why did he become a Conservative? Because, he used to say to me, 'Because Labour holds you back, it doesn't want you to succeed, it doesn't want you to do well.' So these things were all formative influences in me." One of the legacies of such childhood lessons was that "I think I have a very, very strong set of values, but a diminished sense of preconception about how those values should be translated into practice."

Thatcher's 1983 victory rested in part on her military success a year earlier in driving Argentina from the British-owned Falkland Islands in the South Atlantic. The restoration of British rule in the Falklands capital of Port Stanley—against the odds, and against the wishes of some in Ronald Reagan's administration in Washington—had cemented Thatcher's reputation as the "Iron Lady" of Western politics. But the fact that she secured a bigger majority in spite of the deep economic recession of the early 1980s and a sharply rising unemployment rate also testified to the changing shape of the nation's politics. The decline of once-great industries such as coal and steel, shipbuilding, and automo-

bile manufacturing as Britain embraced the service economy was breaking the familiar patterns of political allegiance. The former social and political divisions of a profoundly class-based society were crumbling, and with them the tribal loyalties that had once assured Labour of an army of loyal voters in the nation's industrial heartlands.

Under the sincere but feeble leadership of Michael Foot, the Labour Party was simply not listening. Instead of tacking toward the political center ground in response to what was to become the Thatcher revolution, Foot led his party still further to the left. Extraordinary though it later seemed, Labour fought the 1983 election on a platform of withdrawal from the European Union (dubbed a "capitalist club"), unilateral disposal of Britain's nuclear deterrent, and wholesale nationalization of major industries and banks. The perplexing question, many thought afterward, was why nearly 28 percent of the electorate had actually voted for such full-blooded socialism. Blair would later disavow any personal attachment to the party's manifesto. And, to be sure, there were few points on its unashamedly socialist map that showed up on his personal political compass. In his first, or "maiden," speech to the House of Commons he did defer to the party line by describing himself as a "socialist," a word that would later appear only sparingly in his personal political lexicon. But for an ambitious young politician, climbing onto the first rungs of the ladder demanded awkward compromises, and signing up for a political program that bore more than a passing resemblance to those of Moscow's eastern European satellites had been one of the more painful.

Having looked over the precipice, Blair's party now took a step back. Neil Kinnock replaced the defeated Michael Foot as leader. A politician originally of the left, with the fiery rhetorical style of his Welsh forefathers, Kinnock began to provide brave leadership to a party that had become unleadable as well as unelectable. He confronted the Trotskyists who had infiltrated and taken over many of Labour's local organizations. The 1983 manifesto was torn up, and Kinnock began the painstaking and painfully slow process of constructing a more attractive prospectus.

Blair's arrival at Westminster, meanwhile, coincided with that of a brilliant young Scottish politician, Gordon Brown. The two hailed from entirely different backgrounds—Blair, for all that he had been born in Edinburgh, from the English middle classes, Brown from the hair-shirt tradition of Scottish Presbyterianism. To all intents and purposes Blair was still an amateur in his new trade, a lawyer who had decided to seek his fortune in Parliament. Brown, dark-haired and with the frown and physical build of the rugby player he had once been, exuded the seriousness that marked out those with a political mission. Two years older than Blair, he had prepared for this moment for most of his life, rising through student politics and into the high ranks of the Scottish Labour Party before reaching Parliament. By contrast, Blair, six feet tall but slim and wearing a perpetual smile, seemed to travel light. Brown spent his evenings buried deep in the writings of the prophets of the Labour movement. Blair preferred time with his young family.

This was the beginning, though, of what would become the most powerful partnership in British postwar politics. Fifteen years later Blair and Brown would be neighbors in Downing Street, prime minister and chancellor of the exchequer respectively, and authors of the most sweeping changes in their party's history. Later still, the tensions and rivalry between them would threaten to crack the foundations of the new party they had created. But in these early days they shared a cramped office, more a cubbyhole, tucked behind a corridor in the House of Commons. Brown was the teacher, already steeped in the byzantine ways and well practiced in the endless power games of Labour politics. Blair took the role of the ever-eager pupil turned talented advocate who could grasp instinctively the sharpest points in any argument and present a convincing case before the jury of public opinion. At one in the recognition that Labour had to change or die, they became friends as well as allies in the cause of modernization.

The pair rose swiftly as Neil Kinnock sought to wrench Labour back into the world of political reality. Kinnock was proud of his young Turks. "You watch Blair," he said on one occasion in the 1980s. "He's got guts." The talents that would later propel Blair into the leadership

were already beginning to form. Fresh-faced and unburdened by a left-wing past, he had a style designed to reassure and win over those in the media and in business who had come to count themselves among Labour's natural enemies. His youthful air played to his advantage, for opponents tended to underestimate him, and in the dawning age of personality politics his telegenic good looks made him a natural spokesman for Kinnock's assertion that the party was changing. Successive election defeats had driven Labour back into its Celtic strongholds of Scotland and Ireland. While the party still held seats in England's poorer inner-city areas, there were vast swathes of suburban and rural England where it was impossible to find a Labour MP. These were the homes of the aspirant and the middle classes, and in appearance, accent, and temperament Tony Blair seemed to be on their side. Roy Hattersley, the senior figure in Kinnock's team to whom Blair reported, described him in a newspaper interview as "hugely industrious." He also noted his impatience for victory. "He was always saying that there was no point in doing things if we didn't win."

With experience came the confidence to challenge traditionalists among his colleagues at Westminster. Blair could never match the dawn-to-dark work rate of Gordon Brown–he and Cherie were starting a family–but the MP for Sedgefield had the capacity for hard, concentrated work and the lawyer's talent for assembling his case. In the chamber of the House of Commons, a rowdy, rumbustious place where the reputations and careers of British politicians are made or, just as often, broken, Blair won plaudits for his forensic skills and for his habit of taking opponents by surprise. He had limits as an orator–Brown was the stronger speaker in the mortal combat of House of Commons debate–but Blair knew how to wound his opponents and thus command attention.

Those outside politics who came to know Blair during this time–and he was as assiduous in courting the media as some of his more left-wing colleagues were angrily disdainful of what they saw as a Tory-biased press–caught a glimpse of many of the traits that would later define his

political leadership. In arguments about policy, he had the lawyer's predilection of going back to first principles, an approach he had learned from Alexander Irvine. While others would argue interminably about the detail of this or that policy, Blair would start with a question: What was the party seeking to achieve? Work out the end, he would say, before you debate the means. His constant refrain was that values were what counted. Policies mattered not for their own sake but only insofar as they promised to deliver those values. From that starting point he could challenge the vast accumulation of obsolescent party doctrine. And yet Blair was also a studiously careful politician. Once he had decided to seek to rewrite this or that piece of traditionalist dogma, he would use persuasion to win the widest possible support. Reason, flattery, and guile were deployed in equal measure. He never doubted his own capacity to convince others to accept his position. As Charles Clarke, who served as Neil Kinnock's chief of staff during the 1980s, says, "His great skill as a politician is that he has always believed that getting somewhere depended on making the argument. He knows which corner of the room he wants to get to and works out precisely how to get there. Most politicians are never as clear about their destination and, when they are, they find it difficult to find a way around the furniture." It was also about this time that colleagues began to hear the phrase that would become Blair's leitmotif: change was "the right thing to do."

The ready smile of this fresh-faced politician belied his single-minded determination. Although Blair's rise through the ranks of Neil Kinnock's opposition team during the 1980s seemed effortless, he had to work at it—inside the party and beyond it. The strategy of making friends rather than enemies was a reflection of his ambition. The many contacts he made with the newspaper and television journalists who covered politics from permanent offices at Westminster were central to the plan. Quite suddenly, his was a name to watch. He was widely quoted in the press, regularly interviewed by broadcasters. This was a politician, the columnists and the commentators began to say, destined for the top.

Blair would never be a member of the Labour "tribe." He was separated from his peers by more than a privileged childhood. Two other formidable Labour leaders–Clement Attlee and Hugh Gaitskell–had come from families wealthy enough to send them to prestigious fee-paying schools. With Blair, though, there was a wider cultural chasm, which consciously or unconsciously he had marked out in his maiden speech in the House of Commons in July 1983. Most of Blair's colleagues had always known that Labour would be their chosen party. The roots of their politics were deep, and many hailed from the trade unions. Like Blair's friend Gordon Brown, they were steeped in the history of the left's constant struggle for social justice. From the beginning, the future leader of his party positioned himself as the outsider: "I am a socialist not through reading a textbook that caught my intellectual fancy," he said in that first parliamentary speech, "nor through unthinking tradition." Instead, he had joined the Labour Party because he shared its fundamental values–"cooperation not confrontation, fellowship in place of fear."

Theological discourses about party policy were brushed aside– never mind that for many colleagues this was the very stuff of politics. Blair was badly read in Labour history; his political icons were William Gladstone, Lloyd George, William Beveridge, and other heroes of the once-powerful Liberal Party. Nor was he "clubbable"–while most MPs would happily spend their evenings planning and plotting in the multitude of bars and restaurants at Westminster, Blair preferred to return home. His close friends were as often as not outside the inner circles of politics–Barry Cox, a successful television executive; Charles Falconer, a fellow barrister; Maggie Rae, who would later act as lawyer for the Princess of Wales; Marc Palley, a close friend from student days at Oxford; and Alan Haworth, a senior Labour Party official. These were people with connections to politics but who also had a life beyond it. Shared vacations in France and Italy were family rather than political affairs. And here was one of the ironies of Blair's political ascent. Eleven years later, the Labour MPs who voted for him as leader of the

party would say that one of his greatest strengths was that he was a politician with a hinterland, someone with a life beyond the corridors of Westminster. The image of the young man in denim jeans and casual shirt sitting with his family at the kitchen table at home in the fashionable London district of Islington was just what they wanted. Blair's electoral appeal was to a nation that, after the fall of the Berlin Wall, had lost interest in the old ideology. It no longer wanted leaders obsessed with politics.

In the British political system each government minister–from the twenty or so senior figures in the cabinet to the seventy or more with middle-ranking or junior roles in departments scattered across Whitehall–has a "shadow" in the main opposition party. Within a year of entering Parliament Blair had been appointed to the shadow Treasury team, winning promotion to the post of trade and industry spokesman before the 1987 general election. In the aftermath of that election he was chosen by fellow Labour MPs as a member of Kinnock's shadow cabinet. Still only in his mid-thirties, he was now marked out as one of the fastest-rising politicians in the House of Commons. His style as a spokesman for Labour was distinctive, ever reflecting his distance from the instincts of his own party. In the public mind, Labour had long ago become a party of producer interest groups, chief among them the trade unions. In any conflict between producers and consumers, the presumption was that Labour would side with the former. Since consumers were far more numerous, the electoral consequences were obvious. In his first senior role as Labour's energy spokesman, Blair began to redress the balance. Margaret Thatcher was proceeding quickly with the sale of state-owned utilities. Labour opposed the sales, partly as a matter of ideology, and partly because privatization would weaken the unions in their industrial strongholds. But there were votes for the Conservatives in the disposal of state industries. Shares, or stocks, were sold at a discount to individuals, and Thatcher proclaimed the birth of popular capitalism on the American model. Blair, bound by his party's policy, nonetheless found a way to change subtly the direction of its

criticism. He focused on the threat of higher prices for consumers once hitherto nonprofit businesses like electricity and gas passed into the hands of private shareholders. In the wider scheme of things, this might have seemed a trivial distinction, but it was a signal that the party had begun to address a larger audience.

One way of doing this, as Blair understood, was to draw on the power of the media. Britain's press is deeply partisan, its political tone set by a handful of powerful proprietors. Most newspapers are careless of the distinction between news and comment observed by their American counterparts. During the 1980s Labour could rely on the support of one or two left-leaning newspapers, but most of the popular press was implacably hostile. Margaret Thatcher was lionized in the many newspaper titles owned by the media tycoon Rupert Murdoch, particularly the tabloid *Sun,* and the Australian-born magnate was a regular, honored guest at 10 Downing Street. The prime minister's early assault on the power of trade unions had allowed Murdoch to radically cut costs, and thus to greatly increase the profitability of his businesses. The rules governing concentrations of media ownership were flexibly interpreted to allow Murdoch to establish a satellite television network. For his part, Neil Kinnock was consistently vilified, the attacks as often personal as political. Kinnock understood better than most the political imperative of change, but a hostile press would never allow him to shake off his own past on the left of the party's politics. Now, battered and bruised, he would sometimes refuse even to speak to the Murdoch newspapers.

His young acolyte was less encumbered, however, and knew there was a battle to be fought. While the party leader shunned the *Sun* and the *Daily Mail,* another deeply hostile tabloid, Blair actively courted such newspapers. The odds of winning them over seemed slight, but at least their attacks might be blunted. He found it curious, in any event, that the argument should be lost by default, and that Labour had surrendered to Margaret Thatcher's Conservatives a monopoly on new media techniques and modern political campaigning strategies. Blair also appreciated the ability of television to shape public perceptions in an era when far fewer people felt bound by tribal loyalty. Thatcher's

success in winning the votes of aspirant working-class voters had testi-
fied to this new promiscuity in electoral allegiances. Because the daily
newspapers shaped television's news agenda, Blair secured regular
slots on the op-ed pages to press the case for Labour's new agenda.

For all his personal distaste of the Murdoch press, Kinnock never-
theless recognized that the left had to fight for hearts and minds. In
1985 he appointed a young television producer by the name of Peter
Mandelson as the party's communications director. The grandson of
Herbert Morrison, a leading figure in Clement Attlee's postwar Labour
government, the new recruit would prove himself a brilliant electoral
strategist. With the party leader's encouragement, Mandelson joined
Brown and Blair in what was dubbed "the project" to modernize the
party. He introduced aggressive campaign techniques, including a
sophisticated computer-based strategy to rebut the charges levied at
Labour by the Conservatives. Hugh Hudson, the director of the award-
winning film *Chariots of Fire,* was employed to film Kinnock's political
broadcasts. Working in adjoining offices in a small annex near the
House of Commons, Brown, Blair, and Mandelson became the found-
ing members of what later became New Labour. Brown and Blair
would shape the political strategy, refining each other's speeches, and
orchestrating attacks on the government and shifts in Labour's own
position. Mandelson worked tirelessly to keep them in the public eye.
Brown and Blair—and in those days it was the older of the two men
whose name always came first—were the living proof that the party
really was changing.

Not fast enough, though. In 1987 Mandelson's skills and Brown and
Blair's enthusiasm could not save Labour from its third successive elec-
toral defeat. On June 11, 1987, Margaret Thatcher was returned to of-
fice with a seemingly impregnable, if slightly diminished, majority of
102 in the House of Commons. Labour had fought a brilliant cam-
paign, but the gloss of modernity could not disguise the fact that most
of its members still clung to its old ideology. The judgment of many
political commentators was that the Conservatives were destined to
become the permanent party of government.

Five years later came the general election that could and should have defied that prediction. Instead, on April 9, 1992, against the odds and in defiance of its own expectations, Labour crashed to its fourth consecutive general election defeat. The party woke up on April 10, 1992, to the realization that it had not won an election since 1974. It had been out of office for thirteen years. Now it was destined for another four or five years in the political wilderness. For a young politician as ambitious as Blair, the prospects could hardly have seemed bleaker. Equally dispiriting had been the nature of the defeat. This election had been Labour's chance, and until the last few days of the actual campaign the party had almost convinced itself that indeed it would win. The dismal truth, though, was that it had itself to blame for the Conservative victory, a fact that Blair himself acknowledged in interviews immediately after the election: "The true reason for our defeat is not complex. It is simple. It has been the same since 1979. Labour has not been trusted to fulfill the aspirations of the majority of people in a modern world."

During the closing years of the 1980s the Thatcherite economic miracle had turned into a mirage. The sustained upswing that had filled the pockets of enthusiastic Tory voters and given Margaret Thatcher three successive election victories had, like so many economic booms before it, turned to bust. Interest rates had climbed to as high as 15 percent to contain runaway inflation, the economy had slumped into recession, and unemployment was rising fast. House prices, the source of soaring personal wealth for most of the previous decade, began to fall. Many of the voters who had put their faith in the Conservatives had become trapped in what is known as negative equity. The outstanding loans on their homes totaled more than the properties were worth.

Thatcher, who had been one of Britain's most powerful prime ministers, fell victim to the growing discontent. Her election victories in 1983 and 1987 had filled 10 Downing Street with the dangerous fumes of hubris, and the Iron Lady thought she could do as she would. "She's mad," one of her cabinet ministers was heard to remark in the lobby of the House of Commons after a particularly fraught encounter, "com-

pletely mad." That was an exaggeration born of the moment, but it was true that Thatcher had begun to act without restraint. Nemesis lurked around the next corner. Thatcher's decision to replace progressive local property taxes with a flat-rate "poll tax" to pay for local government services spurred more than a million people to mount an angry protest on the streets of London. The new tax was grossly unfair, demanding, in popular parlance, that a dustman, or refuse collector, pay the same tax on his property as a castle-owning duke. The protests turned to riots, and many voters threatened not to pay the new levy. The increasingly unpopular Thatcher retreated into her "bunker" in 10 Downing Street. The Tory Party, sensing impending electoral defeat, grew restless with its leader. She opened up a second front with her critics by sparking a confrontation with Britain's European partners over their hopes for deeper economic integration. During 1989 and 1990 two of her most senior ministers, Nigel Lawson and Sir Geoffrey Howe, resigned from the cabinet. The most successful peacetime leader in Britain's recent past was finished. Thatcher had thrice won famous election victories, had danced on the world stage with Ronald Reagan, and had stiffened the resolve of George Bush after Iraq's invasion of Kuwait in the summer of 1990. But she had become a political liability. Conservative MPs, more ruthless in their determination to cling to power than grateful to their leaders, deposed her.

John Major, chosen by the party to succeed her, was cut from different Tory cloth. Where Thatcher was imperious, he was consensual; where she was abrasive, Major was a natural conciliator. At home he set about promoting a different brand of "caring conservatism." The hated poll tax was abolished. Abroad, for a time at least, he began repairing broken relationships with Britain's European neighbors. He could not escape immediately the economic storms, but he held out the promise of a different future. It was fear of Labour rather than love of the Conservatives, however, that gave Major his election victory in April 1992. For all the pain of the economic recession and their growing distrust of the Tories, the voters decided that putting Labour into government was too much of a risk. Thatcher's majority in the House

of Commons of 102 in 1987 was cut to a mere 21 under Major. But the voters' decision was still clear enough: the nation had decided to stick with the devil it knew.

Neil Kinnock, a brave politician, had continued the process of modernization after the 1987 defeat. Year by year he had abandoned policies such as unilateral nuclear disarmament and wholesale renationalization of key industries that had locked the party into its ideological past. Ties with the trade unions had been loosened. He had moderated the socialist commitment to the redistribution of wealth, cutting back on plans for more state spending and for accompanying increases in taxes. He had continued to promote the new generation of party modernizers–Blair and Brown–while encouraging Mandelson in the transformation of the communications strategy. Labour's general election campaign had been slick, and many of the relics that seemed to trap the party in the past had been dropped. Labour's new emblem was a red rose, and the old socialist anthem, "The Red Flag," was quietly abandoned.

Not surprisingly, Kinnock faced constant battles against the old ideological guard, with the inevitable compromises. The trade unions, which had founded the party at the turn of the twentieth century, remained a dominant partner because they still provided the bulk of the funding for election campaigns. Sometimes they frustrated Kinnock's plans for change, and they always reinforced the party's image as class-based. Labour's tax and spending plans, published just before the 1992 election, were modest compared to previous proposals. But a plan to raise taxes on those in the higher income brackets sent the powerful message that Labour would still punish those who had successfully climbed the ladder of prosperity. The party's manifesto did not recognize the unshakable demographic truth of the age: the blue-collar workers in industries like coal, steel, shipbuilding, and auto production, who had been the foundation of past Labour victories, had been replaced by the new aspirational classes of a service-based economy. Middle Britain stuck with the Conservatives. The message of the 1992 election was that it was not enough for the party of the left to abandon the past. It had to have something convincing to say about the future.

Blair understood the imperative of radical change within the party. As Labour's spokesman for employment in the shadow cabinet, he had pushed the boundaries of reform to the limit. To the fury of some of the unions, he had abandoned the party's support for the so-called closed shop, the tradition that obliged every worker in some industries to join a union regardless of personal preference or conscience. He had said that Labour should keep some of Thatcher's employment legislation. Blair saw his party's role as the guardian of the rights of individual employees, not of the workplace privileges of particular unions. But the very fact that within the confines of Labour politics the abolition of the closed shop was a deeply controversial change spoke to the huge gulf between the mindset of his party and that of the nation beyond. The issue, Blair told journalists on the weekend after the election defeat, was not "change or no change." It was what type of change. "Nobody should be under any illusion that the route back to power can be achieved without fundamental reform of ideas and organization."

By the autumn of 1992 he was steeped in gloom. As the evenings grew darker with the onset of winter, so did his mood. Those who encountered him in the wood-paneled corridors and vaulted lobbies of the Palace of Westminster found a politician burning with frustration. What was always obvious was his exasperation, sometimes anger. "It's hopeless," he would mutter. "Why don't they realize?" The "they" were his own party's leader and the senior party colleagues around him. Behind his gloom lay the fear that once again Labour was about to squander its chances. The party, he now feared, was heading toward the political oblivion of permanent opposition. Later it would emerge that he was almost as angry with himself as with those around him. In retrospect, it was evident that this had been the moment when Blair's political ambition hardened into ruthless determination.

The strange thing was that he could easily have affected an air of optimism during those last months of 1992. He had recently been promoted again in the pecking order of the shadow cabinet. As shadow home secretary, he now occupied one of the top three jobs in his party, and that at the youthful age of thirty-nine. Across the Atlantic Bill Clinton had just become the first Democrat since Jimmy Carter in 1976 to

win the presidency. The center-left, the New Democrat victory declared, could still triumph in elections. More than that, Clinton had won by building just the sort of broad center-left coalition that Blair understood to be vital to his own party's political recovery. The hegemony of the political right, Clinton's victory seemed to proclaim to a wider world, was not after all a preordained fact of life in post–cold war politics. Although conservative ideas had dominated the 1980s on both sides of the Atlantic, the Democratic White House offered the proof that the middle classes could be persuaded to vote again for progressive policies.

There were other straws at which Blair might have clutched. Within months of its election victory, John Major's Conservative government had become deeply unpopular, following a storm on the international currency markets. Sterling's exchange rate had been pegged since 1990 within the European Union's exchange rate mechanism. But with the economy in recession, a tidal wave of speculative selling by currency traders had forced the pound out of the system. September 16, 1992, was a national humiliation, entering Britain's history books as Black Wednesday. On that day the Bank of England sold tens of billions of dollars from its currency reserves, buying pounds for the dollars in the vain attempt to keep up the value of the pound. George Soros, the international financier, boasted that he had made a profit of $1 billion from the bank's futile intervention on currency markets. The defeat had all but destroyed the credibility of Major's economic strategy. Beyond that, it had fanned the flames of a nascent revolt in his party about Britain's wider relationship with Europe. The opinion polls began to show that Labour was ten, sometimes as many as fifteen, points ahead.

Blair's depression was rooted in his analysis of what had happened six months earlier. Immediately after the April 1992 election he had issued a cri de coeur in the form of an essay published in the left-leaning *Guardian* newspaper. The time had come, he argued, for a bonfire of ideology. If Labour was ever to return to power, it was simply not enough to drop this policy or modify that one. The voters had delivered their verdict on such tinkering. What was needed, he believed,

was a fundamental reimagining of the very purpose of the center-left. Winning the next election would require not a delicate shift in tactics but a vast and visible upheaval in outlook. Labour must embark on a "project" to define its basic values and principles and then refashion each and every one of its policies accordingly.

Tony Blair's political prospectus, visible in outline during the previous decade, was now taking definitive shape. At its core was a belief in the inescapable interdependence of the modern world. Here, Blair believed, three years after the fall of the Berlin Wall had rendered obsolete the old ideological battles between right and left, lay the new dividing line of politics. Liberals as well as Conservatives now had to acknowledge individual aspiration. The issue was how it could best be advanced. Conservatives saw government in almost all its forms as standing in opposition to the freedoms of the individual. It was a necessary evil, but one that constantly had to be reined back. For a modern party of the center-left, the young Labour politician believed, the guiding principle was that people prospered in strong communities. The state could and should be the friend of the individual, a source of security in a fast-changing world. Margaret Thatcher had been right about much in the 1980s, particularly the market economy. But she had been wrong when she had declaimed the idea of society. For its part, though, Labour had lost this argument by default. To Blair's mind, it had confused the concept of community with the idea of a powerful centralized state. In the eyes of voters, its ambition had become the advancement of big government for its own sake. The individual had been forgotten. The left's addiction to the politics of tax and spend had blurred the essential distinction between an enabling state and an oppressive one. Labour's task, as Tony Blair saw it, was to reclaim the idea of community from that of an overmighty state.

Such admonitions fell on largely deaf ears. Neil Kinnock, dogged by a hostile media and exhausted by his efforts at modernization, had resigned after the 1992 defeat. He was replaced by John Smith, a bluff but shrewd Scottish lawyer who had served as Kinnock's shadow chancellor of the exchequer (the British equivalent to the American treasury

secretary). Smith had been responsible for the budgetary plans that many thought had contributed to the election defeat. But he was a powerful politician, an impressive performer in the House of Commons and a figure of reassurance in the country. His solid frame and dark suits conveyed the image of a solid figure—the friendly bank manager or the family lawyer. Because Smith had always hailed from the right, the middle classes, the party hierarchy thought, would see in him a safe pair of hands, a man who could be trusted with the keys of 10 Downing Street.

Therein was Blair's frustration. Even as he pressed the case for change, the new leader's strategy was to wait for victory to come to him. Smith's reasoning carried a superficial logic. After all, Major's party had been badly battered by Black Wednesday. Its reputation for economic competence would soon be dented further when it would be forced to raise taxes to curb a sharp increase in public borrowing. Then there was the growing dispute over Britain's relationship with a fast-integrating Europe. A few months before the 1992 election, Major had signed the Maastricht treaty with other European Union nations, which provided for the creation of the single European currency that would later become known as the euro. The prime minister had secured a specific clause allowing Britain, if it chose, to opt out of the venture. But that was not sufficient for a growing band of so-called Euroskeptics in the Conservative Party, in whom Margaret Thatcher's antipathy toward Europe had hardened into profound hostility. Now in the House of Lords, Thatcher herself fanned the flames of rebellion within the party against the Maastricht treaty. The Conservatives were heading for civil war.

As Smith was reassured in his caution by favorable opinion polls, Blair scarcely hid his dismay. A change in economic circumstances, a new bargain among the pro-Europeans and the Euroskeptics in Major's party, an act of God—all might yet rescue the government. The voters needed specific reasons to vote Labour as well as cause to abandon the Conservatives. More than that, Blair had begun to think about what Labour might actually do if it did win an election. Its existing policies, he judged, simply would not work. Here again, the past cast a

dark shadow. History showed that Labour's victories were inevitably short-lived. Its instincts had led it to tax and spend in government, and then repent in opposition. Even the administration of Clement Attlee, which had founded Britain's welfare state after 1945, had survived in office for only six years. It was scarcely an accident that no Labour prime minister had ever served two full parliamentary terms.

The moment that marked out Tony Blair in the public mind as an entirely different Labour politician was as unexpected as it was horrific. In February 1993 the nation was convulsed by the murder of a two-year-old boy. James Bulger, let out of his mother's sight for just a few moments, was led from a shopping mall in the northern city of Liverpool by two boys who were themselves no older than ten. Taken by the hand to a nearby wasteland, James was then brutally battered to death. The murder sparked anger, revulsion, and incomprehension in equal measure. To a nation already unnerved by the rising rate of violent crime, the death of James Bulger seemed to speak to a collapse in social values, to a fatal tear in the fabric of civilized society. Blair, as spokesman for home affairs and justice, gave his party's response. It took him out from the shadows of Westminster and from the political sections to the front pages of the newspapers—and from there onto the national stage.

Blair declared that the murder did indeed betray a deeper malaise. Society had lost its ethical compass; tolerance had given way to license. The time had come to jettison moral relativism and to reassert the fundamental distinction between right and wrong. Curious though it may seem in retrospect, this approach was entirely unfamiliar territory for the Labour Party of the early 1990s. The instinct of many of Blair's colleagues would have been to express shock and sadness at the murder and then turn to the social ills that must have lain at the roots of the crime—to blame the murder, in other words, on cutbacks in welfare spending. Blair's message was that it would not do to look for excuses for such barbarous behavior. Labour had to be as resolute in punishing offenders as it was committed to tackling the social deprivation in which crime flourished. Marching onto political ground that

had been owned by the Conservatives, he warned of a decisive weak-
ening in the framework of society. Politicans, he avowed in a keynote
speech, must be "unafraid to start talking again about the values and
principles we believe in." In language that carried echoes of the moral-
ity of an earlier age, Blair continued that crime simply could not be ex-
cused by social circumstance. Citizens had rights, but they also had
responsibilities. "We cannot exist in a moral vacuum. If we do not learn
and then teach the value of what is right and what is wrong the result
is simply moral chaos which engulfs us all."

The speech not only caught and carried the national mood, it an-
nounced to Blair's colleagues and to his opponents alike that the Con-
servatives could no longer lay sole claim to the mantle of law and
order. Henceforth, in what became a favorite mantra, Blair declared
that Labour would be "tough on crime and on tough the causes of
crime." It was, Peter Mandelson would reflect, a turning point in the
party's reconnection with the voters of Middle Britain and a seminal
speech for Blair. "He was nervous about making it, as some said it
might be misinterpreted as being redolent of the religious right in
America, and he refined the text right up until the last minute. But he
had found his voice, and more than any other speech this one defined
the man and imprinted his character on the public's mind."

Here was a harbinger of the strategy that Blair would use to redraw
the boundaries of British politics. The Labour Party had always been
proud of its tolerance, of a liberalism that respected social and cultural
diversity and understood the pressures of economic hardship. During
the 1960s the Labour government of Harold Wilson had been in the
vanguard of a social revolution that had seen radical revision of the
laws prohibiting divorce, abortion, and homosexuality. As it happened,
Blair shared the same tolerance toward the social and lifestyle choices
made by individuals. But while he had no truck with the idea that the
state should enter the bedrooms of consenting adults, he thought the
party had then traveled too far in its disdain for social norms. By ap-
pearing to condone antisocial behavior and to explain away criminal-
ity, it had ceded the moral ground of politics to the Conservatives. The
focus on individual rights was at the expense of individual responsibil-

ity; that on sexual choice at the cost of respect for the family. Labour was mistrusted on law and order because it seemed more concerned with the fate of criminals than with that of their victims. Blair proposed a new social bargain, one which he would apply well beyond the field of crime and punishment. Government had a duty to foster opportunity for citizens, but the contract demanded that individuals accept the corresponding responsibility to observe the rules of society. With rights and responsibilities as his mantra, Blair had staked his claim to Tory ground, and to the leadership of his own party.

4. NEW DEMOCRATS, NEW LABOUR

TONY BLAIR'S opportunity came unexpectedly in the early summer of 1994. It was one of those chilling moments that serve as a reminder that politics is never so cruel than at the passing of one of its leaders. John Smith died on the morning of May 12, 1994, the victim of a massive heart attack at the age of fifty-five. Only the night before, the Labour leader had been in ebullient form, celebrating at a fund-raising dinner his party's strong lead in the opinion polls over John Major's government. Smith had had a health warning six years earlier, when a heart attack had put him out of action for several months. As time passed, he had become less respectful of his doctors' insistence that he should work, eat, and drink at a careful pace. The shock of his death was palpable, rippling out from the hushed corridors of Westminster into the nation's living rooms. The avuncular Smith, exuding Scottish decency, had become a popular and respected national figure, and Britain went into mourning. But politics does not wait for due respects to be paid. Within hours of his death, senior Labour figures were quietly discussing the succession. In corridors and corners at Westminster the name most often heard was that of Tony Blair. As he flew back to London from a political engagement in the north of England, Blair himself was deciding that this time he would take his chance.

At first glance, the young politician's ambitions seemed to defy the natural hierarchy of Labour politics. For a decade Tony Blair and Gordon Brown had been a partnership in the project to modernize their party. But for almost all of that time, Brown had been the senior partner. He had shaped the constant flow of press releases to the media that had given the two men a rising public profile; he had crafted the new economic framework that would enable the party to break its ad-

diction to the politics of tax and spend. More than that, Brown had Labour blood in his veins, while Blair, the middle-class lawyer from Middle England, was still the outsider. The leadership was his friend's rightful inheritance. But Blair had changed, as had Labour. Two years earlier, when Neil Kinnock had resigned after the 1992 election defeat, Blair had briefly considered standing for the deputy leadership of the party, while Brown had thought for a moment of fighting John Smith for the top job. Both had ultimately demurred. As Blair's frustration with Smith's wait-and-see approach to party reform mounted over the succeeding two years, he deeply regretted his failure of nerve. In an interview with the *Financial Times* in the autumn of 1993 Blair made no secret of his exasperation: "What I find odd is that after four election defeats and with Labour not having won 40 percent of the popular vote since 1970 that you have to argue the case for change." The argument to which he referred was at its core with John Smith.

Now Smith was gone, albeit in tragic circumstances. Blair resolved he would not make the same mistake twice; this time he would aim for the main prize. He knew the decision would be the cause of great anger and hurt for Brown. His fellow modernizer had been a friend and ally as well as a political mentor. Blair discussed the dilemma at length with his closest aides. They were struck by the steel behind the genuine turmoil. Now politics would catch a glimpse of the ruthlessness that lay beyond Blair's easygoing manner. Brown, Blair decided, would have to concede the leadership, or he would fight him for it. The party took Blair's side, for it was hungry to win a general election. The arithmetic of the electoral college that would choose a new leader said Brown had a chance. But politics is about mood, about scarcely visible but irresistible currents of opinion, and within hours of John Smith's death it was obvious that they were flowing toward Blair. Even some in his party who clung to the old socialist ideology had had enough of losing. Just hours after Smith's death, one Labour MP was asked who he expected would get the leadership. "Tony Blair," came the reply. When asked whom he himself would support, "Tony Blair again." But how could this MP give his vote to someone so out of tune with his own traditionalist beliefs? Blair would jettison almost everything he

stood for. The answer to the question came almost before it was asked. "Blair can put us back in power."

He was right. Only Blair had the lightness of political touch and the persuasive smile that would say to the voters that Labour really had changed. Despite his outward confidence, Brown seemed hunched by comparision, almost as if he was carrying the burdens of his party's past. For all that Scotland was his birthplace, Blair was English, and it was in England that the next election would be won or lost. The two principal contenders struck a bargain of sorts over dinner at a restaurant in the fashionable North London district of Islington where Blair had his home. Brown agreed to stand aside with the promise from his younger partner that he would serve as shadow chancellor of the exchequer in a Blair-led party. Once Labour was in government he would take the mantle of chancellor and assume sweeping authority over a broad swath of economic and social policy, thus keeping his place as the intellectual dynamo of the modernization project. Blair intimated also that he would not be party leader forever. They were both young men; there would be time enough for Brown to take his turn. Their deal, sealed at a restaurant called Granita, would enter the folklore of Labour politics. It established that the partnership of the previous ten years would continue, so that if Blair became prime minister, Brown would all but be his equal in the running of a Labour government. Nothing about the timing or circumstances of a leadership handover was written down that evening, however, and later each would offer a different recollection of what had passed between them—Blair insisting there had not been any precise agreement, Brown intimating otherwise. The disputed terms of the Granita deal were destined to become the subject of intense argument between the two men and would later disfigure Tony Blair's government. Here were two politicians who needed each other. But the trust between them had been badly undermined.

Blair's victory was, in fact, a shattering blow to his friend. Brown, having supped from the cup of politics almost from infancy, had planned his entire life for this moment, only to see the opportunity snatched from him. There was an unfairness about it. Brown's own standing among party activists had fallen since 1992, but only because

he had been ready to take tough decisions to cut back on commitments to higher public spending. His disappointment, the sense that he had been cheated of a rightful inheritance, would henceforth reverberate through the most important relationship in British government. It is one of the clichés of politics that there is no room for personal friendship at the top. On this occasion, though, even Blair's closest friends were surprised at how unsentimental he had been about leaving Brown behind.

In the formal leadership contest that followed, Blair's victory–he secured a comfortable majority over two left-wing opponents, John Prescott and Margaret Beckett, in July 1994–heralded a new realism. The party, or most of it, had realized that it would win only when it assembled a broad coalition. That meant securing the votes not just of the working-class electors who had deserted to the Conservatives but also those of a burgeoning middle-class constituency that had never voted Labour–the voters of Middle Britain. The new leader's colleagues had also understood Blair's powerful personal appeal. He was young, cherished his family, had charm, and looked at the world in a way that was intuitively in tune with the values and aspirations of those beyond Labour's old heartlands.

The political insight that the new leader brought to his party was at once simple and profound. For the previous few decades Labour had defined itself in terms of its policy prescriptions. It knew how much it would spend (more) and where it would set taxes (higher). It had commitments to raise welfare benefits, and a policy to reduce defense expenditure. It wanted more state regulation of business, less restraint on the powers of trade unions. The arguments between right and left within the party had concerned the precise calibration of these policies. Should the highest rates of income tax be raised to 50 percent or 60 percent? Should the state pension paid to the elderly be increased by £5 or by £10 per week? How much extra money did the National Health Service need? Blair declared an end to these arguments. Labour, he said, had left behind its basic values in the tortuous debates about how to achieve them. The party had been founded at the turn of the twentieth century to promote opportunity, fairness, and social justice.

It rested on a belief in community and responsibility. It now had to re-
cover those values–the "ends"–from the introverted disputes about
particular policies–the "means." Thus fairness was more important
than any particular balance between private and public ownership, op-
portunity more relevant than undeliverable commitments to redistrib-
ute wealth. And the responsibility of the individual counted for as
much as that of the state. This was the "back to first principles" ap-
proach that Blair had taken in reshaping the party's platform on law
and order. As leader, he would apply it across the entire policy spec-
trum. Each of the old shibboleths, every relic of the past, would be
tested against the new framework. The binding idea, set out in his
manifesto for the leadership contest, was the notion that the state did
not stand in opposition to the individual, but in support of his or her
aspirations. "Individuals prosper best within a strong, active society,
whose members owe duties to each other as well as to themselves, and
in part at least, depend on one another to succeed." If the phrasing was
inelegant, the meaning was clear: what mattered was not the size of
government but whether the actions of the state widened the scope of
individual opportunity.

Future policies would, of course, also be tested against another
reality–the mood of the electorate. While the public seemed to share
many of Labour's values–by now there had been something of a back-
lash against the free-for-all individualism of the Thatcher years–it re-
mained deeply distrustful of the party itself. Thus opinion polls would
regularly show that the voters wanted more public money to be spent
on the state health and education services, and likewise, most people
said they would accept some increase in their tax bills to pay for better
schools and hospitals, but this apparent support for Labour's prospec-
tus did not translate into votes for the party. The same polls revealed
that although people believed that Labour would indeed increase
taxes, they felt it would waste the extra money rather than spend it
wisely. What Blair had to restore was that most precious of commodi-
ties in politics–trust. He reached the same conclusion that Bill Clinton
and the New Democrats had arrived at several years earlier: the
electoral arithmetic of modern democracies meant that a party that

wanted to stand for office as a champion of the poor and disadvantaged could not win unless it also appealed to the self-interest of a much bigger, middle-class constituency. Labour could preserve the purity of its ideology and lose, or it could modernize—in other words, compromise—and win.

The new leader therefore set out to change the terms of trade in British politics. Since 1979 the Conservatives had succeeded in defining in the public mind not only their own positions but also those of their opponents. In this construct, Margaret Thatcher stood for low taxes, Neil Kinnock for raiding the wallets of the hardworking classes. The Tories backed freedom of the individual, Labour the power of the state. Thatcher wanted to nurture enterprise, Kinnock to put the economy in the hands of the trade unions. The Conservatives were the party of law and order; socialists cared more about the criminals than their victims. Conservatives revered the flag. Labour would destroy Britain's international standing by slashing the defense budget. Blair's response to these stereotypes was informed by Bill Clinton's experience. Philip Gould, Blair's political strategist and pollster, had watched the 1992 Democratic campaign from up close. During a spell in the Clinton headquarters in Little Rock, Arkansas, he had forged a friendship with Stanley Greenberg, one of the candidate's key aides. The story he brought back to Labour politicians was of the contrast between Clinton's victory and Michael Dukakis's defeat at the hands of George Bush in 1988. Dukakis, Greenberg had written in an article for the *American Prospect* in 1990, had failed to articulate any clear set of principles during his presidential campaign. The result was that the voters had been left with a savage caricature, created by the Republicans, of a "Democratic Party short on patriotism, weak on defense, soft on criminals and minorities, indifferent to work, values and the family, and, inexplicably, infatuated with taxes." It was a description, Gould concluded, that could have applied equally well to Neil Kinnock's campaign in 1992.

Blair resolved to redraw the dividing lines, to map out a new political landscape on which the next election would be fought. Dumping the ideological baggage of the past would allow him to redefine his own

party, but he also had to reformulate the Conservative program in the public mind, exposing the false antitheses on which Tory policies were based. These held that a choice had to be made between sound economics and social cohesion, between punishment of criminals and measures to tackle the causes of crime, between helping the unemployed and cutting welfare spending. Blair turned the tables. In his new description, John Major's government believed that social injustice was a price worth paying for free-market economics. Labour, by contrast, understood that a strong economy and a stable, more equitable society were mutually reinforcing. The Conservatives were slashing social benefits; Labour would use the welfare budget to give the unemployed a leg up into jobs. The government claimed to be the party of patriotism, but by isolating Britain in the European Union, it had damaged the nation's strategic interests. Blair thus began to position his party on the territory between the ideology of its past and the unbridled individualism that was Margaret Thatcher's brand of radical conservatism. The two most important words in British politics were "moderate" and "extreme." Ownership of the former was the route to government, and Blair now laid claim to it. The priceless center ground of politics opened up before him.

First, though, he not only had to change his party's name, but to demonstrate to voters that the transformation in its outlook was real and permanent. "It is not enough that we change," he observed soon after he had taken the leader's mantle. "We have to prove we have changed." Moreover, the proof had to be visible to, and accepted by, his own party as well as indisputable among the voters of Middle Britain. In other words, he had to be bold—to show he could defy the traditions of Labour.

Clause IV of the Labour Party constitution was a sacred text, a testament printed on the back of every party membership card. It had been written in an age when Labour defined itself as the representative of a working class engaged in perpetual war with the rapacious owners of land and capital. Penned in 1918 by Sidney Webb, a prominent social reformer, against the backdrop of the Russian Revolution, it reflected

the then socialist view that private ownership of land and industry was intrinsically exploitative. The toil of the poor would always serve to further enrich the wealthy. Clause IV consequently declared that the party's objective must be to "secure for the workers by hand or by brain the full fruits of their industry." To that end it would seek "common ownership of the means of production, distribution and exchange." Even before the ink was dry, the notion of such wholesale appropriation of private property was a fanciful one for all but those who looked to Lenin for their political model, and no subsequent Labour government would seek such a radical program of nationalization. Clement Attlee's administration in 1945 marked out the practical boundaries when it took into public ownership such strategic industries as coal mining and power generation. Nevertheless, Clause IV had become a totem, an emblem of an earlier idealism, a status it shared with the party's commitment to equality—once again an unattainable goal but a cherished ideal. In the past, other Labour leaders had toyed with scrapping the clause—most prominently Hugh Gaitskell, whose efforts to modernize the party in the late 1950s prefigured those of Tony Blair—but the weight of traditionalism scuppered the attempts. Subsequent Labour leaders brushed off Clause IV as a harmless piece of history, an anachronism that had long before become irrelevant. Blair took an entirely different view. In Peter Mandelson's description, "It prevented the party from proclaiming clearly what it did stand for, and it confused the voters about Labour's intentions."

When delegates arrived in the northern seaside town of Blackpool in the autumn of 1994 for Labour's annual convention, they found the leader had given the party a new name. The conference platform declared the creation of "New Labour," and in his first speech as party leader Blair issued an uncompromising call for modernization. As proof of its intent, Labour would rewrite Clause IV. To those beyond the Labour tribe, this might have seemed a small gesture. Germany's Social Democrats, for example, had made much the same pilgrimage when they had come to terms with the market economy at a conference in the German town of Bad Godesberg a full twenty-five years

earlier. But for all its irrelevance to modern politics, Clause IV was part of Labour's inheritance. Blair was challenging his party, obliging it to put its head before its heart, with the explicit aim of sending a powerful signal of change to a much wider audience. The message was that Old Labour (as it soon became known in the leader's circle) had finally been left behind. The goal of the transformed party–and its constant obsession over the next three years–was to regain the trust of the voters.

Blair's alternative wording for the constitution–acknowledging the reality of market economics while setting out a project for a society in which "power, wealth, and opportunity are in the hands of the many, not the few"–was not a piece of political rhetoric to stir the imagination. What mattered, though, was that it signaled that New Labour was serious in its intent. During the months between Blair's conference announcement and a vote on the new constitution scheduled for the following spring, there were moments when it seemed the party might lose its nerve. Trade unions attempted to water down the new wording, steering it away from acceptance of market economics, and two of the biggest unions opposed any attempt to ditch Clause IV. But Blair launched a personal crusade for change. This was the moment, he declared, when New Labour could rid itself of the ambiguities of the past and speak with one voice to itself and to the voters. By the time of the spring conference the party was ready to vote for a different future: Clause IV was buried, and New Labour was born. For its leader, this was only the first step. In the afterglow of that first speech at Blackpool, Blair had confided that he had seen his initial task as teaching his party a new political language. The next step would be to "change the way it thinks." The voters would believe Labour had escaped from the past when it produced a vision of the future.

It was at this moment that those who watched him carefully began to realize that Blair did not share the faith in big government that had sustained his party's beliefs for most of its lifetime. Many years later an official–a civil servant rather than a political aide, who had worked intimately with the prime minister–offered one of the best descriptions of the outlook the new leader brought to his party. "He's a nineteenth-century Liberal rather than a twentieth-century socialist," this official

observed. "He's radical but not ideological. He holds to a set of values—fairness, tolerance, decency. He believes there are things that governments can and should do. But he also believes that it should not interfere in people's freedom."

However similar they appeared, New Labour was not the creation of Bill Clinton and the New Democrats but their younger sibling. The people whom Blair now gathered around him in the Labour leader's office—Gordon Brown; Peter Mandelson; Alistair Campbell, a former tabloid journalist and his press secretary; Anji Hunter from his school days—all had recognized long before they met the Democrat from Arkansas that they had to re-create their party if it was ever to win another election. Words like "community," "responsibility," and "fairness" had peppered Blair's speeches since the 1980s. If any single person could claim authorship, it was the late John Macmurray, the Scottish philosopher whose work had entranced Blair during his time at Oxford University. In any event, history, culture, and the facts of politics meant that there would always be some distance between Labour and the Democrats. Britain owes many of its instincts to its close ties with the United States. But in the broad sweep of attitudes to capitalism, to welfare, to crime and punishment, and the role of government, the British attitude is often as close or closer to that of continental Europe. While Americans, for example, argue about the scope of Medicare and Medicaid, a publicly funded National Health Service, free to all, has long been one of the fixed points of British political life.

Despite all that, Clinton's election victories and the tide of ideas that flowed around them gave Blair and his fellow modernizers both confidence and a role model. New Labour plundered the New Democrats for campaign techniques and political positioning. Clinton adviser Dick Morris's "triangulation" strategy—building new positions between left and right—was ported across the Atlantic. There was policy substance, too, in the transatlantic trade. Clinton's success in turning around the U.S. budget deficit in the first years of his presidency had paved the way for the sustained economic upturn that gave him the financial space to pursue his social agenda. This was mirrored by a New Labour

pledge to do much the same in Britain, as fiscal prudence became the leitmotif of Gordon Brown's promised economic strategy. Brown's decision to give independence to the Bank of England as one of the first acts of Blair's government in 1997 came after close consultation with the Federal Reserve's Alan Greenspan. The Fed chairman had struck an implicit deal with the president that had traded lower interest rates for a tough budgetary stance during Clinton's first term. Brown was to do much the same in Britain. Blair's flagship pledge to be tough on crime as well as on the causes of crime was borrowed from Clinton's determination to reclaim for the Democrats the mantle of the party of law and order. The president's mantra that the purpose of welfare was to give a hand up rather than a handout was soon heard almost as often on the British side of the Atlantic. The earned-income tax credits that Clinton put at the center of his program of tax cuts for America's working families became in Labour's platform the working families tax credit.

The love affair had begun in early January 1993. Steeped in depression after the 1992 general election, Tony Blair and Gordon Brown traveled to Washington to see for themselves how Clinton had won. Jonathan Powell, the young political officer at the British embassy in Washington who had been assigned to follow the Democratic campaign, introduced the two Labour visitors to the architects of the victory. Powell, a rising star in the Foreign Office, was the younger brother of Charles Powell, who had served as Margaret Thatcher's long-standing foreign policy adviser. Jonathan had built strong connections with the Clinton team, and, for all his brother's devotion to Thatcher, his own political instincts were those of the center-left. His meeting with Blair was fortuitous: when Blair became Labour leader the following year he asked Powell to join him as his chief of staff.

For Blair, there would be no meeting with the president-elect on this occasion. Labour was too obscure, and its two young modernizers too junior, to merit an audience with the man who was about to step into the Oval Office. But Blair and Brown heard the account of the creation of the New Democrats from Al From, the director of the Demo-

cratic Leadership Council, and of the successful campaign from Paul Begala, a key Clinton strategist. Blair was struck instantly by the way the Clinton campaign had harnessed the ideas of opportunity and responsibility to a hard-edged social policy that was at once supportive of the disadvantaged and attractive to the wider electorate. For the young Labour politician it was the perfect elision of principle and populism. Blair was smitten. The Clinton campaign, he wrote on his return to London, "set out to identify the concerns of the broad mass of the people, not trying to reconcile all the special-interest lobbies in a rainbow coalition. The program was for a government not a pressure group." The unspoken contrast was with Labour's failure in the spring of 1992. "For a Labour politician," Blair continued, "comparing the fatigue of our Conservative government with the energy and drive of the New Democrats in America, it is hard not to feel more than a little envious." The warmth of this new relationship was meanwhile matched by a distinct frost between the incoming president and John Major's government. Major's Conservatives had advised George Bush's election campaign and, against all convention, agreed to Republican requests to look through British government files for any information from Clinton's time at Oxford that might damage the Democratic candidate. No such dirt was uncovered, but the search was an act of aggression that Clinton would not forget, or forgive.

The January 1993 meetings in Washington marked the start of a burgeoning transatlantic traffic in people and ideas. John Smith, the party leader, was skeptical, and when some of the young Clintonites arrived in London to share their experiences at a trade-union-sponsored conference, there were protests from party traditionalists. Although the new president was viewed with deep suspicion by those on Labour's left, the modernizers were unabashed. Gordon Brown was a crucial link between them. The shadow chancellor of the exchequer was as entranced by the energy and dynamism of American politics as Blair had been by Clinton's campaign themes. Brown, a politician with an immense appetite for political ideas, had a ready introduction to Clinton's economic team through Ed Balls, Brown's own economic adviser. Balls had been taught at Harvard by Larry Summers, who served

as deputy treasury secretary in the first Clinton administration before taking the top economic job during the president's second term. Another point of contact was Robert Reich, Clinton's energetic and often irreverent labor secretary. The shadow chancellor also became a regular caller at the Federal Reserve office of Alan Greenspan. As the range and depth of the contacts were extended, Brown's annual visits to Cape Cod for his summer vacation became a rolling seminar on the economic strategies of the center-left.

Meanwhile, Labour's campaign managers learned from Clinton's experience. On becoming leader Blair made Philip Gould a pivotal figure in his general election team. If he had been deeply impressed by the work of Stanley Greenberg in projecting the New Democrat prospectus, Gould was equally interested in the way that the Clinton campaign had taken the offensive against the Republicans, under the leadership of James Carville. In Gould's almost awestruck words, "James Carville was the Democrat who drew a line in the sand and stopped the Republicans from advancing one step beyond it. . . . Carville turned the Democratic Party from victim to aggressor." The Ragin' Cajun, as he was known, had created the Clinton "war room," had streamlined campaign management structures, and had honed the strategy of "rapid rebuttal." All these would now loom large in New Labour tactics, as would the lesson that the best defense is a good offense. The Conservatives, accustomed to writing the agenda of election campaigns, now found themselves on the receiving end of one of the most sustained and ferocious onslaughts ever seen in British politics. The media was buried daily under an avalanche of press releases, statements, and position papers attacking every decision and announcement from John Major's government.

The media effort was led by Alistair Campbell. A former journalist on a left-leaning tabloid, the *Daily Mirror,* a reformed alcoholic, and a long-standing friend of Neil Kinnock, Campbell transformed New Labour's relations with the press. In the jargon of the time, every party spokesman and member of Parliament was ordered to stay "on message." Announcements, statements, reactions—even, it sometimes seemed, permission to speak—all had to be approved by Campbell. And the "mes-

sage" was brutally consistent: New Labour had broken forever with the past; Tony Blair alone was qualified to set Labour policy; the Conservative government was rotten with sleaze. "Anything I do or say," Campbell remarked before the 1997 election, "is because Tony wants it done or said." The leader's press secretary would soon emerge as Blair's most powerful adviser, one of a small inner circle with the authority to question and shape the leader's judgments—and a man who wielded more authority than most of those who would sit around Tony Blair's cabinet table.

Blair was granted his first audience with Bill Clinton in the autumn of 1995. It was a low-key affair. The president was on a visit to London, a trip that included an address to a joint session of the British parliament. With John Major acting as his official host, the meeting with Blair had to be discreet and so was held not at the Labour leader's Westminster office but at the grand residence of the United States ambassador to the United Kingdom, Admiral William Crowe, in London's Regent's Park. Nonetheless, it gave Blair the opportunity to explain to Clinton how New Labour had moved back into the center of British politics—and to suggest to the president that the two men could lead a broader movement to modernize the politics of the center-left.

That idea was taken further when Blair traveled to meet the president at the White House in February 1996. The leader of Her Majesty's opposition got a warm reception, as well as an hour of the president's time—a stark contrast to the humiliating fifteen-minute dressing down that Neil Kinnock had endured at the hands of Ronald Reagan a decade earlier. It mattered to the voters at home that a Labour leader was taken seriously again in Washington. The aides traveling with Blair returned to London in a state of high excitement: there was nothing the president didn't know; he was so charming, so intelligent, so attentive. And then, of course, there was the raw political power that comes with the tenancy of the Oval Office. It was power that really impressed them—the capacity to do rather than just say. This was the politics for which Blair hungered, and he had other chances on the same trip to savor Washington's heady atmosphere. Sidney Blumenthal, the jour-

nalist who was later to become the president's special assistant, gave a dinner at which Blair met Hillary Clinton and a host of other Washington luminaries. Like his aides, the young British politician was intoxicated. For his part, Bill Clinton saw potential in the relationship. Blair's subsequent election as prime minister, Blumenthal would say in his later memoir of the Clinton years, gave "global perspective" to the president's politics, turning national election victories into an international movement of the center-left. This was the beginning of an extraordinary friendship between the president from the wrong side of the tracks in Hope, Arkansas, and the prime minister from the medieval cloisters of Durham, England.

Back home, Blair continued to take an ax to the old ideology of his party, at the same time that he moved aggressively into Conservative territory. Law and order, defense, the economy–these had long been Tory issues which Blair now reclaimed. To the charge–heard often, if sotto voce, in his own party as well as from John Major's government– that he was stealing Conservative clothes, Blair was indifferent. His answer was that the values he upheld–respect for authority, patriotism, duty, responsibility–had always been those of the center-left. Labour's mistake had been to cede them.

Gordon Brown was an eager accomplice in this effort. Although the Scottish shadow chancellor had been in Labour too long to share Blair's visible delight in burying its past, he was single-minded in constructing a new economic strategy for the party. The dour Brown remained uneasy with the language of New Labour, for own political instincts, at least those regarding poverty and deprivation, were to the left of Blair's. But, in the area that really mattered, he shared the conviction that the party's social ambitions could be achieved only when it had secured long-term stability in the economy. He therefore began to construct a framework for Labour economic policy that would guarantee that stability. Because Britain had no tradition of an independent central bank, the politicians set interest rates, often manipulating the markets for short-term political advantage. Brown, foreshadowing his later decision to put the Bank of England on a footing similar to that of the Federal Reserve, said that New Labour would relinquish

such interest-rate decisions. Past Labour governments had spent and borrowed with abandon. Brown determined to break the spend-and-repent cycle by announcing that budgets would be frozen for the first two years of a New Labour administration. Only when the government's finances were in order would it begin to meet its commitments to pour more money into public health, education, and transport. The same hard edge would be applied to welfare policy. Brown had been brought up in the Presbyterian tradition that said work was the escape route from poverty. The purpose of New Labour's welfare policy would be to put people back into jobs, not to support them in unemployment.

The bonfire of Old Labour policies extended to education and health, as well, where the party had traditionally argued interminably with itself about precise structures rather than standards. Equality had always seemed to count for more than excellence, with Labour seen to be on the side of the unions rather than parents, pupils, and patients. Blair discarded past commitments to scrap selective schools in favor of raising overall teaching standards and pupil achievement. He insisted that the money promised eventually for public health care would be spent only if the fifty-year-old National Health Service modernized its management and work practices. Many of the laws promulgated by Margaret Thatcher to curb the powers of the trade unions would remain in place. More broadly, the language of public ownership was replaced by that of a public-private partnership. Blair spelled out his approach during a series of conversations in 1996. The great ideological battles of twentieth-century politics, he said, were over. "People will look back on the present century and say that, in a curious way, it was an aberration—that you had this war to the death about ideology." The politics of the next century would be less about "some final ideological confrontation and more about the values underpinning government, the objectives of government and the policies it can deliver." His ambition, he said, was recognizably that of Keir Hardie, one of Labour's founding fathers—to extend opportunity and create a fairer society. The difference was, "I am happy to put the policies of left and right in the same pot and pull out the ones that best serve that objective. Frankly, I

don't care whether this or that enterprise is in public or private owner-
ship if the purpose of a more cohesive society is being served. I don't
have any loyalty to the old left-right boundaries."

Inclusive politics meant making friends with business. Trade union
leaders were kept in the background, out of sight of the television cam-
eras, as Blair breakfasted, lunched, and dined with any business execu-
tive who would accept the invitation. New Labour presented itself as
the party of wealth creation rather than redistribution. Employing his
trademark strategy of squaring what had once been seen as circles,
Blair said that said it was absurd to view enterprise and social justice as
standing in opposition. To the contrary, only if business produced the
wealth would government be able to spread opportunity for the less
fortunate. Private capital and expertise would be harnessed to New
Labour's social ambitions as well as to the pursuit of profit. While such
relationships would have been unremarkable in Bill Clinton's party—
indeed Blair held up the Democrats' close ties with the business com-
munity as the role model—it was something new in the politics of the
Labour Party for its leader to be so obviously at ease in the nation's
boardrooms. Blair's courtships had another objective—to reduce the
party's dependency on the unions for its funding. His friend Michael
Levy, who had made his own fortune in the music business, started to
prise open the checkbooks of fellow entrepreneurs and business lead-
ers, with impressive results. Business had contributed less than £1 mil-
lion sterling ($1.6 million) to the party's 1992 election campaign. By
1997 Levy had raised that figure to £15 million ($25 million).

There was an extraordinary, if occasionally absurd, bravura in Blair's
insistence that New Labour's Big Tent would accommodate princes
as happily as paupers. In the autumn of 1996 he gave two newspaper
interviews within a day of each other. The first, to a Conservative-
leaning newspaper, ran under the headline "Making Britain into a Land
for Millionaires." The second, published in a Labour-supporting
tabloid, was headlined, "Why I Will Never Allow Our People to Grow
Old in Poverty." Blair was unabashed; Alistair Campbell was thrilled.
The determination to win over the Tory press—particularly those news-
papers owned by Rupert Murdoch—was underscored in 1995 when

Blair accepted an invitation to speak to the annual conference of leading executives of Murdoch's News Corporation. The simple fact that the invitation had been offered said something important about perceptions of Blair. Murdoch, who had been one of the Conservatives' most stalwart supporters, clearly sensed the turning of the political tide. Just as revealing was Blair's willingness to take a twenty-hour plane journey to Australia to deliver the speech. Blair thought his text–making the case that the task of modern government was to equip its citizens for the new era of globalization–was one of his strongest. Some of his colleagues, however, began to wonder whether there were any limits to his campaign to court the media magnate.

Sometimes it almost seemed as if Blair wanted to goad his party into rebellion to prove to the voters that he was different. To the horror of those still marching under the banner of Old Labour, Blair offered less than guarded praise for Margaret Thatcher's contribution to British politics. "She was a thoroughly determined person, and that is an admirable quality," the Labour leader said in a newspaper interview in the spring of 1995. Had she been right? Well, in part, at least: "Yes, Britain needed change in the 1970s." Even some of Blair's allies found such pronouncements hard to swallow. Thatcher, after all, had all but destroyed Labour in three general elections. But there was worse to come. The Iron Lady, in resentful retirement, returned the compliment: "I see a lot of socialism [in Labour] but not in Mr. Blair. I think he genuinely has moved." He was probably the most formidable leader Labour had had since Hugh Gaitskell more than thirty years earlier, she added. For any criticism this gained Blair in his own party, the benefit in the country at large was immeasurably greater. "If Thatcher says he's different who can say he isn't?" one of his inner circle whispered amid the furor in 1995.

The political tides were with Blair. Clinton's reelection in November 1996 carried a message well beyond America's shores. The president had proved that parties of the center-left could do more than merely win elections. They could govern successfully–and then win again. Clinton, in his State of the Union address that year, explicitly dis-

avowed the goal of "big government." But he had made the case for active government. Above all–and this was the most important lesson taken by Blair and his fellow modernizers–he had shown that a progressive government could run a prosperous, low-inflation economy.

Not everyone on Blair's staff was quite so smitten with the White House. Peter Mandelson, now a member of Parliament as well as a close friend of Blair and his principal campaign strategist, warned of the risk that New Labour might be seen as simply stealing Clinton's ideas. The party's pitch had to be seen as rooted in Britain rather than a different world on the other side of the Atlantic, he argued. Mandelson was careful to ensure that the Clinton aides who traveled to London to advise the New Labour campaign kept a low profile. Yet for all the focus on the United States, many of the new policies crafted by Blair's burgeoning team of policy advisers were borrowed from elsewhere. The reforming Labor governments of Bob Hawke and Paul Keating in Australia were often an important model. It was Keating who warned Blair that the days had passed when parties of the center-left could include tax increases in their programs and still win elections. Other policies were begged, borrowed, and stolen from progressive governments in Europe, such as the Netherlands and Sweden.

The would-be prime minister was a beneficiary of deeper undercurrents in society. The 1980s had been the decade of the individual, a conscious celebration of unfettered markets and the atomized society. But for many of those who had rejoiced in that self-absorption, the 1990s had become the decade of insecurity. Across the industrialized world, the chill winds of the globalized economy had begun to challenge the assumption that the more prosperous in society would always benefit from unrestrained markets. Once-secure white-collar workers suddenly saw their futures under threat from a harsher, more competitive world. These global trends were reinforced in Britain by the experience of John Major's economic recession, as his opponents called it, which had been like no previous downturn–its principal victims had been the white-collar middle classes rather than blue-collar workers. The manufacturing industry had had its shake-out of workers a decade earlier in the first Thatcher years. Now it was the turn of the

junior and middle managers who pushed the pencil or tapped the key-board. The rapid pace of technological change and a tougher employ-ment market suddenly threatened all the familiar assumptions of Middle Britain. The advance of job insecurity into the ranks of the af-fluent marked the end of Britain's postwar life plan: the assumption that the educated employed could rely on a steadily rising and unin-terrupted stream of income throughout their working lives. The mar-ketplace suddenly seemed unforgiving. Perhaps, after all, there was a role for the state. Here lay an important opportunity for a political leader pressing the case for government as the friend of the individual.

The Conservatives made Labour's task easier. The economic failure represented by sterling's ejection from the European exchange rate system in September 1992 had shattered their reputation for economic competence. The tax increases needed to repair the damage to the budget deficit caused by the economic downturn had broken John Ma-jor's promises to the electorate. Worse, the convulsions in the Conser-vative Party over Britain's place in the European Union that had begun with Major's signature on the Maastricht treaty in 1991 had by the mid-1990s turned into civil war. The plan for a single currency agreed at Maastricht was seen by a growing number of Tories as the precursor to a European superstate—a threat to Britain's sovereignty and national independence. Margaret Thatcher had chosen Major as her successor, but she soon grew disenchanted with him as her own views hardened into an uncompromising anti-Europeanism. With a small majority, constantly behind in the opinion polls, and struggling to find his own political compass, Major lurched from crisis to crisis. The Conserva-tives had been in office for too long. They had run out of ideas and grown arrogant in power. One of the symptoms was a spate of scandals surrounding the personal affairs of some ministers and MPs. Tory MPs were found to have taken bribes. Resignations followed, and the gov-ernment found itself tarred with the brush of sleaze. New Labour ex-ploited the scandals mercilessly, displaying a ruthlessness in attacks on individuals that had once been the preserve of the Conservatives. A spate of defeats in by-elections, meanwhile, eroded to nothing Major's majority in the House of Commons. During 1996 and into the early

months of 1997 Blair was seen not as leader of the opposition but as prime-minister-in-waiting.

It was during this time that the various strands that defined his political character began to come together. The Labour leader's office at Westminster was sparsely furnished—he would say that he had no intention of remaining long in the suite reserved for the leader of the opposition. In a harbinger of his style as prime minister, Blair worked through a small team of staffers whose personal loyalty was unquestioned. He was telegenic, perfectly at ease in front of the microphone or under the arc lights. But if it all looked natural, everything had been painstakingly rehearsed and nothing was left to chance. Blair had always said that he wanted to keep his family, his children above all, out of the glare of politics. But the carefully posed photographs of father, wife, and three children somehow appeared at just the right moments in the tabloid press. Boldness was accompanied by careful political calculation. Even as he discomfited party colleagues by striking out into the political center ground, he made careful efforts to mollify the standard-bearers of Old Labour. John Prescott was a constant object of this charm campaign. Elected by the party as deputy leader, the rough-edged Prescott had come from the left of the party. His instincts railed against Blair's modernization, and to a degree he was considered the party's conscience. But as one who had climbed from a life working on the lower decks of a cruise liner to a place near the top of politics, Prescott's ambition was to sit in one of the great offices of state, a desire to which Blair played. As a consequence, others in the same traditionalist wing of the party as the deputy leader more than once shrugged their shoulders in acquiescence when Blair unveiled another policy swerve: if Prescott could go along with it, they reasoned, then so could they.

There were occasional glimpses, too, of Blair's weaknesses. The self-belief, the unerring conviction that he knew this or that decision to be "the right thing to do," militated against consultation. He found it hard to share decisions, and never seemed to doubt the innate "goodness" of his own character. Others were "ruthless"; he was "right." Many of his colleagues found the discipline stifling. For those beyond

the leader's circle, New Labour often seemed a party in which being "on message" counted for more than intelligent debate. Blair and those around him came to view politics as an endless series of almost military campaigns—a style that would later sit uneasily with the more complex demands, and necessarily more measured pace, of government. At times the rhetoric ran away with him. The precise pledges that New Labour made to the electorate were deliberately modest—small enough to be printed on a wallet-sized card mailed to every voter in the land. The bigger promise was that income taxes would not rise and government spending and borrowing would be strictly limited. But the mood music was of transformation, of a New Britain to be cast in the crucible of New Labour. Blair's speeches had a curious staccato quality: a torrent of short sentences devoid of verbs but full of long rhetorical processions. Even some of his own staff winced with embarrassment when he declared, without a blush, that Britain would be remade as "a Young Country." Blair was undaunted. New Labour had to win.

5. <u>ANOTHER COUNTRY</u>

As DAWN BROKE on May 2, 1997, Britain woke up another country. Once in a generation, an election heralds an earthquake that completely alters the contours of a nation's politics. Tony Blair's victory was one of these seismic shifts. Having presided over the longest period of one-party rule since the premiership of William Pitt in the closing decades of the eighteenth century, the Conservatives had now been swept from power. A few days short of his forty-fourth birthday Tony Blair had won the biggest election victory seen in Britain since the 1930s. The Conservatives had suffered their worst defeat in more than 150 years, losing scores of seats in Parliament not just to New Labour but also to the small Liberal Democrat Party. It seemed impossible to imagine how the party of Winston Churchill and Margaret Thatcher could ever recover. With 419 newly elected members of Parliament New Labour had secured a majority of 179 over all the other parties in the 659-seat House of Commons. The Conservatives held only 165 seats.

Yet there was more to the palpable shift in the nation's mood than even these startling statistics suggested. Perhaps it was the weather. Few could recall such a strikingly bright, sunny May morning. Then there was the constant, inescapable beat of New Labour's campaign anthem, "Things Can Only Get Better," by the rock band D-Ream, which seemed to be the only tune heard across Britain. Perhaps, too, it was the new prime minister's youth–Britain had been fighting the Napoleonic Wars when it had last elected a leader so young. In any event, this was more than a change of government. The country felt like a different place. Britain had a government it could trust.

Later it would be obvious that here lay a central paradox of Tony Blair's victory. For the previous three years, and then for every minute, hour, and day of the election campaign that had begun on March 17, his message had been one of constant reassurance. You can elect New Labour, the leader had said a thousand times, because it is safe. To be sure, the rhetoric of a new beginning had sometimes soared, but the specific pledges made to the electorate were as modest as he could make them. The waiting lists for treatment in the National Health Service would be shortened, the size of classes in state schools would be reduced–these were not the foundations of a revolution. Even as the opinion polls predicted a landslide victory, Blair never abandoned his caution. Many years before, he had privately confided that he would have only one ambition for his first term in office–to prove that New Labour was competent to govern. He had not changed his mind by the time of the 1997 campaign. He would run the economy well; income tax rates would not be increased; government spending and borrowing would be curbed; New Labour would be the friend of business; money would be invested in public education and health–but only when it could be afforded.

In truth, the scale of New Labour's victory was as much a verdict on the dismal condition of the Conservatives as it was an endorsement of Blair's New Labour project. John Major's government had been broken by the civil war that raged within it over the question of Europe. A series of financial scandals that would see one cabinet minister sent to prison had buried it in sleaze. While the British economy had actually prospered in the two or three years preceding the election, the Conservatives were not given credit for the achievement. The government had never recovered its credibility after its defeat at the hands of the currency speculators on Black Wednesday in September 1992. Long before the election the voters had decided that Major's administration was no longer fit to lead. Such caveats, though, seemed out of place on a day when nothing could deny Tony Blair his triumph. Euphoria elbowed aside caution. Expectations ran riot. Those who had not voted for him were as eager as those who had to share in the na-

tional celebration. Soon opinion surveys would show that millions more claimed to have backed New Labour than had actually done so in the voting booths.

Changes of government in Britain are brutal affairs, for the nation's unwritten constitution does not allow for a measured, orderly transition from one administration to another. Defeated prime ministers are denied even a brief interlude of a day or two to gather their belongings and depart. The moving vans appear as soon as the people's will is known. Just before midday on May 2 and after snatching only an hour or two of sleep, John Major left his official Downing Street residence for the last time as prime minister to tender his resignation to the Queen. As Major's limousine left Buckingham Palace, Blair's was arriving. Within an hour of Major's departure his successor was standing on the steps of 10 Downing Street, ready to receive the secret codes that would bestow on him immediate authority over the nation's nuclear missiles.

Tony Blair seemed almost disbelieving as he posed in the bright sunshine with Cherie and the three children outside their new home. He had known he would win but had always been superstitious about admitting it. Complacency, he would say to anyone willing to listen, was New Labour's most dangerous enemy. To be seen as overly eager in anticipation of victory was somehow to invite defeat. Such was his superstition before the election that he had entered 10 Downing Street only once during his time as leader of the opposition—and then only because he felt he could not refuse an invitation to attend a state dinner in honor of President Bill Clinton. During the weeks before the election, with every opinion poll predicting a landslide victory, Jonathan Powell, Blair's chief of staff, struggled to get his political master to look ahead to the pressing decisions that would have to be taken during the first weeks of government. "He just won't focus on it," Powell grumbled with obvious frustration as polling day neared. Even during the early hours of May 2 Blair would not accept the margin of his victory until the results pouring in from around the country could no longer be denied. As he flew back to London from his Sedgefield constituency in

the dark hours of the night, his mood seemed as much hesitant as jubilant. "A new dawn has broken, has it not?" he asked the ecstatic party workers who had gathered for a victory celebration at the Festival Hall on the South Bank of the river Thames. Standing at the threshold of 10 Downing Street a few hours later, he seemed as anxious as ever to reassure the nation that it had made the right decision. "I say to the people of this country. We ran for office as New Labour. We will govern as New Labour." There would be no reversion, in other words, to the bad old ways of the left. Having won once, Blair was already determined that he would win twice.

For all such admonitions, the new prime minister was quick to seek advantage in the prevailing mood of national unity. Later in his premiership the distinctive moral tone of Blair's foreign policy would invite frequent comparisons with that of William Gladstone. But it was from Gladstone's bitter rival, the Conservative Benjamin Disraeli, that the new prime minister borrowed a political slogan for these early days in government. A writer as well as a politician, Disraeli had penned a famous novel, *Sybil*, in which he had made the case for "One Nation" politics. If Conservatives were to retain their grip on power, this eloquent thesis said, then they must build a society which offered hope to the poor as well as advantage to the wealthy. Without a blush Blair appropriated Disraeli's phrase as his own: New Labour was the party of One Nation, he declared. Visitors to Downing Street were told that prosperity and social cohesion would henceforth march hand in hand. There was no contradiction to be found in New Labour's program of opportunity for the less fortunate in society and generous reward for those who created the wealth. The false antitheses of the modern Conservative Party had been banished.

The coalition-building that had begun before the election, including the co-optation to his cause of the aspirant middle classes, continued beyond it. Blair pitched New Labour's Big Tent over ever wider ground. True to the promise that the government would be as friendly to industry and commerce as to the disadvantaged, senior business leaders such as David Simon, the former head of British Petroleum, and David Sainsbury, of the eponymous supermarket chain, were given

ministerial offices in the government. The hand of reconciliation was also stretched across previous political divides. Senior Conservatives such as Chris Patten, Kenneth Clarke, and Michael Heseltine were offered places on the many independent commissions set up by the new administration, as was every business leader willing to serve.

The small, center-left Liberal Democrat Party led by Paddy Ashdown was given an unprecedented role in shaping the government's domestic legislation. Blair judged that divisions on the center-left had been a fatal weakness for the progressive forces in British politics. Votes for progressive policies had been shared by Labour and the less powerful Liberals, conferring an automatic electoral advantage on the Conservatives. Now he hoped to bridge the divide. Ashdown and his senior colleagues were invited to join the prime minister around the cabinet table in meetings of a new high-level cabinet committee responsible for New Labour's plans to modernize the British constitution and create new political assemblies in Scotland and Wales. "My vision for New Labour," Blair said in a speech during the autumn of 1998, "is to become, as the Liberal Party was in the nineteenth century, a broad coalition of those who believe in progress and justice. Not a narrow class-based politics but a party founded on clear values whose means of implementation change with the generations."

Although this public disdain for the tribal boundaries of politics shocked many in his own party, the new prime minister initially would have liked to have gone still further. He had decided before the 1997 election to invite the Liberal Democrats into a formal coalition in which Ashdown would have been offered the pivotal role of foreign secretary. In the moment of victory, however, Blair suffered a loss of nerve, fearing a backlash in his own party. Senior members of his cabinet, including Gordon Brown and the newly appointed home secretary, Jack Straw, were vehemently opposed: how could he justify sharing everything with Ashdown when New Labour alone commanded such a huge majority in the House of Commons? Blair still harbored the hope that New Labour and the Liberal Democrats could eventually be merged into a single progressive force in British politics.

Ashdown's published diaries record many lengthy and agonized conversations in which the prime minister searched for ways to circumvent the hostility of senior cabinet colleagues. The irony was that that opportunity had been lost in the very size of his own victory.

Beyond the boundaries of politics the doors of 10 Downing Street were thrown open to many who had never before crossed the threshold of the prime minister's residence. In imitation of Bill Clinton's celebrity style, parties and receptions in the grand state of rooms of the prime minister's residence were peopled by rock stars, soccer players, actors, painters, and writers, as well the more familiar cast of the great and the good. The more excitable among the government's young advisers spoke of a new Camelot. The Blairs, society writers gushed, were the new Establishment. Cherie, for all her humble roots, or perhaps because of them, enjoyed the adulation and often seemed intoxicated by the glamour. If her husband seemed less comfortable in such extravagant company, the glitz suited his politics. Modernity ruled. New Labour was the future, the Conservatives the past. He intended to marginalize those on the right of politics just as surely as Margaret Thatcher had made outcasts of the left. The conceit of "Cool Britannia" was born, first on the cover of *Newsweek,* then in the pages of newspapers and periodicals across the Western world. Blair would protest some time later that it was a phrase he had never used, but he was more than content that others should do so. This was the promised New Britain. So it seemed, anyway, in those heady early days.

The apotheosis came in the wake of the death of Diana, the Princess of Wales, just a few months after the election. The royal family was initially hesitant in its mourning for the lost princess, for Diana's broken marriage with Prince Charles had caused them much grief. But Queen Elizabeth and her courtiers badly misread the national mood. Amid an extraordinary outpouring of popular emotion, Blair interposed himself between a beleaguered monarchy and a tabloid press growing increasingly hostile to the ancient House of Windsor. As the Queen was guided to safer ground, Blair usurped the monarch's role,

speaking for the country in its hour of grief. Suddenly the talk was of President Blair. The appellation was heard inside government as well as beyond it.

The view the outside world has of 10 Downing Street–a small black-painted door with highly polished brass plaque set in a small row of town houses–is deceptive. By the standards of other official residences–the White House in Washington, the Elysée Palace in Paris–that of the British prime minister is indeed modest. But that famous door, and the equally unremarkable white-and-black-tiled reception hall that lies directly beyond it, opens onto a much bigger complex of offices and reception rooms. The present No. 10, which began life in the seventeenth century as a private residence built by Sir George Downing, is in fact two houses merged into one. The prime minister's domain extends through a maze of corridors linking it with the two others in the row and, farther, via an enclosed "bridge," to one of the much larger government buildings on Whitehall. The offices and reception rooms at No. 11 are reserved for Gordon Brown, the chancellor of the exchequer, and Tony Blair's staff occupies No. 12. Across the top floors of the row are two private apartments. As prime minister, Blair took the larger of the two with his family, which happens to be above No. 11. Gordon Brown and his wife, Sarah, were allocated the smaller apartment above No 10. Both look out onto a small, high-walled garden, with views of St. James's Park beyond. This is the quiet sanctuary to which Blair retreats whenever the British weather allows.

John Major had chosen as prime minister to work in the cabinet room, a grand book-lined chamber overlooking the garden. He would sit with his back to the ornate fireplace under the portrait of Robert Walpole, the first British prime minister, at the large boat-shaped table around which senior ministers still gather for the weekly meeting of the cabinet. This was the room in which Winston Churchill had written his stirring speeches during the Second World War and from which he had broadcast his famous radio address announcing victory over Germany. Blair, though, eschewed the gilded ceilings and chandeliers,

settling into a small room that had previously been the office of a lowly political adviser. He had always been uncomfortable working at a desk and was curiously reluctant to embrace the information technology that he declared was at the heart of Britain's future. He wrote speeches and notes to staff in longhand, all the while balancing official papers on the arm of his chair. Later he moved to slightly less cramped quarters, with a door leading directly into the cabinet room. But even this space allowed for not much more than a chintz sofa, two easy chairs, and a modest desk cluttered with photographs of his wife and children. The style of this government, such surroundings said, was relaxed. John Major, a prime minister forever under siege, valued the visible trappings of power as outward proof of his status. Blair, as powerful a leader as the nation had seen, could be indifferent to such symbolism. But the modest room—the prime minister's "den," it was called—also conveyed a more substantive message. Decisions in the new administration would not be taken by the broad collective of senior ministers represented by the cabinet. Instead, policy would be made by the small number of colleagues and close advisers who could squeeze into the prime minister's room. Senior ministers soon discovered that the politics of inclusiveness did not extend to Downing Street's inner sanctum.

The British system of government has traditionally dispersed power across the great departments of Whitehall. Within a cabinet of twenty or so senior ministers, the formal position of the prime minister is that of *primus inter pares*—first among equals. His or her ultimate authority rests on patronage—the right to choose and dismiss members of the cabinet. Once appointed, the senior ministers who run departments like the Treasury, Defence, Health, Education, or the Home Office have their own considerable power bases. The prime minister proposes policy, but relies on these colleagues to dispose. Even before the May 1997 election Blair was distinctly uneasy about the idea of sharing so much power. Clement Attlee, the Labour prime minister who had won the 1945 general election, once remarked that "democracy means government by discussion, but it is only effective if you can stop people talking." Blair was as impatient as any about discussion.

Jonathan Powell gave a preview of the new prime minister's intentions before the election when he compared the distribution of power in the cabinet system to that between the king and aristocracy in medieval England. Under New Labour, Powell said, there would be no place for baronial fiefdoms beyond the walls of 10 Downing Street. Tony Blair's model would be much closer to that of Emperor Napoleon's France.

The prime minister was true to his aide's prediction. Government, he said in an informal conversation soon after his election victory, was about "political will, focus, and energy." That demanded strong command and control from the center—from 10 Downing Street. He had too much to do and, if he was to be certain of that all-important second term, too little time to do it. His answer was to create an office of the prime minister that was of unprecedented authority and reach, more powerful even than that presided over by Margaret Thatcher at her peak. Though New Labour's promise to the public had been to build a Britain in which power and opportunity belonged to "the many, not the few," in Blair's government they were reserved for the few.

Behind this lay the leader's intrinsic mistrust of his own party. The misgivings began with his own cabinet, which one close aide in Downing Street likened to a group of reformed alcoholics—they had signed up for the New Labour agenda but everyone knew that, given the chance, many would relapse into their Old Labour ways. Blair's unease was intensified by an anachronistic party rule that had obliged him to give senior jobs to Old Labour traditionalists. His first cabinet included a clutch of political heavyweights. Alongside Gordon Brown at the Treasury, Robin Cook was appointed foreign secretary, and Jack Straw, one of the earliest advocates of the abolition of Labour's Clause IV, was put in charge of law and order at the Home Office. David Blunkett headed the Education Department. Alexander Irvine, the lawyer who had taught the young Blair how to think when he first left Oxford, took command of the nation's legal system as lord chancellor. Overall, though, the cabinet was raw in its inexperience and less than a celebration of talent. Precious few at the top shared the prime minister's

fervor for the center ground of politics. They had understood the electoral imperatives behind the creation of a new party, but, unlike Blair, they did not *think* New Labour.

Blair therefore governed with the political allies and aides he had worked with closely in the opposition. Gordon Brown was foremost among them—and the single exception to the Napoleonic model. Given the Treasury, the most powerful department in Whitehall because of its oversight of all tax and spending decisions, the dour and fiercely able Brown would soon become the most powerful chancellor of the exchequer Britain had seen in modern times. In accordance with the deal he had struck with Blair when he stood aside in the 1994 leadership contest, Brown's writ ran across a swath of other government departments well beyond his own. Welfare, Employment, and Trade and Industry were swept up into his empire. The new chancellor's intellectual intensity and grasp of political strategy were matched by his ruthless grip on the levers of power. One senior official who worked for him observed that the chancellor was a politician cut from the same unforgiving cloth as Russia's Vladimir Putin, and those colleagues foolish enough to challenge Brown's decisions soon found themselves agreeing with that assessment. The analogy missed, however, the complexity of the second most powerful figure in the government. Behind the iron determination lay disappointment and insecurity. Though his counsel was sought on every important decision—nothing seemed to happen in Downing Street before it had been discussed privately between prime minister and chancellor—Brown could still not accept that the younger man had seized the bigger prize. Before long the friendship between the two men would be pushed aside by rivalry.

If Tony Blair's first telephone call each morning was to Gordon Brown, his second was to Peter Mandelson. Blair leaned on Brown for the intellect and political force he brought to economic policymaking. He looked to Mandelson for his political skills, for his genius as a campaign tactician and strategist, and as a friend and confidant. Mandelson was Blair's consigliere—the person to whom he opened his heart and turned in moments of crisis. Unlike the prime minister, Mandelson came from

a family steeped in Labour history; his grandfather Herbert Morrison had been a formidable figure in Clement Attlee's post–World War II government. But Mandelson's politics looked well beyond the tribal boundaries of the past. He was an enthusiast for a coalition with the Liberal Democrats, and contemptuous of those who clung to the old ideologies. His relationship with Blair had a personal intensity absent in that between the prime minister and the chancellor. With Mandelson, Blair could share his innermost doubts and thoughts. Both had New Labour in their souls.

Beyond Brown and Mandelson, Alexander Irvine, the new lord chancellor, also provided close counsel. Irvine had prospered greatly in the law before being brought into government by his former pupil. He was a man of ferocious appetites and ego, his capacity for hard work matched by an equal thirst for the best French wines and a love of fine paintings. The prime minister, embarrassed by Irvine's lavish use of taxpayers' money to decorate his official apartments, once observed that his former mentor's conspicuous consumption belonged to the age of the Italian Renaissance prince. Irvine was a man who had never had even a passing acquaintance with humility. He rashly likened himself to Cardinal Thomas Wolsey, the corpulent and self-aggrandizing chief minister to England's Henry VIII. Blair lamented his friend's extravagances, but he valued his intellect and authority.

Charles (Lord) Falconer had known Blair for longer than either Brown or Mandelson. Their first encounter, in the early 1970s when the future prime minister was in his last year at Fettes, had been less than amicable. Falconer broke up one of Blair's first serious romances, stealing his girlfriend, Amanda Mackenzie Stuart, the daughter of a distinguished Scottish judge. Falconer recalls that this was not a slight taken lightly. Even then, Falconer says, Blair liked to win: "He was incredibly sweet-natured but not someone who would easily give up." When they ran into each other at social events, the atmosphere was tense. "He was quite hostile," Falconer says. But by the mid-1970s, when their paths crossed again in London, the tension had dissipated. Falconer had already started his career in the law, and the two became good friends, with Blair lodging for a time in Falconer's house. As Blair

rose in politics, Falconer prospered in the law. After his election as prime minister Blair gave his old friend a seat in the House of Lords and a ministerial job. "Charlie," as he was universally known in Downing Street, gained reputation and influence as one of the prime minister's trusted "fixers" in the political battlefields of government and as a cool-headed public face in moments of crisis. His rise through the ministerial ranks was rapid, and, in a touch of irony that none of these three lawyers whose paths had first crossed in the 1970s could have predicted, he eventually replaced Irvine as lord chancellor.

The new prime minister broke with another convention by taking into 10 Downing Street the many political aides who had worked for him in opposition. The British civil service prides itself on an independence that allows it to work for masters of all political stripes. Incoming prime ministers usually bring with them just a handful of policy advisers, relying mostly on the career officials who had worked for their predecessors. Blair, though, was conscious of his own inexperience and of the fact that the officials he would inherit had served the Conservatives for eighteen years. He wanted his own people around him—people, as he put it, "I can trust." The new court was a curious mix. At the center were Alistair Campbell, who had become his press secretary in 1994; Anji Hunter, the friend from school days who had run his office in opposition; and Jonathan Powell, the chief of staff who had first introduced him to Bill Clinton's team in Washington. These were the staffers who felt comfortable calling the prime minister by his nickname, "TB." Later, others would join the inner circle: Sally Morgan as Blair's principal political secretary, and, at times, career civil servants like David Manning, his foreign policy adviser during the Iraq war. David Miliband, the first head of the Downing Street strategic policy unit, and his successor, Andrew Adonis, could also command the prime minister's time.

Alistair Campbell, the most prominent and powerful in this group, was, on the face of it, the very antithesis of the man he served. Everything about him seemed an affront to Tony Blair's Victorian social mores. A recovered alcoholic who had once written for a soft-core pornographic magazine, Campbell came from what the British call the

"rough" end of the media—the tabloid press. He was also godless. As for honoring the traditional family, he had never seen a reason to marry his long-term partner, Fiona Millar, even after the couple had children. His choice of words was colorfully Anglo-Saxon. Tribal in his political views, he often scorned his boss's preference for making friends over defeating enemies. The press secretary saw politics as combat. Yet Campbell was closer to Blair than anyone. He brought formidable talent and ferocious loyalty to New Labour's communications strategy. Having witnessed the Conservative-leaning media set out to destroy Neil Kinnock during the 1980s, the message Campbell had taken was that attack was the surest means of defense. If he could be blunt to the point of rudeness in private exchanges with Blair, he was relentless in pursuit of the prime minister's interests. His relationship with Blair could not have been more intimate. No one else could tell the prime minister, as Campbell was once heard to do, to "get lost." In Blair's projection of New Labour, presentation and policy had become inseparable, which meant that Campbell's writ ran well beyond that of a media adviser. It was often said, not least by aggrieved ministers, that he wielded more authority than the elected politicians with seats around the cabinet table.

Anji Hunter gave Tony Blair another set of eyes, ears, and instincts. As special assistant to the prime minister, she acted as Blair's gatekeeper, adviser, and fixer at 10 Downing Street. Hunter had been the first person Blair called for advice in 1994 when he heard of the death of John Smith. The daughter of an affluent Scottish rubber plantation manager, she had been born in Malaysia but returned to school in Scotland, where she met the future prime minister. Her upper-middle-class background cast her, like Blair, as an outsider in the Labour Party. In Downing Street she was a finger on the pulse of Middle Britain, a role in which she served as a political counterweight to Blair's wife. "Cherie would pull him to the left, Anji would remind him of his bigger constituency," is how one aide described her function. Needless to say, the relationship between the two women was often strained. At once flirtatious and combative, Hunter kept open Downing Street's channels to political enemies as well as friends. And, like Campbell, she

was ready to fight the grubby battles of politics that Blair preferred to imagine never really happened.

Jonathan Powell, the third member of the troika of intimates, brought a more cerebral tone to the deliberations in the prime minister's den. A former diplomat, Powell was publicly self-effacing, preferring the shadows to the limelight. He shared Blair's public-school and Oxford background and had joined the Labour Party only after meeting Blair during the latter's trip to Washington in January 1993. Powell's task was to plug the Blair premiership into the wider government machine. He served, too, as a powerful personal emissary in the tortuous search for a peace in Northern Ireland. His strong Atlanticism and his equally powerful conviction that Britain must come to terms with its European partners had a profound influence on Blair's foreign policy. Powell, with Campbell and Hunter, was among the few who could tell the prime minister hard truths.

Those who lived on the edges of this magic circle marveled at the way the prime minister and his aides interacted. One official who watched them from close up over many years said that they shared a secret, silent language. Intuition often seemed to substitute for the spoken word. Of course, there were disagreements, sometimes loud ones. Yet by some strange telepathy each seemed to know what the other was thinking–and what Tony Blair wanted. Their wholly different characters were bound together in unyielding devotion to the leader. When the government sailed into the murkier waters of politics–into scandals about party fund-raising and ministerial misdemeanors, for example–their first reaction was always to protect the prime minister. Whatever had passed in the government's name could not be allowed to tarnish Tony Blair personally. Everyone else was expendable, even those who might count themselves the leader's friends. What mattered, the only thing that mattered, was that the leader emerge unsullied.

With the serious business of government conducted in the prime minister's den, meetings of the cabinet were occasions where decisions were ratified rather than made. Smaller ministerial groups were tasked

with delivering Blair's policy rather than formulating their own. Serious political players like David Blunkett or Jack Straw did shape the agenda, but they wielded influence in bilateral talks with Blair rather than in any wider forum. John Prescott was given the grand title of deputy prime minister. It was an honorific. Blair listened to Prescott when he found it politically expedient. He stroked his deputy's ego, and in return Prescott guarded Blair's flank against attacks from the party's traditionalist wing. But mostly the deputy prime minister contented himself with the trappings of office.

Just outside the inner circle, the world-weary civil servants in 10 Downing Street who had watched prime ministers come and go with the changing political seasons found themselves at once beguiled by Tony Blair and vexed by his complexities. Their new political master, these veterans of Whitehall soon discovered, was a man of many characters. First was the good-mannered—even sweet-natured—husband who craved more time with his children and enjoyed nothing more than playing tennis or strumming his guitar. Next came the politician whose charm and persuasiveness had never been matched by any previous occupant of 10 Downing Street. Alongside him stood the nineteenth-century public servant, who talked of duty to one's country. Yet another Tony Blair was born to the lights, the brilliant mimic and actor who could turn in an award-winning performance at scarcely a moment's notice. Next to him stood the conviction politician, the brave leader and genuinely pious man whose self-belief and ethics reflected a deep personal commitment to the Christian faith. Then again there was the leader who always shied away from personal confrontations. He had a habit of telling visitors what they wanted to hear, even when that meant saying different things to different people. "He believes everything he says at the moment he says it," was the caustic observation of one insider. Yet, when circumstance demanded it, he could be as coldly single-minded in pursuit of his political ends as any who had preceded him in the nation's highest office. Each and every one of these people was real. And Tony Blair was all of them.

————————

The voters, of course, saw little of this rarefied world of political wheeling and dealing. Their interest lay in how the government would seek to reconcile the reassurance it had offered before the election with the post-election promise of radicalism. Tony Blair and Gordon Brown always intended to invest more in publicly provided services, above all in health and education and in a welfare system to put people back to work. After all, New Labour's central ambition was to reconcile market economics with the decent public provision that would create a fairer society. But a steep change in public spending required tax increases that could not be hidden from the electorate. That in turn was a bridge the government could cross only when it had passed the crucial test of proving it could run a modern economy.

A big part of the government's response to this test came within days of the 1997 election. Even before Parliament had been reconvened, Gordon Brown announced that control over interest rates in the economy would be handed without delay to the Bank of England. This was a defining decision of the first Blair government. While central bank independence may have been the norm in most Western economies, previous British governments had jealously guarded political control of one of the principal levers of economic management. Brown's decision sent an unmistakable signal about the intent of the new administration. Its radicalism lay in the final rejection of the old, Keynesian belief that governments could manage the rate of growth in the economy by manipulating the price of money; the reassurance came in the proof that this decision offered of New Labour's reconciliation with the market economy. An independent Bank of England marked the final exorcism of history's ghosts. Gordon Brown knew how many previous Labour administrations had lurched from reckless post-election boom to fatal pre-election bust. Henceforth, the ambition for a more cohesive society would rest on the firm foundations of a stable economy.

The new chancellor went still further in his embrace of the economic orthodoxies of the times. The Treasury published a plethora of new rules to limit the amount the government could spend and bor-

row. In effect, Brown designed his own budgetary constraints to gain the confidence of financial markets. He would seek to generate faster growth in the economy not through Keynesian demand management but with micromeasures to stimulate enterprise, strengthen competition, and raise productivity. As ever in politics, some sleight of hand was involved. The pledge not to increase personal income taxes still left room for the chancellor to raise additional revenues from indirect and business taxes. He took full advantage of what soon became known as "stealth taxes," and the new budgetary rules were crafted to give the Treasury room where it needed it. The big political picture, though, saw the government following in the footsteps of Bill Clinton's administration, which by eliminating the budget deficit was able to pursue its social objectives. Brown was committed to the redistribution of wealth across society, and before the election had floated the idea of raising the top rate of income tax rate from 40 percent to 50 percent. Blair had overruled him. That disagreement apart, what united the two men was the certainty that competence had to precede compassion.

Prudence was Gordon Brown's favorite word. It was duly rewarded with a resounding vote of confidence from the nation's financial markets. Stock prices rose; long-term interest rates fell. Alan Greenspan, the Federal Reserve chairman, had privately predicted as much when Brown consulted him on New Labour's economic plans just before the 1997 general election. The government had given itself room for maneuver. Within two or three years it could boast of steady economic growth, monetary and fiscal stability, low inflation, and an unemployment rate that had fallen to its lowest level since the 1970s. A large budget surplus in the 2000–2001 financial year provided the platform for an unprecedented series of increases in the funding of key public services. Tony Blair had achieved his central ambition. New Labour was indeed competent to govern.

The other decision that assured this first Blair administration of a place in the history books lay well beyond the realm of economics. Tony Blair will be remembered in his own country as the prime minister

who fundamentally recast Britain's constitutional settlement—above all by restoring to Scotland its own parliament. Scotland's relationship within the United Kingdom—in the Union of England, Scotland, Wales, and Northern Ireland—had become a running sore in British political life. Nearly three centuries earlier the Act of Union that joined the English and Scottish monarchies had placed both under the rule of the Westminster parliament. Scotland retained its own legal system and distinct social mores, but its laws were made in Westminster, where English MPs commanded a large majority of the seats in the House of Commons. The Union had endured, but tensions had grown as the political complexions of the two nations had diverged—Conservative governments at Westminster typically won only a minority of the votes in Scotland. The 1960s and 1970s had thus seen the rise of the Scottish Nationalists, a party committed to complete secession from England—the breakup, in other words, of the Union.

Tony Blair had inherited his party's response to the dilemma when he became leader in 1994. The proposal for limited self-rule in Scotland was one piece of party baggage he felt unable to jettison. Devolution had the backing not just of his own party and of the Liberal Democrats but also of the majority of voters in Scotland. A parliament in Edinburgh, the devolution camp argued, would give Scotland autonomy over its domestic affairs while retaining the essential link with the rest of Britain. Wales, where the pressure for self-government was visible but less acute, could be given an assembly with lesser powers. Most of Labour's Scottish MPs—Gordon Brown prominent among them—were convinced that a new parliament in Edinburgh responsible for Scotland's domestic policies was the only way to prevent a complete schism between the two countries. Others felt that even limited self-government would be a step on the road to complete separation. Over the decades, this divide had provoked as many arguments within political parties as between them. Why should Scotland have its own parliament and England be denied one? asked many English MPs. How could it be fair that Scottish MPs in the UK parliament at Westminster would retain the right to vote on laws affecting England, while

English MPs had no say in Scotland's domestic affairs? Such were the political rocks on which other governments had foundered and which Blair now sought to navigate.

The new prime minister was no great enthusiast for devolution. Although Blair was born in Scotland and had gone to school in Edinburgh, he was English in his outlook and privately shared some of the doubts of other English MPs about the plan. The focus of his strategic ambition was to convert the English middle classes to New Labour's progressive politics. The Labour Party had always prospered on Britain's Celtic fringes, and it always would. Blair's political project was to establish the hegemony of center-left politics in the Westminster parliament—and for that he needed English votes. Too generous a settlement for Scotland could lose him that vital English support. These were doubts, though, that he put aside; better to give Scotland its parliament, he concluded, than be forever dogged by the threat of the breakup of the Union. The seemingly intractable constitutional questions were brushed aside, and it was a measure of the prime minister's extraordinary authority and of the popular mood for change that within two years of the May 1997 election, Scotland had its parliament and Wales its assembly. Blair packaged these changes as part of the modernization of Britain's system of government. They were accompanied by other legislative measures to give Britain its first elected city mayors and to strengthen the role of regional authorities in England. The prime minister never quite explained the apparent contradiction between his desire to centralize power at 10 Downing Street and this dispersal of authority to new political institutions beyond his direct control. In any event, the history books would record that Tony Blair had presided over a revolution in the way that Britain was governed.

These were times when Tony Blair carried all before him. The scale of his 1997 election victory and bold decisions on economic policy and devolution had shown him as a leader who made the political weather. The government provided other emblems of its radicalism. For almost a century those on the left of British politics had promised and failed to remove from the House of Lords the hundreds of its members who

owed their place in Parliament's second chamber to an accident of birth—the viscounts and dukes of the British aristocracy. By the end of Blair's first term, most of these hereditary peers had gone, legislated into the history books. The few allowed to remain pending a more fundamental overhaul of the House of Lords were granted only a temporary stay of execution. At the other end of the social scale, low-paid workers benefited from the introduction of an American-style minimum wage. Before the general election the Conservatives had argued that any interference in the labor market would destroy jobs, while in fact employment rose rather than fell. In any event, Blair was untroubled by the Conservative opposition. The Tories had responded to their 1997 defeat by electing a new leader in place of John Major. But William Hague was lost even before he had set off. The shock of defeat had sent his party into denial, and the Conservatives seemed unable to comprehend why the voters had extracted such revenge for those eighteen years in government. Instead of examining the question, or showing a touch of penitence and humility, the party continued its private wars, Euroskeptics battling pro-Europeans, moral authoritarians fighting social liberals. Hague, young and inexperienced, showed neither the wisdom nor the forcefulness to end the squabbling. Instead of attempting to reclaim the swathes of traditional Tory ground that New Labour had occupied—on law and order, welfare reform, defense and patriotism—Hague took his party further toward the far right of politics, just as Blair had hoped and planned.

Yet even so apparently impregnable a government had its frailties. Those who closely examined the way Tony Blair's administration operated discerned the seeds of later troubles. It sometimes seemed that it swaggered by day and sweated by night, both of which were testimony to its long political exile. In his eagerness to solicit the endorsement of (and financial contributions from) the business community, the prime minister was often naive about the motives of those who wrote large checks to New Labour. He seemed beguiled by the rich entrepreneurs who crowded the corridors and waiting rooms of 10 Downing Street. One close friend remarked early on that Blair, with no experience of his own of the worlds of business and commerce, had a

habit of mistaking "wealth for worth." This friend, himself someone of considerable financial means, thought the prime minister too gullible and too careless of proprieties when supping with rich entrepreneurs. "There's always a price," he said of the business leaders who were contributing to New Labour. Blair soon discovered as much.

In the autumn of 1997 the integrity of the new government was publicly questioned when it was disclosed that one of New Labour's largest benefactors had persuaded the prime minister to change government policy to his advantage. While the particular details of the so-called Bernie Ecclestone affair would soon be forgotten, what would stick in the public mind was that Ecclestone, owner of the Formula One worldwide motor racing business, had contributed £1 million ($1.6 million) to New Labour's election campaign and then seemed to have won exemption for his industry from a proposed ban on tobacco advertising. The donation and the exemption were never linked, the prime minister always insisted, but his explanations were never quite convincing. In any event, because Blair had promised that his government would avoid the appearance as well as the fact of such conflicts of interest, he only added to the problem by being less than candid when the story first broke. By the time the dust had settled, it seemed that this was not a tale of great corruption, but rather one of misjudgment and attempted cover-up. Trust me, Blair asked the nation when he appeared on television to calm the storm: "I think most people who have dealt with me think I'm a pretty straight sort of guy, and I am." In fact, most people did, but at best the prime minister had been careless. On this occasion he was given the benefit of the doubt, but there were other allegations of financial improprieties. Geoffrey Robinson, a businessman-turned-politician who had long been close to Gordon Brown, found his personal business dealings under scrutiny by the House of Commons. As a senior member of Brown's ministerial team at the Treasury responsible for tax policy, he was embarrassed by the disclosure that much of his own wealth was conveniently sheltered in offshore trusts beyond the reach of the British tax authorities.

For all his immensely privileged position at the center of power, Peter Mandelson was twice trapped in these periodic political storms

about the government's financial probity. On the first of these occasions, he was obliged to resign from the cabinet after failing to disclose a large private loan from Geoffrey Robinson. Mandelson had used the money to buy a London house, but he had failed to make the necessary declarations to Parliament and to his senior officials at the Department of Trade and Industry. On the face of it, this was a small infraction, less a possible conflict of interest than the appearance of one. But he was caught by the government's pledge that its conduct would be beyond reproach. In any event, Mandelson's hopes for one of the most senior positions in the government seemed compromised. Reappointed to the cabinet by the prime minister after a short period of penance, Mandelson then became embroiled in a public furor about whether the government had traded British passports for political donations with a wealthy Indian family, the Hindujas. This time, in a moment of political panic, Blair sacked his closest friend in government. Although an independent inquiry subsequently declared Mandelson innocent of wrongdoing, it was too late to reinstate him a second time. Mandelson's career lay in ruins–though not his friendship with the prime minister. Such was the extraordinary intensity of their relationship that these two men remained the closest of friends. Though he was now formally outside the government, Mandelson soon enough resumed his role as prime ministerial confidant. The world beyond Downing Street also caught in this incident a glimpse of Blair's ruthless instinct for self-preservation. Here was a prime minister ready to fire one of his closest political friends to avoid damage to his government. Yet the accumulation of such awkward episodes took its toll. Throughout the early years of his leadership, Blair had understood the importance of rebuilding trust in his party. Now, as the mud thrown by his opponents began to stick, he was losing it.

Passing from the innocence of opposition to the experience of government, Blair would discover how easily strengths could turn into weaknesses. The iron discipline over policy that had been essential to win back the confidence of voters began to resemble something of an obsession with centralized control, as did Alistair Campbell's fight to win every day's headlines. "Control-freakery" and "spin" were charges

that would ultimately damage the government. Blair's presidential style caused needless irritation among his own supporters, not least his habit of continuing to praise Margaret Thatcher's record. "Why does he treat the [Labour] party as his enemy?" one senior minister asked privately in some exasperation in the summer of 1999. In opposition Blair had shown he had the courage to make hard decisions and stick with them. He was less ready to understand that the complexities of government demanded a team effort. "He's a hopeless manager of people," one of the business advisers brought into Downing Street said. New Labour's Big Tent began to spring leaks. Government is about choosing; and choosing creates losers as well as winners. Business grumbled about stealth taxes, voters about the snail's pace of improvement in public services. Conservative-leaning newspaper editors, once charmed by the young prime minister, returned to the attack. The Dome–a vast steel-and-fiberglass structure built beside London's river Thames to celebrate the new millennium–turned out to be an expensive flop. The 1 billion sterling of public funds wasted on the project was early testimony to the hubris of Cool Britannia.

These, though, cast as yet small shadows over Tony Blair's political achievement. He had reduced to political rubble the most formidable vote-winning machine in European politics. The Conservatives–the party of Benjamin Disraeli, Winston Churchill, and Margaret Thatcher–had seemed to own a freehold on power. Now that party lay in ruins. The prime minister had recast the political terrain in his own image, redrawing the old dividing line between left and right. He had also changed the argument in British politics. While the Conservatives had won four successive election victories on a platform of cutting taxes, Blair had made the case for a different balance between taxation and public provision. Above all, though, he had shown that New Labour was competent to govern.

6. THE WORLD AS A STAGE

TONY BLAIR WAS ALWAYS going to be a prime minister eager to play to a bigger audience. While New Labour had been elected to repair the tears in Britain's social fabric, to fix the schools and modernize the hospitals, his temperament, self-belief, and sense of personal mission cast Blair as one of those leaders for whom domestic politics would inevitably be too small a theater. All postwar British prime ministers had agonized about the nation's role in the world—the retreat from past glories had been a painful experience. But the nineteenth-century politician in Blair felt more acutely than most a need to reassert British influence. "That's my job," he once confided: "to promote and project British power." A high-ranking official would later remark of the prime minister, "He is moved by world events in an extraordinary way. Sure, he works at domestic policy. He has to. But that's *applied* energy. The world is what really excites and energizes him." Those who talked to Blair in his Downing Street study took away the same impression. Although he would typically go out of his way to say how much time he was devoting to education, health, or welfare reform, it was a case of protesting too much. Even before the upheavals in international affairs caused by the war in Kosovo and the terrorist attacks on America of September 11, 2001, foreign policy was what animated him. At home, Blair's prospectus was drawn from the set of values he had carried with him from Oxford, though in immodest moods he would say that these same principles had universal application. If individuals could thrive only in strong societies, so nations would prosper only in a secure international community. The notion of interdependence, at the heart of his domestic politics, applied equally in world affairs—the more so as globalization tore down the boundaries between nations.

Self-image also demanded that the New Britain Blair had promised the electorate would hold its head up in the world. Margaret Thatcher had shown how it could be done. Before her fatal collision with other European leaders she had restored the nation's standing abroad, whether by winning the war in the Falklands or sharing the limelight with Ronald Reagan. If it often seemed that Blair's habit of praising Thatcher was tactical–designed at once to taunt his own party and to prove to a wider audience that Labour really had changed–his admiration for the Iron Lady was at times genuine. The challenge of adding luster to his country's reputation in the world appealed to the new prime minister's sense of self-confidence in spite of his inexperience in the domain of foreign affairs. Nearly forty years earlier an American secretary of state, Dean Acheson, had famously described Britain as a nation that had lost an empire but had failed to find a role. In the summer of 1997, as he pored over the thick folders of foreign policy briefings handed to every incoming prime minister, Blair was soon aware that nothing much had changed in the interim. Even in the late 1990s the burden of past greatness sat heavily on the shoulders of a nation that had never quite understood why it had won–albeit with indispensable American help–World War II and yet somehow had lost the peace. Germany and France had prospered greatly in the postwar years, and even Italy had begun to catch up with Britain economically. For Britain, the fifty years since 1945 had been at once a period of lost empire, diminishing influence, and a refusal to admit the new realities of world power. Blair saw an opportunity to refashion the public mood to create a nation at ease with itself. There was no time for nostalgia; Britain could no longer pretend to be the "Great Power" that Winston Churchill had imagined. It could, however, in its youthful leader's phrase, reposition itself in the world to become a "Pivotal Power."

Two sets of relationships lie at the heart of Britain's foreign policy. The first is the "special relationship" with the United States, the nexus of historical, cultural, economic, and security ties, alongside a shared language, that binds Britain to an Atlanticist outlook. The second is defined by the close links–geographic, economic, and political–between

Britain and its European neighbors in the European Union. The grand theory of Britain's strategic posture holds that these twin associations are mutually reinforcing. The stronger Britain is in Europe, the more clout it will exercise in Washington, and vice versa. But the reality has rarely been thus. The very term "special relationship," coined by Winston Churchill, has often overstated Britain's standing in a distinctly unequal partnership with America. Engagement in Europe, meanwhile, has been a constant struggle between the emotional instinct to stand aloof from the enterprise and the realpolitik that says that Britain cannot afford to exclude itself from decisions taken on the European continent.

Britain's ties with the rest of the world have never quite emerged from the shadow of Suez. In 1956, Britain and France—both engaged in the painful withdrawal from empire—invaded Egypt to secure the Suez Canal. The proximate cause was the decision by Gamal Abdel Nasser, the intensely nationalist Egyptian leader, to seize the Suez Canal from its private "European" owners. In London and Paris, Nasser's act was seen as an unacceptable challenge to British and French power in the Middle East. The flimsy pretext for the Anglo-French invasion was that the two countries were seeking to impose a cease-fire after the Israeli army had marched into Egyptian territory, but the deception did not stand scrutiny. The Israeli incursion was contrived, an integral part of the plot, agreed in advance to provide the excuse for the intervention. This was a war grounded in self-delusion, a desperate effort by Britain and France to reassert their dwindling power on a stage increasingly dominated by the superpower rivalry of the United States and the Soviet Union, and it provoked an international outcry. In Washington, President Dwight Eisenhower reacted with fury and demanded the withdrawal of the Anglo-French force. Faced with American anger and universal condemnation at the United Nations, the two countries were obliged to retreat in ignominy, Britain first and then France. The latter accused the "perfidious Albion" of caving in too readily to the United States, a resentment that would continue to burn in the relationship between Paris and London for decades to come. Amid political uproar in England at the debacle, Anthony Eden, the British prime minister, was forced to resign.

The failure of the expedition taught Britain that it could no longer project power in the world without the support, or at least the acquiescence of, the United States. It was another awkward reminder, too, that, for all the friendship between the two nations, Washington saw the relationship through the prism of America's own national interest. The British conceit at the close of the World War II had been that, in the new international order, it would act as Greece to America's Rome—British wisdom would buttress U.S. strength. But there had already been signs indicating that America would decide its own priorities. Harry Truman had failed to keep a bargain struck between Winston Churchill and Franklin Delano Roosevelt on the sharing of U.S. nuclear technology. There had been arguments about the speed of Britain's withdrawal from its former colonies, about the economic arrangements that survived empire, and about American policy toward the Communist regime in China. When Acheson discovered that State Department officials were working with Britain's Foreign Office to put down on paper the terms of the special relationship, he ordered a halt to the talks and all copies of "the wretched paper" destroyed. There could be nothing exclusive about the relationship, Acheson decreed. Britain would have to take its place among America's other allies.

The lesson drawn in London was that it, too, would have to seek wider influence. Bridges had to be built across the English Channel to the European continent. In 1955 six European nations, led by France and Germany, had gathered at a conference at Messina in Sicily to plan the creation of the European Union. Anthony Eden had turned down an invitation to participate, for Britain saw itself as too grand for such projects. (One senior minister airily dismissed the Messina talks as "some archaeological excavations" in an old Sicilian town.) But France and Germany were deadly serious in the endeavor to construct a Europe that would preclude forever the option of another war between the two countries. By the early 1960s Harold Macmillan, the Conservative prime minister who succeeded Eden, realized the British mistake, and it was he who shaped the post-Suez strategic doctrine that would guide Tony Blair forty years later. The relationship with the United States, this doctrine said, would henceforth be the sine qua non

of British influence. On the big issues of strategic security Britain had to stay close to Washington. During the 1980s, Margaret Thatcher had concluded that the lesson of Suez was that Britain could not afford to position itself on the opposing side to the United States when its own national interests were at stake. Although he took a much more favorable view of Europe, Blair essentially agreed. But Macmillan had decreed that the relationship would not be exclusive. Britain also had to play a full part in the European Union. Above all, the guiding principle of Britain's foreign policy was to avoid making a final choice between America and Europe. Instead, in the metaphor that Blair would adopt, Britain would act as a bridge across the Atlantic.

By 1997 the tensions inherent in such an approach were abundantly obvious. During the 1960s France had delayed Britain's formal entry into the European Union for more than a decade in retaliation for its rapid withdrawal from Suez at America's behest. By the time Britain did join in 1973, the rules of the European club had already been established by France and Germany. The French "Gaullist" view of Europe as an alternative center of power to America did not sit easily with London's concept of a triangular relationship in which Britain would be the linchpin. There had been transatlantic storms, too, which had strained one or other of Britain's twin relationships—over the Vietnam War, over Ronald Reagan's "Star Wars" program to take the arms race into space, over American policy in the Middle East. Politics, a distinguished Labour politician once remarked, is "the language of priorities." Britain found it hard to avoid making the choices Macmillan had feared.

Tony Blair came to these strategic issues with a mixture of innocence and advantage. The innocence lay in his own inexperience in foreign affairs, which had featured only occasionally in the many speeches that, in opposition, had established the parameters of New Labour. Nor had the new leader traveled widely. His annual holidays were taken in Italy or in the south of France, and he had visited New York and Washington in pursuit of the collaboration with the New Democrats. He had spent time in Paris—and learned the language—but other European capitals were something of a mystery. As one aide would re-

mark, the new prime minister's knowledge of Italy was limited to the Tuscan hills so beloved of British tourists; he had never been to Rome. This was not a leader closely acquainted with the political geography of the world, nor was he an eager student of diplomacy.

On the other side of the balance sheet, he had an advantage in the strength of his political position relative to other players in the international arena. The great figures of European politics in the 1980s–François Mitterrand of France, Helmut Kohl of Germany, and Jacques Delors, the president of the European Commission–had by the late 1990s left the stage. In France the Gaullist president Jacques Chirac was obliged to govern in cooperation with a Socialist administration led by Prime Minister Lionel Jospin. Gerhard Schröder, Kohl's successor as German chancellor, lacked the experience and stature of the leader who had presided over the reunification of Germany. Since its inception as the Common Market, the European Union had been driven forward by a Franco-German motor, but by the time New Labour took office the motor was stalling. Blair's political position, meanwhile, was impregnable. His stunning electoral victory and huge majority in Parliament gave him a personal standing among other European leaders disproportionate to his experience. His very youth seemed an advantage, for here was a leader with energy and ideas in a continent that seemed to be losing its way. He was a "modern" politician in an era increasingly obsessed with modernity. Blair, it seemed, was the zeitgeist. The British economy was booming. London had become one of the world's most fashionable cities. Such factors, albeit intangible, shape the mood of foreign affairs.

For all his inexperience, or perhaps because of it, the new prime minister started out with Harold Macmillan's dictum in his pocket. "The two main partnerships for Britain are the European Union and the transatlantic relationship," he said in 1995 during one of his few foreign policy speeches as opposition leader. "We need to use them to maximize our influence so that we can promote and protect our interests around the world, because we cannot do so alone. But to be effective we have to participate fully in each partnership." The relationship with the

United States was "essential," he remarked on another occasion during the same year. "Whatever disagreements there may be from time to time ... what binds us together is infinitely more powerful than anything that divides us." The essential truth that lay behind this assessment was that for fifty years Britain's security had been anchored to the American guarantee provided through the North Atlantic Treaty Organization. Although the cold war had ended, in the eyes of British strategic thinkers that guarantee was still vital. And yet decisions were also being made in Europe that would have an enduring impact on British influence and power. So, as Blair put it, "If it is to maintain its historic role as a global player, Britain has to be a central part of the politics of Europe."

As he stepped out into the world in 1997, it was Europe that demanded the new prime minister's immediate attention. The weather over the Atlantic was calm. A rough semblance of peace had been restored to the Balkans after the murderous war in Bosnia, which had badly strained the transatlantic partnership during the first half of the 1990s. Saddam Hussein's Iraq was already a problem on the near horizon as the regime sought to defy and disrupt United Nations sanctions. But Blair's blossoming friendship with President Bill Clinton would keep the lines open between London and Washington. The English Channel, by contrast, was thick with the fog of acrimony. In the dying years of the previous Conservative administration, Britain had become at best a semidetached member of the European Union, as resentful of its EU partners' plans for more economic and political integration as it was determined to stand aside.

Under Margaret Thatcher and then John Major, Britain had moved to the edge of influence in the councils of the European Union. As the Conservative Party fought its civil war during the 1990s over whether to accede to integration or seek to reclaim more of Britain's national sovereignty, the rest of Europe closed its ears. Major's government did secure parliamentary ratification of the Maastricht treaty, the agreement signed in 1991 as the basis for the creation of a single European currency. But Britain had an "opt-out" from the new currency, allowing it to decide not to participate if it so chose. And during the closing

years of his premiership Major found himself held hostage to the swelling ranks of Euroskeptics in his own party. For those Conservatives who sided with the deposed Margaret Thatcher against the vision for Europe of nations like France and Germany, the Union had become a threat to Britain's sovereignty and, indeed, to its very nationhood. Major, with only the smallest majority in the House of Commons, became a prisoner of such sentiments, forced to oppose each and every new step forward by Britain's European partners. The public mood often mirrored the resentments of the Conservative Euroskeptics, and in much of the press the European Union had come to be seen as an anti-British conspiracy.

Tony Blair arrived in 10 Downing Street an instinctive European. "Europe is not something that happened to us in 1973 [the date of Britain's entry to the then Common Market]," he had said while still in opposition. "We are Europeans. We are made up of wave after wave of settlers who came to these islands from Europe: Celts, Romans, Anglo-Saxons, Vikings, and Normans." The new prime minister was of the first generation of political leaders without personal memory of World War II or of the economic privations that followed in the aftermath of 1945. As such, he had been spared the nightmares of those of the previous generation who had never quite understood how Britain had contrived to lose the peace: how the defeated Germany and the occupied France both seemed more prosperous and content. When Anthony Eden's Suez failure had closed the final chapter on Britain's imperial pretensions Blair was still only three years old. Upbringing and experience had left him comfortable in the company of Europeans. He had spent part of a gap year between school and university learning French while working in a bar in Paris. So when he addressed the National Assembly in Paris in the spring of 1998, he did so, to considerable effect, in the language of his hosts.

Blair was unimpressed by the theological disputes about national sovereignty that lay at the heart of the battle between Euroskeptics and pro-Europeans in the Conservative Party. For those, like Margaret Thatcher, who had come to see the European Union as an enemy, each step along the road to a more united Europe represented another

assault on the sovereign authority of the Parliament at Westminster: the governance of Britain was passing from its own elected representatives to that of a new European "superstate." Blair judged otherwise. The absolute sovereignty that the Euroskeptics sought was a chimera. Sovereignty had already been eroded by the realities of strategic power in the world; by the march of globalization, with its vast flows of goods and capital; and by Britain's relative decline. Interdependence was the way of the modern world. Community–that favorite word again–was as important in international relations as in domestic politics. What mattered, the prime minister would say, was the pursuit of national interest. If that was best achieved in concert with other European nations, then so be it. He recalled the metaphor of Michael Heseltine, the pro-European Conservative and former deputy prime minister, who had toppled Margaret Thatcher. A man alone in the desert is truly sovereign, Heseltine would say. He is also powerless.

There was nothing sentimental though about Blair's Europeanism. He could justly claim to be Britain's first intuitively pro-European prime minister since Edward Heath, the Conservative leader who had negotiated entry into the European Union in 1973. But he shared little of the dream of a "United States of Europe" that had been at the heart of the vision of the French and German founding fathers of European cooperation in the 1950s. Jean Monnet, the Frenchman who had been the principal architect of the new Europe, had spoken of an "ever closer union" of the peoples of the Continent. Blair's Europeanism, in contrast, was grounded in English pragmatism and realpolitik. The case, as he emphasized in a speech in Warsaw in the autumn of 2000, was about "projecting collective power." For Britain, "being at the center of influence in Europe is an indispensable part of influence, strength, and power in the world." The continent, he said in the same speech, could be a "superpower" but not a "superstate."

Influence, strength, power–these were words that had a central place in the vocabulary of Blair's foreign policy. They spoke to the coincidence of temperament and ambition. It was his "duty" (another of those favorite terms), he would say, to maximize British influence abroad. He understood the connection between the international and

the domestic stages: a government that was respected abroad would command more support at home. And a government strong at home, in turn, would have a louder voice abroad. Rebuilding relationships in Europe, nourishing the ties with Washington, intervening in Kosovo, sending British troops to Sierra Leone in West Africa, fighting along-side George W. Bush in Iraq–all were undertaken in the central pur-pose of projecting British power.

Foreign policy, Blair soon discovered, is also the place where today's political leaders can escape the confining and frustrating straitjacket of what is known as the machinery of state–that great cumbersome body of ministers, officials, and obdurate bureaucracy that always seems to stand in the way of bringing about change at home. A British prime minister who wants to reform, as Blair did, the public health or educa-tion systems soon finds himself in a quagmire of political controversy. There are no simple levers to be pulled. Power is dispersed through the system across a swath of political and other vested interests, each with its own reason to resist change. The world of international summitry is entirely different. Leaders travel without their bureaucracies. They can make their own decisions and commitments–and, by and large, deliver on them. Blair, a prime minister with all the impatience of his youth, enjoyed the experience of taking his place at the table with other world leaders. Untutored in government–unlike his postwar predecessors, he had had no experience of high office before reaching 10 Downing Street–Blair was more frustrated than most by the cumbersome ma-chinery of domestic policymaking. To be abroad was to be liberated–and, usually, respected. Harold Macmillan had once remarked that "at home you always have to be a politician; when you're abroad, you al-most feel yourself a statesman." Blair shared the sentiment, telling friends how refreshing it was to "sit around with a group of people and know none of them want my job." He had always practiced the politics of personal relationships, enjoying the process of building friendships and alliances. He was utterly confident in his capacity to persuade oth-ers of his case, and coldly calculating in his blandishments. He was a well-practiced public speaker but no great orator; where he excelled

was in smaller, more intimate groups. With his distance from the old ideological divides of right and left in politics, he was also entirely at ease with those of a different political persuasion. Those who would later be surprised by the way he struck up a friendship with George W. Bush had not paid close enough attention to his personal diplomacy in Europe during the first years of his premiership.

By the time his government lost office in 1997, John Major had become an isolated, often scorned, figure in the company of other European leaders. The nadir had come after a dispute over exports of British beef products when the nation's cattle were found to be infected with a lethal disease known as bovine spongiform encephalopathy (BSE), popularly known as "mad cow disease." The rest of Europe, along with most of the world, barred imports of British beef. In futile retaliation, Major blocked the normal business of the Union. At regular summits with his counterparts, the British prime minister found himself all but ignored. Blair quickly set about making friends—as many as he could. Thus in these early years he built a cordial, if not exactly warm, relationship with French president Jacques Chirac, all the while making painstaking efforts to establish a parallel rapport with Lionel Jospin, the French prime minister and Chirac's principal political rival. The friendship with Germany's Gerhard Schröder, as leader of that country's Social Democrats a natural ally on the center-left of politics, was matched by a close relationship with José María Aznar, the right-of-center Spanish prime minister. Blair was assiduous, too, in courting the leaders of Europe's smaller states—there were frequent joint initiatives with the prime ministers of Sweden, Portugal, and the Netherlands. There were visits also to Warsaw and to the capitals of other central and eastern European nations that had applied to join the Union. The texture of these relationships varied. With Schröder, it was relaxed. Blair's personal rapport with the German leader—the two would talk at length about their family backgrounds as well as about politics—came closer than any other to his relationship with Clinton. With the imperious Jacques Chirac the situation was more formal, although, curiously enough, the president of the French Republic made a hit with the British prime minister by fussing over baby Leo during his visits to 10

Downing Street. Sometimes Blair's promiscuity irritated other European leaders. Lionel Jospin of France could never quite understand how a politician of the center-left could be so eager to strike up friendships with those on the opposite end of the spectrum. When the media magnate Silvio Berlusconi formed a government in Italy, Blair was among the first to offer congratulations, horrifying many in his own party. Blair, though, was unrepentant, explaining that it was just "politics." Another charge that would often be heard at home–that the prime minister preferred to tell people what they wanted to hear rather than to confront their awkward differences–found echoes in European capitals. Occasionally a touch of hubris appeared during Blair's excursions to the continent. In a speech to fellow center-left European leaders in the Swedish city of Malmö during the first months of his premiership, he slipped into the old Churchillian rhetoric of Britain's "leadership" in Europe. The professorial Jospin, a politician less than impressed by Blair's claims to have reinvented center-left politics, saw his British counterpart as something of an upstart, a master of presentation but not an intellectual. And Blair, like all of his postwar predecessors, underestimated the enduring strength of the Franco-German alliance as the linchpin of European cooperation.

There was substance, though, as well as charm in this new Europeanism in 10 Downing Street. Blair signed two treaties with his European partners–at Amsterdam in 1997 and Nice in 2000–that pushed forward the process of integration and opened the door to the Union's eventual enlargement to include the former Communist states of eastern and central Europe. There was nothing radical in either of these agreements–the exchange of national sovereignty for shared decision-making was modest. But the absence of acrimony in the negotiations between Britain and its partners and of political controversy at home testified to a decisive break with the Europe-is-the-enemy years of Margaret Thatcher and John Major.

Further proof of the new approach came with two of Blair's own European initiatives. The first was in defense, an issue that had vexed the Continent almost since the Union's foundation. Nearly forty years after the Messina conference, Europe's failure to halt the mass killing in

Bosnia during the early 1990s had brutally exposed its lack of military capability. If the United States hesitated in becoming involved, the Balkans war had shown, Europe was powerless to make the peace in its own backyard. The European Union had agreed to what was optimistically called a Common Foreign and Security Policy but provided nothing in the way of "hard power" to support it. The idea of an independent European military force had always fallen victim to differences between Britain and France and to related anxiety in Washington. Successive French governments wanted to assert the continent's independence from the United States, while Britain was determined that any European capability should not undermine the security guarantee provided by America in the North Atlantic Treaty Organization. Since Britain and France were the only two European nations with significant military forces, the result had been a deadlock.

In 1998 Blair resolved to break the impasse. In advance of a Franco-British summit at the French port of Saint-Malo, the prime minister instructed his officials that he intended to strike a deal with President Jacques Chirac. If compromises were needed, they would be made. This was a classic example of his preference for personal diplomacy over lengthy formal negotiations. To the surprise of his hosts, Blair agreed to a proposal to create a 60,000-strong European Rapid Reaction Force. One senior British official later recalled that he had warned Blair that the text of this new Anglo-French entente would be badly received in Washington, which remained deeply suspicious of European efforts to develop its own defense capabilities. The American position was that, yes, European nations should individually spend more on their armed forces to share with the United States the burden of safeguarding Western security; but, no, it should not have enough independent capacity to engage in conflicts of which Washington might disapprove—echoes again of the Suez crisis. Despite his close friendship with Bill Clinton, Blair took the view that the creation of the new European force would be an important assertion of British leadership in Europe. "I'll sort out Clinton," was his response to the worried officials. To be sure, many of the difficult questions posed by the agreement—particularly about the extent to which the new force would

operate within the framework of NATO–were left unanswered at Saint-Malo. A certain ambiguity was part of the price of the bargain. But Blair had understood that the long-held goal of a common European foreign policy was a pipe dream unless the continent could deploy at least a modest military force in the cause of its own security. Saint-Malo was a harbinger, too, of the British's leader's readiness to take risks in the pursuit of strategic objectives.

The second effort to write Europe's agenda came in the area of economic policymaking. Here the British prime minister saw a chance to mediate between two different models of market capitalism–the American preference for laissez-faire economics, with its emphasis on low taxes and freewheeling competition, and the continental European model with its countervailing preference for close cooperation between big corporations and labor unions and high levels of social protection for employees. The Thatcherite economic revolution of the 1980s had tilted Britain firmly toward the American tradition. Now Blair sought to move the rest of Europe in the same direction. The economic reform initiative was launched in June 1998 at a meeting of European leaders hosted by Blair in Cardiff, the capital of Wales, and given substance two years later at another summit in the Portuguese capital of Lisbon. Blair described what became known as the "Lisbon process" as a "sea change in Europe's economic thinking." That characterization included more than a hint of hyperbole, yet it is fair to say that it did result in Europe's beginning to move toward a more market-oriented economic policy. Voices in Germany and France still called for more state regulation and harmonization, but Blair's initiative went with the grain of globalization. Competition, welfare reform, enterprise, and innovation began to appear on the agendas of every European government.

The European balance sheet showed one big debit. January 1999 saw the launch of the euro, the single European currency that had been foreshadowed eight years earlier by the Maastricht treaty. Eleven of the fifteen European Union nations joined the Franco-German project.

Across the continent French francs, Italian lire, German marks, Spanish pesetas, and the rest gave way to the euro. With the new currency came a single interest rate, set by the new European Central Bank in Frankfurt. Britain was alone among Europe's large nations to not take part in a project that effectively merged the management of the Continent's economies. If the circumstances had been propitious Blair would have liked to join, for he understood that, in the medium term, Britain could not hope to exert influence in Europe if it remained outside the Union's most important economic project. The history of Britain's relationship with its Continental neighbors had typically been one of hesitation at the start of each new project, followed by belated and reluctant acquiescence; in the interval France and Germany set its rules. This was a point Blair himself made frequently in his speeches. In an important address to Britain's European Research Institute during the autumn of 2001, he listed many such occasions. The result, he declared, was that "the history of our engagement with Europe is one of opportunities missed in the name of illusions—and Britain suffering as a result."

Yet, in spite of good intentions, as far as the euro was concerned, he ultimately proved almost as cautious as his predecessors. He judged the project a step too far for the first years of his premiership. In the autumn of 1997, Gordon Brown, the chancellor of the exchequer, announced that Britain would retain its own currency, the pound sterling, for the duration of the parliamentary term, which would run until mid-2001. After that it would swap the pound for the euro only if, on the basis of five stringent economic tests, the performance of Britain's economy was aligned with those in the new euro bloc. There were good reasons and bad for this decision. Blair and Brown could argue with logic that, in the closing years of the 1990s, Britain was unprepared to surrender control of much of its economic policy to the European Central Bank. While other European nations had calibrated their economic policies during the preceding years to the explicit goal of joining the euro, the Conservative government of John Major had made no such preparations. Measured in terms of interest and inflation

rates, trade, economic growth, and the exchange rate, the performance of the British economy had not sufficiently converged with that of its European counterparts. Joining the euro at the outset would be a significant economic risk.

But the decision to stand aside was framed as much by timid politics as by solid economics. For all his stated determination to clear the fog from the English Channel, the new prime minister was fearful of the public mood in his own country. He had promised a referendum on the issue of euro membership, but after more than a decade during which Margaret Thatcher and John Major had characterized the European Union as a conspiracy against Britain, he now feared he might lose such a plebiscite. Here, for all his seeming confidence and his unprecedented parliamentary majority, the prime minister showed a glimpse of his timidity. The Conservative-leaning newspapers—notably those owned by Rupert Murdoch—that the New Labour leader had courted so assiduously while he had been in opposition were implacably opposed to the new economic model. Now, as prime minister, Blair was unwilling to make enemies of his newfound friends. Sensitive to this equivocation and swayed by the relentlessly hostile stance of the Conservative Party, public opinion became more rather than less antipathetic to the idea of replacing sterling with the euro. And by stipulating that Britain would join the project only "if" the economic conditions were met, Blair cast Britain almost as a bystander.

To be fair, Blair would have liked a more positive formulation. But as time passed, the euro became entangled in a political struggle much closer to home. Blair, for all his caution, remained an enthusiast for the project, while Gordon Brown harbored more serious doubts. Brown was proud of the new framework for economic management he had put in place in Britain, judging it far superior to that under which the Eurozone countries operated. In any event, Brown considered that under the terms of the deal that he had struck with Blair all those years earlier after the death of John Smith, this was a decision in which he rather than the prime minister should have the final say. He still expected to succeed Blair as prime minister, and a miscalculation over the euro—defeat in a referendum, an economic downturn—could jeop-

ardize his claim to the leadership. The "five economic tests" formulation that he had announced in the autumn of 1997 as the yardstick for entry became Brown's veto over the decision, and one he refused to surrender.

There was scarcely a hint before Tony Blair took office in 1997 of another hallmark of his premiership–a readiness, even an eagerness, to deploy military force in pursuit of his foreign policy ambitions. On the surface he seemed an unlikely warrior. His only experience of the military had been during his school days and even then he had been a reluctant soldier. Fettes had required that all new pupils enroll in the school's military cadet force during their first three years, and the young Blair duly donned his fatigues. But as soon as his compulsory service ended he opted for the alternative of joining the school's community program. Thirty years later the nation's military commanders were distinctly nervous as they contemplated the prospect of a Labour government headed by this unenthusiastic cadet. However much he made the right patriotic noises, Tony Blair was an unknown, unschooled in the ways of the military, and there was nothing in the party's general election manifesto to indicate that the new government would look kindly on defense spending. The military budget had already been cut sharply as John Major's administration spent the post–cold war "peace dividend." Now the suspicion among the generals, admirals, and air vice marshals was that the incoming government would seek even deeper reductions to pay for extra spending elsewhere. After all, only a decade earlier Labour had been committed to scrapping Britain's independent nuclear deterrent, not to mention the fact that most of the incoming cabinet–including, to his own embarrassment, Blair himself– had at one time or another been members of the Campaign for Nuclear Disarmament. Nor did the generals expect sympathy from Gordon Brown, who as chancellor of the exchequer was responsible for public spending. The body language of this Scottish socialist said he would be at best uncomfortable with the military.

To look through the lens of the past, though, was to misread the new prime minister. Tony Blair relished the idea of surprising people–

not least colleagues in his own party. His preoccupation with Britain's place in the world—and the determination to recast his own party in the public mind as one with as strong a claim to the mantle of patriotism as the Conservatives—argued against cuts in the defense budget. Bill Clinton's presidency had gotten off to a bad start with the U.S. military, a mistake the British prime minister did not intend to make. Tony Blair would be the generals' friend.

General Charles Guthrie, the chief of the defense staff, was Britain's foremost military commander. Silver-haired, immaculately dressed in or out of uniform, with a string of medal ribbons and the cut-glass accent of the English upper classes, he might have walked out of a 1950s Hollywood movie. But he was a man who defied first impressions. Guthrie's rise had between through the Special Air Service, or SAS, the elite of the elite among special forces. He had seen plenty of action, much of it in the deserts of the Middle East as Britain fought Soviet-backed Communist insurgents in its former colonies. He spoke little of his experiences—the SAS prides itself on its secrecy—but, in the words of an army colleague, he knew all about fighting "close up." He was also an intelligent soldier, one who understood the ways of politics as well as war. He first met Blair over breakfast at Claridges, one of London's smartest hotels, while the Labour leader was still in opposition. His pitch to the future prime minister was well judged: the year-by-year cuts in military expenditure under the Conservatives, he argued, had been made without reference to Britain's security requirements. There was a mismatch between the nation's strategic interests and its military capabilities. A Labour government should look at both sides of the balance sheet and decide what was wanted from the military before fixing the budget.

Blair was receptive to the idea. Once in government he gave the military further assurance by appointing George Robertson as defense secretary. Robertson, one of the few Labour politicians with a good grasp of foreign and security issues, had a long track record of opposing unilateral nuclear disarmament and was well thought of in Washington. (Later he would move to Brussels to become secretary-general of the North Atlantic Treaty Organization.) Blair also announced the

strategic defense review that Guthrie had requested, and its outcome was as good as the military could have hoped for: the defense budget was stabilized and guaranteed for the next three years. Gordon Brown had demanded deep cuts. But he was rebuffed by Guthrie and ultimately overruled by Blair.

This superficially curious relationship between the prime minister and the favored general flourished. Blair saw in the military an organization that got things done. "Ask a minister to do something," he was heard to remark in 1999, and "there are a dozen reasons why it is impossible." The armed forces were different, he believed. Given a task, they got on with it. The defense review served Blair well when, more than once in the following few years, he sent British forces into action overseas. Those who read the review carefully would have seen a clue to the moral impulse that would frame the prime minister's later decisions to go to war. Britain's strategic ambition, the review proclaimed, was "to be a force for good in the world." There was a hint of what later became known as the doctrine of preemptive or, more properly, preventive military intervention overseas: Britain should not wait for crises to develop but should be ready to demonstrate leadership by acting preemptively. In the following years, these principles would take British troops to war in Kosovo, Sierra Leone, Afghanistan, and Iraq.

7. FINDING A THIRD WAY

BY THE SUMMER OF 2000, Tony Blair and Bill Clinton had traveled together for three years along what they called politics' Third Way. Now the Clinton presidency was drawing to a close, besmirched if not derailed by the Monica Lewinsky affair. A part of Blair thought Clinton had squandered his second term. But during a conversation in the garden of 10 Downing Street, Blair was fulsome in his praise. "Clinton is the most brilliant, the most brilliant politician I have ever met. That's what I have always thought and I still think it."

Three years earlier the American president had stood in the same garden, among the very first of the distinguished visitors after Tony Blair's election victory in May 1997. The prime minister had bestowed on his guest the rare honor of addressing a full meeting of the British cabinet. Even those in this group of senior ministers who had never felt comfortable with the "Clintonization" of Labour politics listened to the master with a certain breathless reverence. "They were like eager puppies," one Downing Street official said later. When the two leaders moved into the garden for a joint press conference, it was an occasion for lavish mutual praise. They represented, Blair told reporters, the new generation of political leaders: "This is the generation that prefers reason to doctrine, that is strong in ideals but indifferent to ideology, whose instinct is to judge government not on grand designs but by practical results." Clinton, harried at home by congressional opposition to his budget plans, took time more than once to voice his envy at Blair's 179-seat majority in Parliament. The British system of government spared the prime minister most of the checks and balances of the U.S. Constitution. Yet, for all Blair's famous victory and soaring rhetoric and Clinton's troubles over Paula Jones, the awe was on the British

side. For some of Blair's staffers a handshake with Clinton fulfilled the ambition of a political lifetime. The British political press, not generally known for its politeness, was deferential in its questioning. The small lawn at the back of 10 Downing Street was not quite the White House Rose Garden, but there had been no event quite like this in John Major's time. For the new prime minister, to act as host to Clinton was to prove that he had made it to the international as well as the national stage. That evening the two leaders and their wives eschewed the grand but stuffy staterooms of Downing Street and dined instead at Le Pont de la Tour, a fashionable and youthful restaurant on the South Bank of London's river Thames.

Back in the first half of the 1990s, when New Labour had raided the New Democrats for policy ideas and campaign slogans, Clinton had beguiled by showing that a modernizing party of the center-left could win an election. By 1997 he had done something even more impressive in the eyes of his British hosts—he had defied Newt Gingrich's Republican Revolution and won the White House a second time. *Winning twice*—this is what impressed Blair above all else, for it echoed his own burning ambition. No Labour government had previously served two full parliamentary terms—a maximum of five years each, under the British system. Clement Attlee had won two consecutive elections in the aftermath of World War II, but his administration had collapsed exhausted and divided after six years. Harold Wilson had also been in power for six years during the 1960s. But Conservative administrations typically ran for eight or ten years, often more. Blair's stated ambition for his first term was to govern with sufficient confidence and competence to be sure of winning a mandate for a second. When Clinton was asked by a reporter what advice he might offer the British prime minister, Blair interjected with his own response: "Well, he [the president] did one thing very right, which was to win again, and I hope I repeat that." Winning again—that would be the leitmotif of Blair's first term.

There was something else about Bill Clinton. In broad terms, political leaders fall into one of two camps. There are the people politicians, the great communicators, the leaders with easy charm and an intuitive

grasp of the emotional pulse of an electorate. Then there are the ideas people, the politicians who find their inspiration in history and philosophy, the intellectuals who draw their energy and motivation from late-night wrestling bouts with political and economic theory. Such characterizations are schematic, but a rough version of them could be seen in Tony Blair's government between the prime minister and Gordon Brown. Blair was the election-winner, the consummate communicator who spoke the language of Middle Britain, a master at building personal relationships, the politician whose effortless guile turned enemies into friends. Blair's brilliance, his chief of staff Jonathan Powell had once been heard say, lay in his powers of persuasion. Brown, surrounded by great stacks of books, wrestling with the latest economic treatises and delivering lectures about something called neo-endogenous economic growth theory, was the intellectual.

Bill Clinton broke this mold. What made him a leader so admired and envied was that somehow he contrived to be both characters–the brilliant populist and the policy wonk wrapped into one. No one was better at empathizing with the voters, making each and every one in a room of fifty or a hundred people feel that he or she alone was the object of his interest, delivering a speech that would crack the resolve of even the most cynical audience. But Clinton's intellect was as sharp as his capacity to articulate the public mood. He devoured history, economic theses, and the works of political thinkers past and present with the voracious appetite many thought he reserved for hamburgers. It sometimes seemed that he knew more about Europe than some of that continent's own leaders. In 1999 the president and prime minister had one of their rare disagreements when Clinton resisted Blair's demands that the U.S. mount a more aggressive military campaign to force Serbia's Slobodan Milosevic to withdraw from Kosovo. The lament among Blair's staffers was that Clinton, the president from the backwoods of Arkansas, had read too deeply into the history of the Balkans. His grasp of the ethnic and historical forces that had so often plunged that region into bloody chaos had persuaded him to tread carefully. Blair himself was startled by, and admiring of, the president's historical insights–if

deeply frustrated for a time that they were getting in the way of decisive military action.

For his part, Clinton saw Blair's victory as an endorsement of his own politics. He had been the architect of the new incrementalism of center-left politics, of the notion that government could be active and enabling without being over-mighty. That Blair had just won such a resounding victory in Britain on a markedly similar platform reflected well on the occupant of the White House. It put him at the head of a movement that defied the boundaries of Washington politics, and provided him with a welcome distraction from the Republican onslaught at home. Sidney Blumenthal, the president's special assistant and a pivotal figure in building his relationship with Blair, would later remark that the parallel politics of the two leaders "gave Clinton's presidency a new sense of coherence and depth, and ratified its course." The ties also promised–and all leaders fret about their place in history–that the new politics of the center-left might endure beyond Clinton's term. In that May 1997 visit Clinton saw the opportunity to build a network of progressive leaders. He mentioned Portugal's prime minister, Antonio Guterres, and Wim Kok of the Netherlands as two other like-minded modernizers. A few months later Hillary Clinton led a delegation of American policymakers to Chequers, the prime minister's country house, for a meeting that would turn an idea into a project. In Blumenthal's account, Blair set out the challenge: the similarities between the two parties were striking, but something was missing. "We win power, but not the battle of ideas. The right wins, even though they're not in power. Unless we define our new type of politics, people will become disillusioned with us." Clinton and Blair would soon set off on a journey along the highways and byways of what they called politics' Third Way.

If Tony Blair owed a debt to Clinton he repaid it during a four-day visit to Washington in February 1998, his first trip as prime minister to meet the president at the White House. Clinton, already beginning to sink into the mire of the Lewinsky uproar, made sure that his guest was greeted in spectacular fashion. As a head of government rather than

head of state Blair did not technically merit full state honors. But no one would have noticed that the nineteen-gun salute at the White House was two shots short of the twenty-one that would have greeted a visit by Queen Elizabeth II. The White House dinner that evening was among the most glittering events in Washington's social calendar—as star-studded, some would say, as anything seen since John F. Kennedy's Camelot presidency. In honor of their British guests, Bill and Hillary Clinton played host at an evening that saw Barbra Streisand rub shoulders with Steven Spielberg, Harrison Ford jostle with Tom Hanks, and Warren Buffett sit down with John F. Kennedy Jr. Stevie Wonder delighted Blair's wife, Cherie, with the authentic version of the British couple's favorite song, "My Cherie Amour." Elton John joined Wonder onstage for a duet. The society columnists had rarely seen such a feast. The *New York Times* reported that the cost of the food, wine, and service for the evening was estimated at $200 per person—and that didn't include the flowers, place cards, invitations, and cocktails. The partying was followed by politicking—a seminar on the Third Way philosophy of the new center-left. Then the Blairs were whisked off to the presidential retreat at Camp David in the Maryland mountains, a rare honor for foreign visitors during the Clinton presidency. The prime minister could hardly be blamed for seeming a little starstruck.

There was serious business on the official agenda, including Bosnia, Northern Ireland, and the future of the North Atlantic Treaty Organization. Above them all loomed Iraq, once again seeking to hamper and evade the efforts of United Nations weapons inspectors. Much later—after September 11, 2001—it sometimes seemed that Saddam Hussein's regime was the obsession of the new partnership of George W. Bush and Tony Blair. Often forgotten is that it loomed large in almost every meeting between Clinton and Blair. And if the then U.S. president was not promising regime change in Baghdad, Blair as early as 1997 and 1998 was offering British participation in military action to clip Saddam's wings. Thus Clinton declared after the February 1998 talks that "if Saddam does not comply with the unanimous will of the interna-

tional community, we must be prepared to act—and we are." For his part, Blair was already preoccupied with Iraq's weapons of mass destruction and the obstacles being put in the path of the United Nations weapons inspectors. A few days before his visit the British government had published a dossier on Saddam's WMD capabilities. Now, standing next to Clinton, Blair announced the deployment of further British fighter planes in the Gulf. "If the [UN] inspectors are prevented from doing their work," he said, "then we have to make sure, by the military means of which we are capable, that, insofar as possible, that capacity ceases."

What mattered most in the fevered atmosphere of Washington in February 1998, though, was the body language between the two men. Above all, how would Blair respond when asked, as he was sure to be, whether the brewing Lewinsky scandal would affect his relationship with the president? The prime minister did not let his host down. When the inevitable question was posed at their joint press conference, he was unequivocal. "I've worked with President Clinton for some nine months as British prime minister. I have found him throughout someone I could trust, someone I could rely upon, someone I am proud to call not just a colleague but a friend." Blair could have sidestepped the question or been tactfully evasive. Before the trip there had been much discussion among his aides as to precisely where the line should be drawn between polite support and needless entanglement in the president's woes. Some urged caution. But Blair had made up his mind to be unstinting in his praise. The evening before, at the White House dinner, the visiting prime minister had even appeared to take a swipe at Clinton's Republican opponents: "I know I'm not alone in supporting you. I know the American people support you, too." Clinton was duly appreciative: "I think, the people who stand up and say things they believe, when it would be just as easy to walk away, show a certain kind of character," he replied. "And I'm very grateful that Tony Blair has done that." Five years later, in circumstances as different as it was possible to imagine, George W. Bush would say much the same about the character of the British prime minister.

The Third Way was an idea much derided by commentators and con-
servatives alike—and in its more grandiose manifestations as an entirely
new theory of politics, rightly so. Some of the intellectuals who climbed
onto the Clinton-Blair bandwagon seemed to believe they could reinvent
politics' wheel. But president and prime minister had a serious political
purpose. Both men had won elections on a platform that promised
to banish the ideology of the past. They had rejected politics' two
extremes—the free-market, get-government-out-of-the-way ideology
of the right, and the statist tax-and-spend solutions of the left. They
had the beginnings of a language for a different brand of progressive
politics whose mantras were community, opportunity, rights and re-
sponsibilities, and social inclusion. But neither Clinton nor Blair had as
of yet woven this into a persuasive political narrative—a positive affir-
mation of what the New Democrats and New Labour stood for, as op-
posed to what they were against. It was fine to say that they were
sweeping aside both the old left's over-mighty state and the atavistic
individualism of the new right. It was much harder to describe the con-
tours of the new landscape, and to translate values into policies.

The task was more pressing for Blair. Clinton was soon to enter the
twilight years of his presidency. He had been elected five years ahead
of his British colleague and his record, to a large extent, spoke for itself.
Blair was at the start of what he hoped would be at least two terms in
Downing Street. His party, though grateful to the leader for its un-
precedented victory, was no longer quite sure what it stood for. Old
Labour traditionalists feared that modernization was simply a cloak for
compromise, for the triumph of pragmatism over principle. There is a
long tradition in British politics that sees many on the left cry "be-
trayal" as soon as their leaders confront the realities of power—better to
be pure in opposition than corrupted in government. New Labour had
already eschewed higher personal income taxes, and Gordon Brown's
Treasury had imposed an initial squeeze on government spending as
tough as any applied by the Conservatives. The market economy, the
government said, was here to stay. Old Labour had been the ally of the
producers in the trade unions; New Labour was the friend of the con-

sumer. It was also on the side of business. Blair made no secret of the fact that he was far more at ease with the entrepreneurs and business leaders who now trooped regularly through the front door of 10 Downing Street than with the trade union leaders who had thought that the election victory would give them a privileged place at the government's table. Gordon Brown's political heritage, rooted more deeply in the traditions of the Labour movement, meant that the union chiefs received a rather warmer reception at the Treasury. But he, too, seemed more interested in enterprise, competition, and innovation than in restoring power to the old producer groups.

The question inevitably asked, inside as well as beyond the new administration, was what made this government any different from a moderate Conservative one. Sometimes, that uncertainty spread to the senior ranks of the government. In the summer of 1998 one of Blair's ministers arrived uncharacteristically late for lunch at a central London restaurant. Flustered and agitated, this minister explained that he had been unavoidably delayed in a heated policy discussion with the prime minister. He was utterly perplexed by the line Blair was taking in this particular debate. Even Conservatives, the minister said, would have considered the prime minister's stance too far to the right. "Sometimes," he confided, "I wonder what kind of government I am in."

There were counterindications to this general air of conservatism, many of them in policies borrowed from Bill Clinton's program. Within the overall squeeze on the government budget, more money was found for schools and hospitals. Education, education, education—they were the government's three priorities, Blair had declared many times. The route to opportunity and a fairer society started in the classroom. A new tax on the profits of utilities such as electricity and gas provided funds for employment programs. Gordon Brown called it the New Deal, though the allusion to Franklin Roosevelt greatly exaggerated its scope and scale. Rights and responsibilities in welfare meant that the government would provide more opportunities for those out of work but would make welfare payments conditional on people taking those opportunities. Another tax increase, this time on pension funds, gave Brown the resources to raise payments to the poorest re-

tirees and to introduce in-work benefits for those on low incomes. Funds, too, were found from the so-called stealth taxes for the National Health Service, the free health-care system that had been starved of necessary money by the Conservatives.

Privately Blair lamented the absence of enemies. Margaret Thatcher, he would tell visitors to his Downing Street study, had had the Soviet threat, over-mighty trade unions, high income taxes. Fighting such foes had helped give definition to her project. But who was to challenge him? The Conservative Party, still reeling from its election defeat, had all but given up on the task of opposition. For a time, the prime minister gave public vent to his frustration by identifying as New Labour's enemies the "forces of conservatism," a catch-all phrase that included anyone and everyone who did not share the goal of a "modern, progressive Britain." Phantom opponents and purposeful incrementalism, though, did not add up to a persuasive political narrative, not least because, for all its high-flown rhetoric about transforming Britain, the government was curiously timid. The tension between radicalism and reassurance was ever present.

At times the government seemed disbelieving of its own authority—of the political reality that, with a majority of 179 seats over all other parties in the House of Commons, New Labour could more or less do as it pleased. Blair never stopped looking at the opinion polls. In the mind of this government the past lived on. The dire electoral consequences of Labour's profligate economic policies when it had last been in office during the 1970s were etched on New Labour's collective consciousness. The nation's economy had been rescued only when the then government had gone cap in hand to the International Monetary Fund. Blair could not escape the shadow of the eighteen grim years in opposition that had followed. It was almost as if one false move, one small mistake, would banish them again to the political wilderness. The prime minister privately acknowledged this fearful caution. "Some cabinet ministers still think government is just a dream," he remarked in the summer of 1999. "They are afraid they will wake up in the morning and find that we did not win at all, that we are still in opposition." Although he applied these sentiments to the mindset of his colleagues,

they seemed an equally apt description of his own instincts in these early years. Roy Jenkins, a distinguished former cabinet minister who had left the Labour Party to found the centrist Social Democratic Party in 1980, put it well. Jenkins, who by the 1990s was leading figure in the Liberal Democrat Party, had become a friend and mentor to Blair. The elder statesman admired the young prime minister, who in turn often sought the older man's wisdom. Jenkins told him he was too cautious. Blair, he said, sometimes behaved with the agonized anxiety of an elderly museum curator carrying a priceless Ming vase across a newly polished floor. Leaders should invest their political capital. Blair was hoarding it.

The Third Way was intended to provide a rationale for such caution—to demonstrate that, for all the government's pragmatism, its program for change was still connected to the fundamental principles of the center-left. With center-left politicians in power on both sides of the Atlantic, they needed a shared theory to underpin the practice of government. Blair had experimented with other descriptions of what he saw as, in its essence, the marriage of the generosity of liberalism with the hard realism of conservatism. He had toyed with the idea of calling this the "stakeholder society" and had often pronounced himself a politician of the "radical center." Neither rubric caught the public imagination.

The first of the Third Way excursions took place during the February 1998 visit to Washington. The politicians and their aides were joined for an afternoon by distinguished business leaders, academics, and political consultants. The goal, in the president's words, was to create a progressive agenda for the twenty-first century. Participants recall much talk about harnessing the forces of globalization and the technological revolution to the cause of wider opportunity, of labor market and welfare reform, and, of course, of education. Security was the recurring theme. The voters did not want big government; they did want an assurance that government would extend a helping hand in the harsh winds of change. The two sides shared lessons, too, on winning elections—and, of course, on winning twice. But, for the British side at least, Clinton, obviously exhausted by his political troubles but none-

theless showing flashes of his intellectual brilliance as the seminar wore on, was the main event.

Others joined the club of progressives in a regular circuit that would take the Third Way caravan to cities as diverse as Florence and New York. The newly elected Gerhard Schröder of Germany signed up in the autumn of 1998. Fernando Henrique Cardoso, the president of Brazil, and Bulgarian president Petar Stoyanov were two further recruits. Romano Prodi, Italy's prime minister, joined the cast when the disciples of the Third Way convened in New York in September 1998. The leaders drew common themes from the exchanges of experience across different continents. Education always loomed large as the lever of opportunity. A mix of tough qualifying conditions for welfare along with increased government spending on training and in-work benefits was part of another emerging consensus. There was a serious, and interesting, discussion about the implications of globalization and technological advance–and of the need to change the left's traditional opposition to competition and market liberalization. Behind the discussions lay a shared conviction that, as President Clinton had declared in his 1996 State of the Union address, the era of big government was over–the challenge was to make slimmer government effective. The campaign strategists and the pollsters meanwhile debated how governments of the center-left could sustain in office the broad coalitions of popular support they had constructed in opposition.

Tony Blair sought to give the process an intellectual framework by publishing a personal Third Way credo coinciding with the gathering in New York. Its title was less than modest: "The Third Way, New Politics for a New Century" was as much a personal as a political tract. As ever, Blair sought to demolish what he called the false antitheses of the old ideological debate–sane economics versus fairness, law and order versus social cohesion. His brand of politics, the pamphlet declared, was "founded on the values which have guided progressive politics for more than a century–democracy, liberty, justice, mutual obligation and internationalism." It was a Third Way because "it moves decisively beyond an Old Left preoccupied by state control, high taxation and pro-

ducer interests; and a New Right treating public investment and often the very notions of society and collective endeavor as evils to be undone." Blair concluded, "The Third Way stands for modernized social democracy, passionate in its commitment to social justice and the goals of the center-left, but flexible, innovative and forward-looking in the means to achieve them." Gerhard Schröder took much the same approach during the following year when he published his own *Neue Mitte*–a call for Germany's Social Democrats to emulate the New Labour example by modernizing the party's economic and social policies. In spite of a backlash within his own party, Schröder acknowledged his debt to his British counterpart. "When it comes to fairness and equality," he told his Social Democrat Party's annual convention in 1999, "it really is as Tony Blair had phrased it. We are not about equal earnings. We are about real equality–equal chances for fulfillment, equal access to knowledge, equal opportunities to flourish."

In Britain, Blair oversaw practical application of the new "mixed-economy" approach to the role of the state. His government would soon pour unprecedented amounts of taxpayers' money into state-financed health and education initiatives. But the private sector was given an ever bigger role in the provision and management of these services. The Labour tradition had been to demand not just the public financing of universal health care and education but also their provision by the government. Blair made the important political distinction between the two–in his mind, it was enough that the government provided the money for such services. Private as well as public enterprises should have a role in delivering them. The dilemma remained that many of these new approaches seemed to say more about how New Labour had escaped its past than about a brand-new vision of the future. The insights into the constraints imposed by political and economic realities were much sharper than the promised exposition of a new system of political beliefs. In areas where the government did make a decisive break with the Conservatives–in greatly increasing, for example, welfare payments to the elderly poor and to low-income working families–it seemed fearful of trumpeting the change. If announced too

boldly, this modest redistribution of income might have offended the middle classes of Middle Britain. Blair had erased the old ideological dividing lines between right and left, but now he discovered how difficult it was to redraw them. If Old Labour had held to a belief in equality that owed more to romanticism than to reality, that ideal had provided the party with a destination, however illusory. The New Labour travelers on Third Way were still scouring the map.

The struggle to translate Third Way values into a framework for government testified at times to Blair's inexperience. The new prime minister was hugely practiced in the arts of opposition politics. Out of office, political leaders have nothing but words with which to paint a picture in the minds of the voters, a task Blair accomplished brilliantly. He was slower to realize that governments describe themselves by their actions. Voters listen occasionally to the rhetoric of their rulers but most make their judgments based on the experience of their daily lives, and they expect less of government than the politicians often imagine. A more experienced prime minister might well have described his administration as one committed to sound economic management; to improving the life chances of the less fortunate with a modest redistribution of wealth; to repairing over time the decay in the public health, education, and transport services; and to rebuilding relationships with Britain's European partners. That would have been an accurate, if not entirely complete, account of Blair's early years in office. But it did not quite fit the rhetorical imperatives of a leader who had promised to build a "New Britain." Here, Bill Clinton's influence was less benign. New Labour had prospered in opposition by borrowing the campaign techniques pioneered by the New Democrats. Clinton, under the tutelage of James Carville, had taken the fight to the enemy. New Labour did the same, only sometimes it borrowed the wrong lesson.

Dick Morris, the pollster and political consultant, was credited with rescuing President Clinton's electoral prospects from the midterm mire that had seen Newt Gingrich's Republicans sweep to power in Congress in 1994. Morris, who once polled 10,000 Americans to decide

where the Clintons should spend their summer vacation, was the author of "triangulation," the campaigning strategy that saw Clinton retaliate against Gingrich by shamelessly robbing the Republicans of their more attractive clothes. Morris's spell as Clinton's pollster-as-consigliere ended in 1996 when news broke of his dalliances with a prostitute in Washington's Jefferson Hotel. Presidents can survive sexual indiscretions; pollsters, even the best, are expendable. But Morris's influence lived on in Tony Blair's government, surfacing in a memorandum written by Philip Gould, the prime minister's own polling adviser, which was leaked to the press in the summer of 2000. Gould's memorandum quoted approvingly from the "The New Prince," a Morris treatise that declared that the rules of politics had permanently changed. The old rules of representative democracy, with its traditional party ties and political allegiances passed down through the generations, Morris had claimed, were over. Political leaders were playing in a different game. The new paradigm said that leaders had constantly to hold up a mirror to the anxieties and prejudices of public opinion. To remain in power, Gould summarized the argument, leaders must win "a daily mandate in which strength comes from popularity," a sentiment with which Blair seemed to agree. A second leak to the media, this time of a memorandum written by the prime minister himself, revealed his thirst for easy applause. The government, he said in the private note to staff written in April 2000, was being seen as weak on issues like crime, the family, and defense. "It is bizarre that any government I head should be seen as anti-family," he wrote. What was needed was "a series of eye-catching initiatives." And, he continued, "I should be personally associated with as much of this as possible." Translated, the prime minister wanted more headline-grabbing initiatives and wheezes to keep him in the public eye.

As a bald description of politics in the post–cold war era, the Morris-Gould appraisal had some merit. The defeat of the Communist alternative to market capitalism had indeed weakened the tribal allegiances on which politicians had once relied. The numbers of undecided voters were growing at every election, as was the proportion of the population that did not even bother to cast a ballot. But as a guiding principle

of government, the idea of perpetual populism was deeply corrosive, encouraging the elevation of "spin" over substance and of presentation over policy. Tony Blair was sometimes seduced, and, seen from the perspective of No. 10, government was too often a battle for the lead item on the evening television news. Long-term strategy was elbowed aside by short-term tactics. Later in his premiership Blair would learn the truth of a painful paradox: the voters preferred conviction and purpose from their political leaders, even sometimes at the cost of unpalatable decisions, to a daily drive to win approval.

As Blair had predicted during the summer of 2000, he and Bill Clinton stayed close friends after the president left office, though the nature of the relationship changed. As Clinton took to the lecture circuit, Blair was growing in confidence and experience. One of the prime minister's close aides said that Clinton had started out in the role of a wise uncle to Blair, but by the time he departed the relationship was more akin to that of elder and younger brother.

When the U.S. Supreme Court gave the presidency to George W. Bush in December 2000, Blair was among the scores of world leaders to put in a telephone call to the president-elect. Bush returned the call during a visit by Blair to the University of Warwick in the Midlands. As chance would have it, the prime minister's guest on this particular trip was Bill Clinton, saying his last good-byes as president to his closest ally. When he took the call from Bush, Blair seemed sanguine about the apparent awkwardness. After congratulating the new president he explained that he was not about to throw over his friendship with Clinton, a relationship that he assured Bush would not be an obstacle to the enduring strength of the alliance between Britain and the United States. Bush, according to Blair's aides, said he was entirely comfortable with that.

Whatever passed between the two men during the telephone conversation with Bush, Blair, as he had been on that first visit to Washington in February 1998, was full of praise for the departing president. Clinton, he told an audience at the university, had brought prosperity to America and peace to many parts of the world. He had been a bul-

wark of the transatlantic relationship and, personally, a friend and counsel. As for the president-elect, Blair said he had spoken to Bush about "Britain's special friendship with America." Britain's role as America's closest ally and a leading partner in Europe was "to be a bridge between the two." Without a hint of embarrassment, Blair added that Bush was "a man who shares our values and who wants Europe and America to stand side by side in the world." The prime minister's big tent, it seemed, could accommodate both Clinton and Bush.

If that notion seemed slightly absurd, time and events proved it otherwise. With his daughter, Chelsea, studying for a time at Oxford University and time on his hands, Bill Clinton was a frequent visitor to England during the following two years–and a frequent guest at 10 Downing Street and Chequers. The two men, one of Blair's friends said, never stopped talking politics–the more so after the events of September 11, 2001. The relationship was more equal now, but as he shaped his own thinking about the new international order, Blair frequently sought Clinton's counsel and more than once his direct assistance. In the autumn of 2002 as the drums of war began to beat faster, the former president was the honored guest at New Labour's annual conference in the northern English town of Blackpool. A down-at-heel resort that, in October at least, has more rain than sunshine, Blackpool is a bleak setting. Clinton loved it, or pretended to. The conference loved him. His brilliant speech there upstaged the prime minister's own keynote address. But that hardly mattered. The former president was there to help an old friend for whom he was generous in his praise. "When the prime minister spoke yesterday I said to myself, I hope I'll be able to give a speech like that when I grow up. It was unbelievable." Responding to the growing disquiet in Labour ranks, he urged Blair's doubtful party to back its leader in calling Saddam Hussein's "bluff." Clinton distanced himself from the Bush administration but heaped praise on the prime minister for his efforts to secure a new United Nations resolution. "I appreciate what the prime minister is trying to do in terms of bringing America and the rest of the world to a common position," the former president told an audience held spellbound by the fluency of his rhetoric. "As an American, and a citizen of the world, I

am glad that Tony Blair will be central to making the call. . . . If he weren't trying to do this, I doubt anyone else could. So I am very, very grateful." It was an endorsement that Blair badly needed. Later that evening Blair spoke to Bush from a secure communications room in his hotel on Blackpool's seafront. The first draft of the resolution on Iraq that Washington had prepared for the UN Security Council, the prime minister told him, would never fly.

8. MAKING PEACE

NORTHERN IRELAND WAS the place where Tony Blair's self-belief fused with political courage, his instinctive inclusiveness with infinite patience. For more than thirty years the province had been scarred by terrorist violence. Some 3,000 people had died and many thousands had been maimed—that in a population of only 1.6 million. The Irish Republican Army's war against the British state had been mirrored by a murderous campaign against the Catholic community by self-styled Protestant "loyalists." London and other cities in mainland Britain had been bombed by the IRA when the conflict periodically crossed the Irish Sea. This was a war, the new prime minister judged, that belonged to the darker annals of the nation's history. The cost in human lives lost and broken had been dreadful enough. In the brutal sectarianism that pitted Protestant Unionists against Catholic Nationalists Blair also saw a terrible corruption of his own Christian faith. Northern Ireland was an ugly stain on Britain's international reputation. How could Britain serve, as Blair intended it should, as a beacon for progress and democracy in the wider world while such a conflict raged within its borders? The task he faced was to reconcile the irreconcilable—the IRA's insistence on a united Ireland with the implacable determination of the Unionist majority in Northern Ireland to remain citizens of the United Kingdom. The negotiations would test to the limits his lawyer's powers of persuasion. Blair seemed to relish the challenge. William Gladstone, the nineteenth-century prime minister so admired by his successor in 10 Downing Street, had moved political mountains in his efforts to solve the "Irish Question"—and failed. The new occupant of Downing Street judged that the time would never be more propitious to finish Gladstone's work.

So it was to Belfast, the capital of Northern Ireland, that he paid his first official visit as prime minister. In a speech on May 16, 1997, he set out a framework for peace. Every sentence was crafted to navigate the treacherous shoals of suspicion and hostility on which previous efforts had foundered. The message to the IRA and its political leaders in Sinn Fein was that Republican violence was as futile as it was abhorrent: they would never bomb the British out of Northern Ireland. But he offered them an opportunity: if Republicans renounced terrorism they would be invited to join the political process in the province. The past was the past. The prime minister would be ready to shake the hands of former terrorists. They could make their case for a united Ireland through the ballot box. "The settlement train is leaving," he said to leaders of the Republican movement. "I want you on that train. But it is leaving anyway and I will not allow it to wait for you. You cannot hold the process to ransom any longer. So, end the violence now."

The offer to Northern Ireland's Unionist community was calibrated with similar precision. The Unionist majority, Blair said, had to face up to the legitimate aspirations of those who sought a united Ireland through political means; Irish Nationalism deserved parity of esteem with British Unionism. But he gave Unionism a guarantee–Northern Ireland would retain its links with Britain unless and until a majority in the province decided otherwise. For decades past the Unionist reflex had been to say "No" to any suggestion of change. Here was a chance to move from the back to the front foot by testing the Republicans' commitment to politics over violence. The third player in the process was the Republic of Ireland. Relationships between London and Dublin were also soaked in the suspicions of history. The Republic's constitution had never accepted the partition of Ireland some three-quarters of a century earlier. It still asserted its sovereignty over the six counties of Northern Ireland, a territorial claim that fueled the paranoia of many Unionists. Blair asked the Irish government to amend its constitution to drop the claim. In return, a new political settlement would give the Republic a say in the governance of the province.

Blair had prepared the ground for his initiative before the general election. His own party had traditionally favored the Nationalists in

Northern Ireland. Though it abhorred Republican violence, Labour had long endorsed the goal of Irish unity, albeit through peaceful means. The policy had sat uneasily with the democratic principle that the citizens of Northern Ireland had the right to determine their own destiny. The pro-Nationalist bias had also fueled Unionist fears that a Labour government would sell out their interests to the Irish Republic. Blair had abandoned this old approach while still in opposition and declared that a New Labour government would be neutral. The destiny of the province would lie with the wishes of its people, Unionists and Nationalists alike. "This principle of consent," he now said in his Belfast speech, "is and will be at the heart of my government's policies on Northern Ireland. It is the key principle." The challenge to Republicans was to swap violence for politics; for Unionists it was to set aside their opposition to power-sharing in a new Northern Ireland parliament. The framework had a compelling logic. Unionists would retain their veto over the constitutional allegiance of Northern Ireland for as long as they remained in the majority. Nationalists—and their militant cousins in the Republican movement—would be given the political and civil rights they had long been denied, as well as the assurance that Britain would not stand in the way of Irish unity if, at some point in the future, that was the wish of the people of the province. The Irish Republic meanwhile would have a voice in shaping the future of its neighbor.

Bringing peace to Northern Ireland, though, required more than calm logic. The province's politics had been poisoned by its history. Nationalists had never forgotten the oppression of three centuries of British occupation, nor forgiven the final act of partition when the British left most of Ireland in 1921. Unionists, crowded into the North after partition, had felt at once threatened by the Irish Republic and forgotten by governments in London. Thus beleaguered, they had trampled on the Catholic community in the North. The bitterness and suspicions had hardened into hatred during the thirty years that the IRA and the loyalists had waged their terrorist campaigns. Belfast had become a city in which Protestants and Catholics threw bricks, Molotov cocktails, and worse at each other over the walls and barbed wire that divided their communities. The biggest of these structures was called,

with more than a touch of macabre irony, "the Peace Line." The streets of Northern Ireland were patrolled day and night by British troops in flak jackets and armored vehicles–the whole place a tinderbox into which extremists on both sides would regularly add the sparks of religious sectarianism.

Another prime minister might have issued the ritual calls for peace, gone through the motions of negotiation, and then quietly walked away. That was the cost-free option. Northern Ireland was not a place where British leaders scored political points. Sad though it was to say, for most people in mainland Britain, the Irish Sea might have been an ocean. They had grown inured to the violence–killings and bombings in Belfast or Londonderry had long before been relegated to the inside pages of English newspapers. Even when the IRA occasionally brought its murder to London, Birmingham, or Manchester, the popular response was one of weary resignation. Among senior British politicians the sentiment most often expressed in private was that the warring factions in Northern Ireland deserved each other. There were no votes for Tony Blair to be gained in the search for peace. Only the risk that he would fail.

To be fair to his Conservative predecessor in Downing Street, Blair was not starting from scratch. For all his domestic troubles–perhaps sometimes in order to escape them–John Major had struggled valiantly to broker an Irish settlement. There had been signs that the leadership of the IRA was slowly reaching the conclusion that its terrorist campaign was indeed futile. Gerry Adams and Martin McGuinness, the most prominent figures in Sinn Fein, had served as young men in the armed brigades of the IRA. Now approaching middle age–and watching the heavy toll inflicted by loyalist terrorists on the Catholic community–they seemed to have wearied of war. For fifteen years the Republican movement had pursued the twin-track strategy of seeking political support in Northern Ireland while waging its terrorist war against the British. But those growing old in the conflict increasingly preferred the ballot box to the Armalite rifle. Demography also spoke for a negotiated peace. The birth rate among Catholics in the province was higher than that among Protestants. Those who wanted a united

Ireland could hope that in thirty, forty, or perhaps fifty years' time, they rather than the Unionists would be in the majority. John Hume, the leader of the Nationalist Social Democratic and Labour Party (SDLP), which sought a united Ireland by peaceful means, had worked tirelessly to secure a cease-fire, acting as a broker between Republican leaders and politicians in London and Dublin. Major's government had tried hard to draw Sinn Fein into the political process. Working with the Irish government, for a time it had had some success. Bill Clinton's administration had also lent its weight to the effort—a critical factor because the Republicans drew most of their financial support from Irish Americans. Clinton had initially irritated Major's government by welcoming Sinn Fein leaders at the White House. But the differences had been settled, and a trip by Clinton to Belfast in late 1995—the first to Northern Ireland by a serving president—gave a fillip to the political process. The strategy seemed for a time to be working, but the attempt foundered on the argument between Major's government and the IRA about paramilitary weapons. Major sought the decommissioning of weapons as a precondition to admitting Sinn Fein fully into political negotiations on a new Northern Ireland constitution; the IRA refused to give up its huge stocks of guns and explosives. In February 1996 the stalemate was broken when the IRA ended an eighteen-month cease-fire with the spectacular bombing of an office complex at Canary Wharf in London's financial district.

In the late summer of 1997 Blair was fully committed to peace. "If you ask me if the Republicans have definitely decided to give up violence for good, the answer is probably no," the new prime minister privately admitted. "But I do think that the more they are drawn into the political process the harder it gets for them to return to violence." There was another dimension to this approach. "It is essential to show—to the United States, to the Irish government, and to the Nationalists in Northern Ireland—that if the IRA remains wedded to violence, that is their decision: that they have rejected the opportunity for peace." Here, then, was the strategy. If it worked, Sinn Fein would be pulled step by step into a political process that would decisively undercut any justifi-

cation for violence. If it failed, it would be clear to all—and above all to Republican sympathizers in the United States—just who was to blame. To the same end, he appointed Marjorie Mowlam, one of the government's most popular and robustly candid politicians, as Northern Ireland secretary. Mowlam, still recovering from treatment for a brain tumor, trampled on ceremony, made friends with ordinary people on the streets, and spoke to the toughest of the province's politicians in their own earthy language. She also took risks, famously stepping into Belfast's notorious Maze prison to convince face-to-face some of the province's most hardened loyalist terrorists of the case for peace. Her breezy honesty meanwhile brought a new atmosphere to the government's relationship with the IRA. In a calculated double act, Blair focused his attentions on offering reassurance to mainstream Unionists.

The gamble paid off. Within two months of the election, the IRA had called another cease-fire. By the autumn of 1997 a Sinn Fein delegation—including some who had formerly served prison sentences for terrorist offenses—joined talks among the other political parties on the creation of a new power-sharing government. The talks were chaired by former senator George Mitchell, who had been appointed by Bill Clinton as his special envoy to Northern Ireland. At John Major's behest, Mitchell had chaired an international commission on how best to secure the elimination of terrorist weapons from Northern Ireland. The commission had also set out a series of conditions—the so-called Mitchell principles—that would allow paramilitary organizations from both sides to participate in political negotiations. The most important of these conditions demanded that Republicans and loyalists had first to renounce violence and commit themselves to exclusively democratic means before they would be permitted to sit at the negotiating table. The destruction of terrorist arms dumps could then proceed in parallel with talks.

Mitchell understood that the political process had to be insulated from those still committed to violence. In the past, the terrorists had held it hostage—an outrage perpetrated by one or the other group had been enough to derail any progress toward a political settlement. The former senator insisted that negotiations between the peaceful major-

ity should continue regardless of the actions of those who chose to remain on the outside. Mitchell employed an element of bluff here–the truth was that the participation of the IRA would be vital to any eventual deal–but his approach intensified the pressure on Republicans and loyalists alike to sign up to the renunciation of violence.

After Blair's Belfast speech Mitchell assumed a central role in the search for an overarching political settlement. Progress over the next few months was painfully slow. Unionists refused to talk to Republican leaders they held directly responsible for the killing of friends and relatives during the IRA's war. There was deep mistrust within each of the province's two communities as well as between them. David Trimble, the leader of the moderate Ulster Unionist Party (UUP), proved himself a more courageous leader than his political past would have suggested. He was willing to try to make negotiations work. But inside and outside the UUP, there were Unionists who saw any compromise with Republicanism as a betrayal. And if Trimble had to persuade his own community that a political settlement would actually strengthen Northern Ireland's position within the United Kingdom, Adams and his negotiating team had to do the opposite–to convince militant Republicans that politics rather than violence was the surer route to a united Ireland.

Blair was playing a game of multidimensional chess. The province's political leaders were negotiating not just with each other but with their own constituencies. In the case of Gerry Adams that meant with the IRA, which still included senior figures who continued to believe that what they called the "armed struggle" would eventually drive the British from Ireland. For his part Trimble had forever to look over his shoulder not just at the doubters within his own party but also at the viscerally anti-Catholic Democratic Unionist Party (DUP) headed by Ian Paisley. Paisley's fiery rhetoric–he denounced Blair as a "liar" determined to destroy the Union and Trimble as a "traitor"–testified to the visceral sectarianism that still infected large sections of the community. The DUP boycotted negotiations, denouncing the proceedings as a Republican plot. As for Blair, he had to find a formula for the Irish government's involvement in the affairs of the province that was

at once acceptable to Nationalist politicians in Dublin and to Unionists in Belfast. He brought to bear the full talents of persuasion he had once deployed as an advocate in the courts, revealing himself as a master of the art of what one British official called "constructive ambiguity." Ingenious formulations, often drafted personally by the prime minister, allowed negotiations to circumvent the many roadblocks to an agreement. Mitchell, too, showed infinite patience, though every now and then even so good-humored a politician could not entirely contain his frustrations. "People here are nice and friendly," he remarked toward the end of 1998. "They're just not friendly to each other. Centuries of conflict have generated hatreds that make it virtually impossible for the two communities to trust each other." For all that, Mitchell persevered. Alongside his forbearance sat Tony Blair's determination.

Peter Mandelson, who later did his own stint as Blair's Northern Ireland secretary, saw that the tortuous search for peace in the province was a perfect fit with the prime minister's political strengths. Blair's habit of taking any argument back to first principles meant that he avoided the dense undergrowth of past suspicions and hatreds. Rather than addressing the rights and wrongs of history, he projected a vision of a different future. The process of negotiation appealed to a supreme confidence in his own powers of persuasion and his skill in building relationships across political divides. A close friendship with Bertie Ahern, the Republic of Ireland's prime minister, was crucial to a new political settlement. Ahern, like Blair, was a politician willing to take risks, and the two men established a rapport that set aside the ancient enmities of Anglo-Irish relations. Equally important was the trust Blair established with David Trimble on one side and Gerry Adams on the other. Sometimes he would tell each of them what they wanted to hear. Sometimes his approach to solving a problem was simply to push it further into the future. But even those who disagreed with him never doubted his commitment. "He's never more engaged and absorbed than in the midst of an argument that he needs to win," one of his close friends observed. And that was never more true than in Northern Ireland. George Mitchell was generous in his subsequent, published account of the peace process, observing that "Blair possesses

the elements of effective leadership in our era. He is intelligent, articulate, decisive, and photogenic. . . . His coming to Northern Ireland was a big gamble. There was no assurance of success and most political consultants would have told him to stay away. But Blair came, and he had an immediate impact."

In the autumn of 1997 Blair became the first British prime minister since Irish partition in 1921 to meet the leaders of the Republican movement. Traveling to Belfast to give impetus to the multiparty negotiations—which now included representatives of loyalist paramilitaries as well as of the IRA—Blair shook the hand of Gerry Adams. To the hard-line Unionists who demonstrated outside the talks it was an act of betrayal. "Traitor!" they shouted when the prime minister emerged. In deference to Unionist sensibilities, television cameras were barred this first time from catching the handshake on film. But a line had been crossed, and a few weeks later Adams would be walking through the front door of 10 Downing Street. Martin McGuinness, an avowed IRA commander during the 1970s, was soon another regular visitor to the prime minister's office. Blair was once asked how he could trust someone who had waged such a cruel war against the British state. Whatever had happened then, he replied, he trusted McGuinness to keep his word now.

The strategy of drawing the Republicans inexorably into the political process soon began to bear fruit. Each time Gerry Adams and Martin McGuinness sat down to negotiate with Tony Blair they took another step away from the violence of the previous thirty years. Throughout the negotiations Blair was helped by Bill Clinton. Northern Ireland became central to the friendship between the two men, for a settlement seemed as important to the president as to the prime minister. Occasionally there were tactical disagreements. Blair sometimes thought Clinton was too biased toward the Republicans. But the leaders of Sinn Fein came to value greatly their access to the White House and to Capitol Hill. They enjoyed the limelight and their newfound celebrity status in Washington—which was part of the plan. Clinton made sure he extracted a price for his hospitality, applying pressure on Blair's behalf to persuade Adams and McGuinness to harden the IRA's

commitment to a political deal. In March 1998, just ahead of an Easter deadline set by Blair and Mitchell for a new settlement, the leaders of all the main Northern Ireland parties attended the annual White House celebrations of St. Patrick's Day. When the glasses had stopped clinking, Clinton took them all aside to impress on them his personal investment in achieving peace.

"Historic" is a much overused word in political discourse. Tony Blair had been gently mocked in the British media when he arrived in Northern Ireland a few days before Easter saying that the "hand of history" lay on the shoulder of those seeking a settlement. But, for once, "historic" was indeed a fitting description of the bargain struck in Belfast on Good Friday, April 10, 1998. The Belfast Agreement, setting up a new political assembly in which Unionists and Republicans would share power, marked the moment that Northern Ireland stepped out of the dark shadow of its history. This was one of those occasions, too, that cast politicians in the unfamiliar guise of heroes. For four days and nights Tony Blair and Bertie Ahern worked tirelessly with George Mitchell and the province's political leaders to secure the accord. Bill Clinton intervened from the White House at critical moments, telephoning both Republicans and Unionists to urge them to make the necessary compromises. Most important, David Trimble and Gerry Adams turned their backs on the past—the one to acknowledge the legitimacy of the aspiration of a united Ireland, the other to accept that the goal could be achieved only through the ballot box.

The architecture of the agreement was much as Blair had set out immediately after the May election. A power-sharing assembly in Belfast gave Northern Ireland self-rule within the United Kingdom. New institutions were established to foster cooperation between the province and the Republic of Ireland. The Catholic community was assured of greater civil rights and reforms to the judiciary, as well as the policing service to safeguard those rights. The Dublin government pledged to revoke its territorial claim to Northern Ireland. This dry constitutional detail, however, understated the significance of the mo-

ment. The television images of the leaders of Unionism and National-
ism, loyalism and Republicanism gathered around the same table were
as remarkable as any seen in the history of Ireland. It would take more
than a day—more, probably, than a decade—to draw the bitterness and
mistrust from the politics of the province. There would be plenty of
stumbles on the road beyond it. The agreement, though, restored dem-
ocratic politics to Northern Ireland—the essential first step to peace. For
Gerry Adams and Martin McGuinness there was no going back.

The making of the accord had seen everyone take risks. Blair found
himself negotiating not just with the leadership of Sinn Fein but di-
rectly with the IRA's military command. "They brought in people who
were obviously members of the Army Council," Marjorie Mowlam
said later. "You don't ask names—you just say hello and you get on with
it." These were people directly responsible for the killing of British sol-
diers and police officers and the murder of civilians. Only fifteen years
earlier the IRA had attempted to assassinate Margaret Thatcher and
her cabinet when it had bombed a hotel in Brighton on England's
south coast. Now her successor was obliged—in a condition as impor-
tant for the loyalist paramilitaries as for the IRA—to agree to the phased
release from prison of those convicted of terrorist crimes. Later he
would admit privately that he had found that particular decision as
personally distasteful as it was politically hazardous. There was no easy
answer to the letters from relatives of the victims of past atrocities as to
why people who had murdered and maimed their loved ones were be-
ing released in the name of peace. Brutal as it was, the only response
was that the emptying of the prisons was vital to the process of recon-
ciliation. Blair was conscious that if the IRA ever broke its cease-fire,
political opponents would charge him with having blood on his hands.
These were gambles he was ready to take, perhaps because his own
commitment to the cause was personal as well as political. The mother
he had lost when still a young man had been born and raised in
Ireland—a Protestant in the mainly Catholic Republic. As a child he
had spent his summer vacations at his mother's family home and drunk

his first pint of Guinness there. The visits had ended with the start of the "troubles" in Northern Ireland. How proud she would have been of a son who brought peace to the island of her birth.

Six weeks later the Good Friday deal won the overwhelming endorsement of the Irish people in simultaneous referendums in Northern Ireland and the Republic. Blair campaigned tirelessly in the North, a central plank of his strategy throughout the peace process being to appeal directly to the people as part of the aim of locking the parties into an accord. The referendums marked the first time that Ireland had spoken as a nation since 1918, when, under British rule, Sinn Fein had won a majority of the Irish seats in the Westminster parliament. The principles embedded in the accord–above all that Northern Ireland's future would be decided only with the "consent" of its people–were now inviolate. The Belfast Agreement was a beginning rather than an end. The enmities and mistrusts in Northern Ireland ran too deep to be washed away even by so remarkable a document. Some problems, the issue of IRA weapons most prominent among them, had been relegated to future negotiations rather than finally resolved. Everything in the history and folklore of Republicanism said that the IRA would never give up entirely its caches of Semtex. Meanwhile the extreme Unionists, represented by Ian Paisley's Democratic Unionist Party, seemed unwilling or unable to accept that the province's Nationalist community deserved parity of esteem. To Paisley, Blair was the "liar" who had sold out Unionism.

In the summer of 1998, just months after the agreement had been signed, a splinter group of Republicans reminded the world again of the terrible violence that the province's communities could inflict on one another. The so-called Real IRA had broken away from the main Republican movement following the signing of the Belfast Agreement. These fanatics remained wedded to violence as the only means to secure Britain's complete withdrawal from Ireland. In August a group of its recruits took a massive car bomb into the town of Omagh, near the border with the Republic. The supposed warnings given before

the bomb was detonated were misleading and garbled. Twenty-nine people–Catholics as well as Protestants, two Spanish visitors, women, children, and unborn twins among them–were killed when the explosion ripped through the town center. Even by the standards of past atrocities the Omagh bombing was shocking. For a moment it seemed that everything gained during the previous few years might be lost. But the outrage seemed to stun mainstream Republicans as much as Unionists, and it was roundly condemned by Gerry Adams. Two weeks later Tony Blair and Bill Clinton visited Omagh to meet with the bereaved, arguing that such horrifying acts of violence strengthened rather than weakened the case for the peace process.

Translating the Belfast Agreement into durable political structures was not easy. David Trimble and Gerry Adams had in their different ways challenged the sacred canons of their respective traditions, and there were points beyond which neither could or would go. It took until the autumn of 1999 to actually establish the new political assembly envisaged by the accord. Trimble was appointed the province's first minister, and, in an extraordinary reflection of how far Northern Ireland had traveled, the former IRA commander Martin McGuinness became education minister. Through the following years, however, the new assembly would be suspended, reinstated, and suspended again as Unionists and Republicans continued to argue about the fate of IRA weapons. More than once the IRA opened its secret arms dumps to inspection by the independent decommissioning body established by the agreement. In the autumn of 2001, just weeks after the terrorist attacks on the twin towers in New York, the independent body supervised the destruction of a portion of the weapons. But Unionist suspicions that the IRA was determined to keep open the option of a return to violence were heightened by the arrest in Colombia of three Republicans who were alleged to have been working with that country's left-wing rebel group, the FARC. Ongoing strains between the doves and hawks within Republicanism stood in the way of a decisive act of decommissioning. On the Unionist side, David Trimble found himself the constant prey of Unionists who would never be reconciled with the

power-sharing at the heart of the Belfast Agreement. The tensions within Unionism and Republicanism often seemed more dangerous than the divide between them.

The frustrations of those who had cajoled the parties into the agreement were often evident. At one point Bill Clinton likened Unionists and Republicans to a pair of drunks leaving a bar for the last time after promising to dry out: "When they reach the swinging doors they turn right round and go back in and say, 'I just can't quite get there.'" Tony Blair, though, persevered. The prime minister returned again and again for day-into-night meetings with political leaders at Belfast's Stormont Castle. Gerry Adams and Martin McGuinness continued their visits to 10 Downing Street and Chequers. "He [Blair] knows Adams better than most of the ministers in his cabinet," an official was heard to remark after one grueling set of negotiations. The prime minister's personal commitment had been reinforced by the hands-on role in negotiations of Jonathan Powell, his chief of staff, and the choice of his close political ally Peter Mandelson as Northern Ireland secretary in the autumn of 1999. The ebb and flow of what often seemed a permanent negotiation, though, continued to absorb large amounts of Blair's own time. The IRA's refusal to make a decisive move to rid itself of all its weapons proved a constant stumbling block.

So the peace was imperfect, the political progress prone to reversals. Some of the former paramilitaries on both sides turned to gangsterism in place of terrorism. By the standards of British cities, Belfast remained a violent place. Yet even such setbacks could not undermine the historic achievement. If some parties in Northern Ireland remained committed to violence while others were still wedded to Protestant supremacy, the truth was the Belfast Agreement had robbed the conflict of its rationale. British troops withdrew their armored cars from the streets of the province. Catholics were encouraged to join a reformed police force. However disruptive the activities of a few fringe groups, the war was over. Many people could claim a significant share of the credit—John Hume, David Trimble, Gerry Adams, Bertie Ahern, Bill Clinton, and George Mitchell among them. But at the heart of the bar-

gain struck on Good Friday 1998 lay Blair's personal commitment and dogged determination.

In November 1998 Blair had become the first ever British prime minister to address the Irish Dail, or parliament, in Dublin. Almost tucked away in his speech was an insight into the mindset—the back-to-first-principles approach—that had begun to unburden Northern Ireland of its history. "It is all about belonging," he told the parliament. "The wish of Unionists is to belong to the UK. The wish of Nationalists is to belong to Ireland. Both traditions are reasonable. There are no absolutes. The beginning of understanding is to realize that." Sometimes during this arduous process, he made mistakes. His dislike of confrontation and constant desire to please occasionally saw him avoiding hard choices in favor of telling people what they wanted to hear. Now and then he seemed to think that simply wishing something to happen was enough. But he was correct in his essential judgment that the war belonged to the past. For all the troubles that still lay ahead, Blair had taken Northern Ireland to the beginning of understanding.

9. WAGING WAR

TONY BLAIR COULD SCARCELY RECALL a bleaker moment in politics. He was spending the Easter vacation weekend at Chequers, but this was hardly a time for relaxation. Ten days earlier, in late March 1999, American, British, and other NATO warplanes had begun the bombing of Kosovo in the Balkans. The campaign was intended to halt Serbia's ruthless suppression of the province's ethnic Muslim Albanians, but the strategy was failing. Instead of being cowed by the West's military might, Serbia's Slobodan Milosevic had stepped up his strategy of purging Kosovo. A river of refugees had turned into a flood. Blair watched the television pictures of terrified and exhausted Albanians clamoring to cross Kosovo's border into Macedonia. The top-secret briefings Blair had received from his military commanders were relentlessly depressing. There had been some who had hoped that two or three days of bombing would drive Milosevic back to the negotiating table. The Serbian leader, after all, had been bombed into submission a few years earlier when air strikes had ended the war in Bosnia. This time, though, the alliance had underestimated Milosevic's determination and overestimated its own capacity to inflict damage on Serbia's military machine.

The daily reports to the prime minister of the British military's strike rate told a dismal story. At the start of the conflict, the Royal Navy had fired four of its submarine-based cruise missiles. Each one of the American-supplied million-dollar missiles had missed its target, exploding uselessly somewhere in the mountains of the former Yugoslavia; apparently the computer-guidance systems of the surface-skimming missiles had been "overprogrammed." The results of the Royal Air Force's bombing sorties over Kosovo were hardly more successful. Everything

that could go wrong was going wrong. Some planes were being forced to turn back from their missions with engine trouble; others could not find their targets. Those that managed to reach them found they could not drop their bombs because of a low cloud cover. To add to the misery, the confidential reports Blair received from NATO headquarters in Brussels suggested that NATO's supreme allied commander, the American general Wesley Clark, was allowing the political and presentational complexities of the operation to interfere with its military effectiveness. In short, a war being fought in the name of halting ethnic cleansing was actually accelerating it. The aides and officials who spoke to the prime minister that weekend remember his mood as bleak. "He was angry, frustrated, deeply upset," one of them recalled. "Everyone felt awful. We felt we had contributed to this [the tide of refugees] and there was nothing we could do about it." In retrospect, though, this was also the point at which Blair began to understand the strategic error that the allies had made, and the moment when he began to say that having started, NATO must now finish the job.

Kosovo was not the first occasion Blair had ordered British forces into action. That had come three months earlier when British warplanes had joined the American bombing of Iraq in "Operation Desert Fox." In late 1998 United Nations inspectors had announced that the Baghdad regime was continuing to obstruct and evade the search for weapons of mass destruction. Britain's spymasters had alerted Blair at the very start of his premiership to Iraq's lethal weapons programs. By the time he entered Downing Street, the enforcement of the UN resolutions that had followed Operation Desert Storm had become an American-British operation. Royal Air Force warplanes flew alongside those of the United States Air Force to police the no-fly zones over southern and northern Iraq. The new prime minister's concerns about the Iraqi situation were reflected in a foreign policy speech he made to the City of London Lord Mayor's Banquet in November 1997, a few months after the election. The government's determination to force Iraq to comply with UN resolutions, he said, was "unshakable."

Privately, Blair was confiding to other political leaders that he was

alarmed by the assessment of Britain's intelligence chiefs. One such conversation took place with Paddy Ashdown, then leader of the Liberal Democrat Party in Parliament. Ashdown, who went on to become the international high representative in Bosnia, recorded the exchange in a diary entry for November 15, 1997. Blair's observations at that time–on the differing views of Western allies as well as the threat from Saddam–later seemed almost a premonition of the heated controversy about the justification for war in early 2003. "I have now seen some of this [intelligence] stuff," he told Ashdown. "It really is pretty scary. He is very close to some appalling weapons of mass destruction. I don't understand why the French and others don't understand this. We cannot let him get away with it. The world thinks this is just gamesmanship. But it's deadly serious." Ashdown suggested that the government needed to get more of the intelligence information into the public domain. Blair agreed: "I said exactly the same to Clinton. I know he is thinking about how it might be possible to do that." A few months later, the government published the first of its Iraq "dossiers" detailing Saddam's capabilities. Another sign of Blair's determination to support Clinton came in August 1998, when, almost alone among world leaders, he supported American missile attacks on what were alleged to be Al Qaeda facilities in Sudan and Afghanistan.

Iraq's cat-and-mouse game with the inspectors continued through 1998. By February Blair was sufficiently concerned to seek Parliament's approval for military action against Iraq through a vote in the House of Commons. The vote saw two dozen of the government's own MPs oppose any action but was carried by an overwhelming majority of more than four hundred. What was significant here was not the rebellion of party members, but the fact that a vote had been taken at all. The prime minister did not require explicit backing from the House of Commons before authorizing military action. The decision to go to war was one traditionally taken on the government's own authority and that of the head of state, the king or queen. During the previous few decades British prime ministers had sent troops into action in Korea, Egypt, the Falkland Islands, and the Gulf without parliamentary approval. By breaking

with tradition, Blair gave added legitimacy to any action against Saddam, but he had set a precedent—one that would come back to haunt him four years later when he faced a huge revolt in his party about the decision to invade Iraq. In December 1998, though, when the UN chief weapons inspector Richard Butler reported that, for all the warnings and threats, Saddam was still not complying, the decision to join the United States in a series of air strikes was relatively straightforward. Some Downing Street advisers did think that the timing of the bombing—on the eve of the impeachment proceedings against Clinton in Washington—was at best awkward, and one senior British official remarked that Clinton had shown "amazing cynicism." But this was not a last-minute decision. Only a month earlier, a planned bombing raid had been halted when American and British planes were already in the sky after Saddam had promised, duplicitously, that he would at last comply with UN inspectors. That had been his final chance. Blair decided that action could not be postponed indefinitely because of the impeachment trial and dismissed as "grotesque" the accusation that he had connived in a plan to divert attention from Clinton's domestic troubles. "I want to deal with one thing straight on," he told the House of Commons. "There are suggestions that the timing of military action is somehow linked to the internal affairs of the United States. I refute this entirely. I have no doubt whatsoever that action is fully justified now. That is my strong personal view. I know that President Clinton reached the same conclusion for the same reasons. Had he acted differently, out of regard to internal matters of U.S. politics, that would have been a dereliction of his duty as president. Instead, not for the first time, he has shown the courage to do the right thing and he has my full support."

Four days of bombing Iraq's military facilities hardly rated as a full-scale conflict, and the prime minister made the decision without fuss. One of those present in his small study on December 16 when he formally gave the go-ahead to General Charles Guthrie, the armed forces' chief of staff, recalled that Blair was remarkably calm, almost matter-of-fact. A few minutes later he was standing in Downing Street telling the world of the decision. Aware of the political sensitivities surrounding

his impeachment, Clinton had agreed that Blair would announce the bombing ahead of his own Oval Office address. For all Blair's composure, the decision to send the nation's forces into combat marked an important psychological moment, as he learned for the first time that war placed the occupant of 10 Downing Street in a position of command unique in the normal life of government. In every other realm of policymaking, the prime minister sets the strategy and leaves the operational issues to others. In times of conflict, he or she deals personally—up close—with the military. The prime minister approves each choice of target and receives detailed scorecards on the success or otherwise of every operation. A small "war cabinet" of senior political colleagues will include the defense and foreign secretaries and the government's senior law officer. But, once shots are being fired in anger, the chain of command and line of responsibility run straight from the battlefield to the prime minister. For Blair, as for his predecessors, the sense of burden was mingled with a curious excitement. Never is a British leader quite so powerful.

The air strikes did not have the specific approval of the United Nations, for neither Russia nor France would have given their backing. Blair was unapologetic, arguing that Saddam's defiance of previous UN resolutions provided sufficient legal grounds. He was a multilateralist by instinct, and like his European counterparts was keen to see a revival of international institutions. But his support for such bodies was conditional. A few weeks after this first experience as a warrior prime minister, he visited South Africa. Nelson Mandela, the outgoing president, had been sharply critical of the raids, arguing that Washington and London should have acted only with UN backing. Speaking to the country's parliament in Cape Town, Blair defended the fact that the two governments had acted alone. "When the international community agrees on certain objectives and then fails to implement them," he said, "those that can act, must." Here, though it was scarcely noticed at the time, were the antecedents of a new doctrine of international intervention that would soon see Blair take Britain to war in the Balkans.

The crisis in Kosovo had unfolded in parallel with that in Iraq during 1998. Like Saddam Hussein, Slobodan Milosevic was a master of pre-varication and equally adept at exploiting divisions in the international community. Each time his repression of the Kosovo Albanians reached a point at which he risked military intervention by the West, Milosevic would take half a step back. Richard Holbrooke, appointed by Clinton as a special envoy to the region, joined a distinguished line of Western negotiators who had been duped by the Serbian leader. By the begin-ning of 1999, in spite of the presence of European observers, Milose-vic's reign of terror had extended well beyond efforts to defeat the Kosovo Liberation Army, the insurgent group that had gathered grow-ing support because of the West's inaction in the face of Serbia's atroc-ities. The previous autumn, in an attempt to unnerve the Serbian leader, NATO had put its air forces on full alert for a potential strike on his troops, but the threat had brought only a brief respite. In January of 1999 the world was still watching from the sidelines when Serbian po-lice and paramilitary troops killed forty-five fleeing Kosovar civilians near the village of Racak. Television pictures of this latest carnage were soon being beamed into living rooms around the world. Milosevic was obliged to send representatives to what would be a final round of ne-gotiations with the KLA at Rambouillet, near Paris.

The Rambouillet negotiations were led by Madeleine Albright, the U.S. secretary of state, and Robin Cook, Britain's foreign secretary. The two worked well together. Albright, who had pressed in vain during the first Clinton administration for earlier and more decisive U.S. ac-tion to end the carnage in Bosnia, was determined that Milosevic would be restrained. Cook hailed from the wing of the Labour Party that had a long tradition of supporting humanitarian interventions. Soon after the May 1997 election, the new foreign secretary had been pilloried in the media for suggesting that Britain's new foreign policy would henceforth have an "ethical dimension." Britain's thriving arms trade with some of the world's more dubious regimes soon raised some of the obvious contradictions, but Kosovo was nothing if not an ethical issue. As Albright and Cook launched a "last chance" round of diplo-matic negotiations in February 1999, Blair was distracted by other is-

sues, though he had been one of the leaders most vocal in calling for an end to the ethnic cleansing during 1998. By the following month, when it was clear that Milosevic was immune to any new threats, the prime minister had become fully engaged. As he prepared to attend a summit meeting of European leaders in Germany, one of Whitehall's senior career officials privately warned Blair that some governments were still looking for a solution short of war; the Germans, Italians, and others remained at best skeptical of military action, and Russia's Boris Yeltsin was enraged by the idea. Clinton might yet prefer some compromise. Shouldn't he climb back a little from the end of the limb on which he was now rather precariously perched? the official asked the prime minister. Blair was adamant: "If there's going to be a fudge, I am not going to be part of it."

In the event, NATO held together and Yeltsin's sound and fury turned out to be just that. Blair would soon discover, though, that diplomacy had been at the expense of the military planning. His priority had been to hold together the NATO coalition. Far less attention had been paid to the strategic calculations behind the air campaign. There was an unspoken assumption that a few days, maybe a week, of strikes would bring Milosevic to heel. General Charles Guthrie had warned Blair at the outset that it was impossible to predict the course of events. But, in the words of another prime ministerial intimate, "There was an air of quiet complacency around the place. We were all tired. Easter was coming up. We just didn't focus enough." The lack of contingency planning became all too clear to Milosevic when NATO ruled out the use of ground troops to fight their way into Kosovo, a cautious move that seemed good politics at the time. Meanwhile, Bill Clinton was facing significant opposition to another foreign entanglement. Most Americans, his advisers told him, had scarcely heard of Kosovo. The Pentagon was against anything but a bombing campaign. Republicans in Congress were vocal in their opposition to putting U.S. forces in harm's way to sort out another of Europe's messes. In any case, five hundred NATO warplanes should be sufficient to achieve the goal. Consequently, at the very start of the campaign the president declared, "I do not intend to put our troops into Kosovo to fight a ground

war." NATO forces would enter to keep the peace only when Milosevic had withdrawn. Tony Blair's statement to the House of Commons was not quite as categorical, but it carried much the same message: "Let us be clear: we are not going to send in 100,000 or 200,000 ground forces with the consent of others, for no such consent exists."

During the days that followed that bleak Easter weekend, Blair began to realize how grave had been their misjudgment. Milosevic knew that if he could withstand the bombing—and Western public opinion would always place limits on the NATO strikes—he could complete the ethnic cleansing of Kosovo. In the jargon, he would create irreversible "facts on the ground." Blair summoned Charles Guthrie, George Robertson, the defense secretary, and other senior figures for the first of a series of intensive meetings to review the strategic options. These were the discussions, one participant would later muse, that should have taken place before the conflict. Still, now that he understood the gravity of the situation, Blair was determined and resourceful. The situation at NATO headquarters was still one of argument and confusion, and at times the lack of clear coordination seemed almost farcical. Blair's aides discovered, for example, that the Americans, whose planes made up the overwhelming bulk of the NATO strike force, were actually hitting two sets of targets. The first was drawn from the set agreed upon during the daily painful wrangles among the allies at NATO. The others the Americans were choosing on their own, without reference to anyone else within the alliance. British officials thought it extraordinary that neither the prime minister nor the military had been informed by the Pentagon about this second group. Embarrassed by their ignorance, they eventually decided to pretend they had been told. As for NATO, for all the doubts among British officials about Wesley Clark, the prime minister concluded that it was essential to give the American commander his full support.

By the time the House of Commons returned from its Easter break on April 13, there were signs that the air campaign was having some effect. Under American and British pressure the scope of the targets had been widened to include more of Serbia's military infrastruc-

ture. Blair, meanwhile, was pressing the point with NATO colleagues that this was a war that none of them could afford to lose. If NATO failed in Kosovo, it would no longer have any credibility as an effective military alliance. Updating Parliament on the course of the conflict, the prime minister also sought subtly to change the terms of the international debate on ground troops. NATO ground forces, he said, could enter Kosovo when the bombing had created a "semi-permissive environment." He was deliberately vague as to what he meant by that latter description. In private conversations with Paddy Ashdown, Blair went further. Ashdown records the prime minister saying that NATO had prepared for "all eventualities." The alliance had been publicly reticent about the use of ground troops, the prime minister explained, for fear of further antagonizing the Russians. But, Blair reassured Ashdown, "when conditions are semi-permissive we will use ground troops whether Milosevic agrees or not. And by semi-permissive I mean when the risks to troops on the ground have dropped to acceptable levels."

In fact, such assurances owed more to hope than reality. There was no consensus on the use of NATO troops except, as had been envisaged at the outset, to police a negotiated agreement between the Serbs and the KLA. Blair was employing one of his favorite strategies—of trying to make things happen by stating that they already had. He had, for example, already sought to delineate the terms of any eventual peace agreement with Milosevic by saying publicly that it would have to include the return to their homes of all the refugees from Kosovo. Some thought such pronouncements naive: prime ministers could not operate on the basis that reality might at some point or another catch up with their hopes. Others, though, saw a courageous politician determined to shape events by creating his own "facts on the ground."

Kosovo was the first war that NATO had engaged in in its fifty-year history. It was also unlike any other conflict in Europe's bloodiest century. The battle was not being fought over territory but to uphold a set of values. In that respect, it marked a profound challenge to the international system that had prevailed since the founding of the United

Nations. That system, for obvious reasons of history, had been founded on the principle of noninterference in the sovereign affairs of independent states. As long as they did not violate international frontiers, the presumption was that governments could do as they pleased. There had always been notional qualifications to this principle in the form of international conventions against, for example, torture and genocide. But internal repression was not a casus belli. Tony Blair now argued for a more fundamental reshaping of the international order to reflect the growing interdependence of the modern world. He made the case in a speech to the Economic Club of Chicago on April 24, en route back to London after the fiftieth-anniversary celebrations of NATO in Washington. Early drafts of this new "Doctrine of International Community" had been produced by Lawrence Freedman, a distinguished British academic and lecturer in war studies. Blair, though, wrote most of the final speech himself. It called for a radical overhaul of international rules and institutions to reflect changing global realities: in a world of porous borders where chaos and conflict quickly spilled over from one nation to its neighbors, moral purpose and enlightened self-interest argued for more assertive intervention. The post–cold war world, he said, needed a broader definition of security than that applied during the confrontation between the West and the Soviet Union. Calling for "internationalism in place of isolationism," Blair argued that states that persecuted their own populations could no longer expect the rest of the civilized world to stand idly by. The West had done precisely that during the ethnic slaughter in Rwanda and, for several years, during the civil war in Bosnia. Now the most powerful nations should accept an explicit responsibility to prevent such massacres from happening again. When oppression in one country "produces massive flows of refugees which then unsettle neighboring countries, then they can properly be described as threats to international peace and security." Thus the sovereignty of states was conditional on their acceptance of a series of basic and universal rules of behavior. The speech was carefully crafted–it was not, Blair insisted, a call for the West to use military force to right every wrong in the world. But in its emphasis on global interdependence and the marriage of values with national interest, it was an im-

portant precursor of Blair's response to the events of September 11, 2001.

The bargain over Kosovo that defused what might have turned into an ugly public argument between Bill Clinton and Tony Blair was struck by the president and the prime minister in a White House bathroom. Before traveling to Chicago and on the eve of the NATO anniversary meeting, Blair had met with Clinton in Washington. Both were aware of the danger that any public split in the alliance would further encourage Milosevic to hold out against the bombing campaign. But Clinton was no closer to agreeing to deploy ground troops, and Blair was increasingly frustrated by the apparent failure of the air campaign. General Guthrie, who was also in Washington for the talks, had told the prime minister that the allied forces were running out of targets. The bombs, in the general's words, were "turning big craters into bigger craters and rubble into smaller pieces of rubble." Meanwhile, the exodus of Kosovar Albanians had become a humanitarian catastrophe. Some 200,000 had already left the province as a result of the Serbian tyranny during the previous year. Now up to a million more were being driven out over the borders with Macedonia in a matter of weeks. So when Blair sat down with Clinton that evening at the White House, each flanked by several senior officials, the atmosphere was tense. The meeting started with Clinton asking for his guest's assessment. Blair dispensed with the usual preliminaries. NATO, he said, could not be sure it was winning. Public opinion had been shaken by the accidental bombing of innocent civilians. Milosevic gave little indication of retreating. The alliance's posture would be credible only if NATO indicated it was ready to put "boots on the ground." It was a message that Clinton did not want to hear. By now, he had had his own serious doubts about the hostage to fortune he had offered at the outset by ruling out ground forces. But Sandy (Samuel) Berger, the national security adviser and author of that initial pledge, remained firmly opposed to any shift in position. Others on the U.S. side—with the notable exception of Madeleine Albright—believed the political risks of committing troops too high. The Pentagon, conscious of the hostile geography of

Kosovo, was deeply reluctant to step into the Balkan quagmire and preferred to keep on bombing from 15,000 feet.

According to the British officials present, the discussion went to and fro in this vein for nearly an hour. Then Blair broke the stalemate by excusing himself to go to the bathroom. Clinton, too, got up and left the room. There was nothing choreographed about their exit, but ten or fifteen minutes passed before the two men returned, this time together, and put an end to the argument. The agreement they had reached in this most private deliberation was a compromise. The communiqué at the end of the next day's NATO summit would leave the issue on the table, but with a slight tilt in Blair's direction. On the one hand, Clinton insisted there could be no specific promise to commit ground troops. On the other, a land invasion would be an implicit option in the military review being conducted by Xavier Solana, the NATO secretary-general. This was less than Blair wanted, but the best he could get–the sort of "constructive ambiguity" that both men were familiar with from their negotiations with the political leaders of Northern Ireland. Most importantly, the alliance had maintained the appearance of unity.

Back in Europe, Blair continued to raise the rhetorical temperature. The bombing continued into the early weeks of May with little visible effect–save for the disastrous destruction of the Chinese embassy in Belgrade by a mistargeted American missile and the mistaken bombing of a civilian convoy. The prime minister's language became increasingly emotive. More than once he compared the expulsion of the Kosovars with the Holocaust fifty years earlier: "It is time for my generation to reflect on the fight of our parents' generation against Hitler's regime," he wrote in one newspaper. At the same time, he very deliberately closed off the option of any compromise with Milosevic. By now, he had decided that peace in the Balkans depended ultimately on the Serbian leader's removal. It was not enough for Milosevic to be driven back to the negotiating table; he had to be roundly defeated. In the middle of May, Blair traveled to Germany to accept the prestigious Charlemagne Prize for his contributions to Europe. Again, he was un-

equivocal; there would be no half-measures in dealing with the brutality of Milosevic: "No compromise. No fudge. No half-baked deals."

With Bill Clinton hemmed in by political opposition, Blair seemed to have eased into the president's place as spokesman for the forces of civilization, and he enjoyed the limelight. The righteousness of the cause appealed to the prime minister's moral conscience, the lead role on the international stage to his political vanity. Paddy Ashdown recalls congratulating Blair on his forcefulness after one particular radio interview, at which Blair preened himself: "I have been giving a lot of interviews in the U.S., too, and they seem to have gone down quite well," he replied. "If you think that our press is being nice, you should see what the American press is saying!" The conviction politician and the actor were thus as one when he flew to the Balkans. His appearance at a refugee camp with Cherie had been carefully planned for maximum media impact, yet it was clear that both were deeply moved by the horror that confronted them. On a trip to the Bulgarian capital of Sofia, the prime minister did not wait for others to make the comparison with the iconic William Gladstone. He reminded his audience of Gladstone's famous "Midlothian" campaign to bring to world attention the atrocities committed against Bulgarians during the 1870s. "The parallels between then and now are all too tragically clear. Today we face the same questions that confronted Gladstone over one hundred and twenty years ago. Does one nation or people have the right to impose its will on another? Is there ever a justification for a policy based on the ethnic supremacy of one ethnic group? Can the outside world simply stand by when a rogue state brutally abuses the basic rights of those it governs? Gladstone's answer in 1876 was clear. And so is mine today." The parallel, of course, was inexact—Gladstone had railed against the persecution of Christians by Turkish Muslims, while NATO was defending Kosovar Muslims against Serbian Christians—but to Blair's mind it was a distinction without an important difference. And to underline his own resolve he ordered the progressive reinforcement of the British troops based in Macedonia. When NATO forces finally entered Kosovo, they would be under a British commander, General Michael Jackson.

Bill Clinton watched all this from Washington with some frustration. While Blair got the press plaudits, American forces were waging the war. Even when the British reprogrammed their cruise missiles to hit their intended targets, the U.S. military effort was what mattered. In truth, the French were flying more bombing sorties than Britain's RAF. Blair, though, was the leader in the spotlight, constantly applying the pressure on the rest of NATO to agree to ground troops. In mid-May Clinton's frustration boiled over during a late-night telephone call to Blair. Alistair Campbell, the president said, had been "spinning" to reporters from the *New York Times,* contrasting Blair's resolve with the White House's supposed hesitations. It had to stop, the president told the prime minister in a rare moment of anger with his British friend.

In the end Slobodan Milosevic withstood seventy-eight days of bombing. When the Serbian leader finally announced on June 3 that he was ready to capitulate, he took everyone by surprise. A week later the air strikes were halted as Serbian forces began their withdrawal from Kosovo. There was much speculation as to what had finally broken Milosevic's resolve. Some said it was the unrest in Belgrade, as the war took its toll on the nation's economy. Russia's Boris Yeltsin also seemed to have lost patience with his fellow Slav. But in Blair's mind the crucial factor had been that Clinton had finally agreed, at the eleventh hour, to begin serious planning for a ground invasion. Milosevic's surrender had come on the very day that the president was meeting with his military commanders to draw up plans to put American forces in the region. That, the prime minister thought, could not have been a coincidence.

The Kosovo war thus confirmed Blair's view that the United States had become the indispensable power in the post–cold war era. His own emerging vision of a more ordered world, in which the West recognized an enlightened self-interest in liberal interventionism, depended critically on American engagement in the international system. There were other legacies, too, of this first modern war fought to preserve a set of moral values. Impressed as he was by American power, Blair was equally dismayed by the shortcomings of Europe's military.

Privately, he said that he had been appalled by what he learned during the planning to send troops into Kosovo. On paper, the European Union had two million servicemen and -women. In reality, it could not deploy even 50,000. The EU's armies had no heavy-lift capacity, no command and communications worthy of the description, and nothing that could be termed a rapid reaction force. He also anticipated the strains to come in the relationship between Britain's European allies and Washington. France had fought alongside America and Britain in Kosovo, but now it was worried that Britain might want to bolster NATO at the expense of the Anglo-French plan to develop Europe's capabilities. While Blair understood the French concerns, he explained during one conversation that, "My basic point, even if it sounds simplistic, is that the big potential security threats–from Russia, China–are containable if Europe and the U.S. are together. That's my starting point. That's why I try to get the Europeans involved in the Third Way discussions with Clinton–to show them the United States is not some hostile power. Where I agree is that the relationship has to be more equal." The other strategic conclusion he had drawn was the imperative of bringing Russia closer to the West. When Vladimir Putin replaced Boris Yeltsin less than a year later, Blair was the first to visit him.

The war also had a profound effect on Blair's political personality. The initial despair of that Easter weekend gave way to a determination and self-assurance that would endure. He gained little if any immediate electoral advantage from the Kosovo war, but the prime minister's resilience in the face of adversity and the impact he had made on the international stage conferred on him an aura, overturning–for a time at least–the perception of him as a politician tossed to and fro by the winds of public opinion. Yet his missionary zeal remained a puzzle: Why was a leader so cautious at home so willing to take risks abroad? Part of the answer lay in the very nature of military action, the way in which it puts power directly in the hands of the prime minister; another part rested in the close relationship he established with Charles Guthrie. Blair "has a lot more faith in Guthrie than in the cabinet," one aide remarked laconically. Most importantly, though, the Kosovo conflict matched his gifts as a politician with his moral purpose. Blair,

more than any other leader, made the case that defeating Milosevic was simply the right thing to do.

The postscript to Kosovo came a year later in the war-ravaged West African state of Sierra Leone. Here was another test of Tony Blair's belief that enlightened self-interest should lead the West to intervene in failed and failing states. Sierra Leone, a former British colony, had descended into a bloody and chaotic civil war. In 1998 Blair's government had been embarrassed by the disclosure that it had given tacit approval of mercenary operations in support of the deposed government of President Ahmad Kabbah. By the summer of 2000 the Kabbah government had been restored. But a United Nations peacekeeping operation in the country was on the verge of collapse in the face of the advance of rebel forces backed by the Liberian leader Charles Taylor. The rebels controlled many of the richest diamond-producing areas, and, in May 2000, they took as hostages five hundred UN peacekeepers. With the capital of Freetown under threat, Blair dispatched nearly a thousand British troops to oversee the evacuation of foreign nationals.

That was about as far as most people thought Britain's responsibilities should go. But faced with the realization that Sierra Leone was on the brink of another full-scale civil war and that the UN mission was close to collapse, Blair ordered British troops to stay on in support of Kabbah's government. Again, the risks were large and the potential political rewards at home negligible. But UN peacekeeping in Africa had suffered a string of failures, and Blair took seriously the advice of those who argued that Sierra Leone was a last chance for the international community in Africa. If the UN failed in West Africa, it might as well pack its bags and leave. The prime minister's gamble looked as if it would fail when members of a British army patrol in turn found themselves taken hostage. The opposition Conservatives called for the withdrawal of British forces, a view echoed in much of the media. Blair authorized a perilous operation to free the captured British soldiers. After a dramatic firefight in the rebels' jungle camp, the hostages were rescued by British special forces and paratroopers. The operation, which cost the life of one British soldier, had been a tough call. Blair

knew, because Charles Guthrie had warned him in such terms, that the casualties might be much higher. Several hundred British soldiers remained in Sierra Leone to bolster confidence in Kabbah's government and to retrain the country's army, and the UN mission survived. It had been a small war but an important one. As Blair put it in a speech in November 1999, "On Sierra Leone there were those who said: what's it got to do with us? But I am sure that Britain's and Europe's long-term interests in Africa are best served if we intervene ... to do what we can to save African nations from barbarism and dictatorship. And be proud of it." History's wars had been fought over territory. In Tony Blair's reworking of Gladstonian moralism, they were now about values.

10. <u>EVENTS</u>

As is so often the case in politics, the long anticipation proved sweeter than the actual event. Tony Blair's ambition had always been to win two elections. Breaking a pattern of history that had always deprived his party of two full terms was the key that would unlock a different future for British politics. This was a prime minister who wanted time to change things and who knew that his own place in history's pages depended on a second, decisive general election victory. On June 7, 2001, the dream was made reality when Britain's voters returned New Labour to office with another huge majority. It was an extraordinary result, laying to permanent rest the demons of his party's past. Clement Attlee's six continuous years in office after the Second World War had been as much as any previous Labour government could achieve. With a second decisive mandate from the voters, Blair could feel assured of at least eight or nine years in Downing Street.

Yet the mood at the moment of this second triumph bore no comparison with that of 1997. The country that had celebrated with such extravagant abandon four years earlier gave Blair his second term willingly but without enthusiasm. The raw statistics of the victory were almost as good as they had been in 1997. New Labour had a majority of 167 over the combined strength of all the other parties in the House of Commons. (At the apogee of her authority the best Margaret Thatcher had managed was 144.) But sobriety had replaced euphoria as the predominant tone. Only 60 percent of the electorate had bothered to cast their ballots, the lowest figure in Britain since the introduction of universal suffrage in 1918. Abroad Blair was seen as the leader of the moment, the most powerful figure in Europe, a politician whose courage during the Kosovo conflict had stiffened the West's moral backbone. At

home New Labour had lost its luster, the shine of optimism dulled in the harsh climes of government. The prime minister had acknowledged the change during the election campaign. "New Labour, New Britain" had been the stirring platform pledge in 1997; "The Work Goes On" was the altogether more prosaic call to arms four years later. The first had promised transformation and instant gratification for a nation disenchanted with Tory rule. The second acknowledged the dull truth that Blair had failed to find a magic dust to sprinkle on the intractability of modern government. His own response to the confirmation of his historic victory was equally downbeat. "Four years ago we were elected as a government with some euphoria after eighteen years of Conservative rule," he said from his Sedgefield constituency in the early hours of June 8. "The judgment may be a more sober one, and the mood is different now. But I believe it is a more reasoned judgment because it is based on a record in office." The prime minister seemed almost depressed. "When I heard him on the radio I thought we must have lost," one of his senior ministers remarked only half-jokingly a few days later.

Blair's assessment was true so far as it went. The government had indeed reaped the electoral rewards of economic prosperity. But it needed more time to keep the second part of New Labour's promise—to modernize the nation's dilapidated public services. During the year preceding the election, the fanciful confection that had been Cool Britannia was finally shattered. In the autumn of 2000 a spontaneous revolt by truck drivers over the high price of diesel fuel had all but brought the country to a standstill. For a time, the government had seemed frozen in the headlights of the protest. A prime minister who had grown accustomed to shaping the nation's mood was nonplussed by the popular support for the truckers. For the first and only time during its initial term, New Labour had fallen behind the Conservatives in the opinion polls. Then, in the opening months of 2001, the farming industry had been struck by a virulent outbreak of foot-and-mouth disease. For week after week the images beamed nightly into the nation's living rooms--and to the world beyond--were of rural roadblocks, quarantined farms, and the acrid black smoke of burning livestock car-

casses. Tourism collapsed, and along with it confidence. Blair had originally planned the election for May 3, 2001, but felt obliged to postpone it for a month until the foot-and-mouth outbreak was under control. To add to the gloom, a series of fatal accidents had badly disrupted the country's aging and decrepit rail system. Only yesterday, it seemed, Tony Blair's Britain had been the envy of the world. Now it felt not so much the "Young Country" of his earlier, hubristic description as one sinking under the weight of its past.

Yet just as the unbridled euphoria that had accompanied New Labour's first victory had raised vastly exaggerated expectations, the sobriety that accompanied the second election victory understated its significance. If Blair's first term in office had fallen short of the more extravagant rhetoric of creating a New Britain, it had wrought enduring changes to the nation's political complexion. Independence for the Bank of England; new political assemblies in Scotland and Wales and Northern Ireland; a bill of rights enacted through the incorporation into British law of the European Convention on Human Rights; exile from the House of Lords of the hereditary earls and dukes; the introduction of a minimum wage and new welfare-to-work programs—all these marked important, often permanent, shifts in the life of the nation. A second landslide election victory provided the proof that Blair had changed the argument in British politics. William Hague, the young Conservative leader who had succeeded John Major in 1997, fought the 2001 campaign on a platform to cut taxes, reduce public spending, and pull Britain back from Europe. This was Margaret Thatcher's tried and tested formula, the key to the party's success during the 1980s. In 2001 it failed dismally. The Conservatives' tally of 166 seats in the House of Commons—only one more than in 1997—left them in circumstances as dire as they had seen since the party had split in the mid-nineteenth century. The voters' willingness to give Blair such a huge second mandate reflected the ruinous irrelevance into which the Conservatives had fallen. Hague, like John Major in 1997, was forced to resign as party leader in the immediate aftermath of the election. But the ills ran deeper than the hapless inexperience of its leader. Hague's successor, Iain Duncan Smith, inherited a party that, a

year later, would be described by one of its own senior figures as "nasty, moralizing, and hypocritical."

The problem Tony Blair now faced was the gap between the rhetoric of transformation and the grinding reality of government. He remained a master of the politics of vision, but he was untutored in the ways of the government machine, exasperated rather than energized by the task of managing such a cumbersome bureaucracy. He had the lawyer's habit of applying intense bursts of concentration to one problem at a time, rather than the juggler's skill of keeping several in the air simultaneously. In the metaphor of his political friend and mentor Roy Jenkins, the government resembled nothing so much as a lighthouse, "its revolving beam alighting for a time on this issue or that before moving on to the next." This was a style that suited the pressing demands of foreign policy much better than the mundane complexities of government at home. Even to those who inhabited the corridors of power, it sometimes seemed there were two prime ministers living in 10 Downing Street. The first, the confident moral missionary, took his place with verve and courage on the international stage. The second seemed hesitant and careworn as he grappled with the obstinate obsolescence of the nation's health and education systems. The government meanwhile continued its extraordinary obsession with managing the media, which gave the prime minister's court an unpleasant air of arrogance. Yet this constant quest for popular acclaim spoke of nothing so much as its fearfulness. Alistair Campbell, Blair's closest confidant and adviser in Downing Street and his director of communications, came under increasing fire from the Conservative-leaning press as the architect of a new age of political "spin." Many of the attacks reflected little more than Tory rage at Campbell's strategic genius. But there remained the sense that New Labour had yet to learn the old adage that for those in power the best politics is good government. Blair still lacked the wisdom of experience, the price of which was a steady erosion of the trust that he had so painstakingly accumulated during the years of opposition.

The broader discontent of the electorate reflected the dismal condition of public services. New Labour's embrace of the economic orthodoxy of the times proved a two-edged sword. Resources used to reduce levels of public borrowing and to cut the national debt was money not spent on the schools, hospitals, and transport networks the government had promised to modernize. Gordon Brown's much-vaunted financial prudence–particularly the pledge not to raise public spending in the first two years after 1997–had come at the price of continuing neglect of the nation's infrastructure. Even though the spending strictures had loosened in the subsequent two years, hospitals remained dirty and overcrowded, and schools lacked modern facilities and sufficient teachers. At the core of Blair's prospectus had been the promised marriage of economic efficiency with the social justice of a refurbished welfare state. The voters who looked with envy to the sparkling modernity of trains, schools, and hospitals elsewhere in Europe were still waiting at the altar.

The prime minister who returned to Downing Street in June 2001 understood the challenges facing him. He came to the task a different politician. His first term of office had often seemed a series of separate, albeit virtuoso, performances, played for the next morning's reviews. The second saw a prime minister with his eye on the history books. The judgment of history had always been central to Blair's self-perception–he would tell friends that he had always regretted studying law rather than history at Oxford. Now he was driven by an urgency to shape the terms in which the future would record his own premiership. He would probably fight a third election, with every chance of winning it. But it was the second term that would define his legacy, and he was looking for a bigger role in history's pages than merely that of the political leader who had taught his party how to win elections. Those who worked with the prime minister noticed he was tougher, surer of his own judgments, less inclined to seek the quiet life over confrontation. He had always been self-sufficient, convinced that it was his unique responsibility as prime minister to find the answers. Others could suggest and advise, but he had to reach his own conclusions.

Now he became surer still of his judgments. "He knows that the second term is his chance to make a difference," one close aide remarked in the summer of 1991. "You'll see a much tougher leader from now on." Blair himself was reluctant to admit any of the mistakes of the first term–humility was never central to the culture of New Labour–but his demeanor said he had changed. He had become a more determined and less indulgent politician, no longer beguiled by the opinion polls and focus groups, and more ruthless. Here was a prime minister so determined to get his way that in the summer of 2003 he would summarily dismiss from his cabinet Alexander Irvine, the man who had given him his first chance in the law and introduced him to Cherie. Irvine's crime–opposing the prime minister's plans to modernize the system of judicial appointments–scarcely seemed a capital offense. But Blair was in no mood to compromise. "The right thing to do" was a phrase that had always echoed through his leadership. Now it was a constant refrain.

He had stepped out at last from Margaret Thatcher's shadow. The politician who had once used the Conservative leader's popularity as a stick to beat the tax-and-spend traditionalists in his own party declared on the eve of the 2001 election, "The Thatcher era is behind us and not a moment too soon." With the Conservatives in disarray, it was safe to return to his party's social democratic roots. New Labour's platform had promised a quantum leap in the quality of public services. The specific pledges included the hiring of another 30,000 doctors and nurses and an additional 10,000 teachers, new funding for the police, and the rebuilding of the nation's rail network. Behind the prime minister's mantra of "delivery" lay the political gamble of his career: the calculation that the middle classes of Middle Britain–the heart of his New Labour coalition–would readily pay higher taxes in return for first-rate public services.

It fell to Gordon Brown, the chancellor of the exchequer, to unveil this new covenant to the voters in the spring of 2002. Brown's budget announcement of unprecedented new investment in state health and education provision alongside large increases in the budgets for transport

and law and order marked out New Labour's new direction. Brown declared that he was increasing payroll taxes to finance the extra funding. This was the first time in three decades that a British government had raised personal taxes from choice rather than necessity. Now that New Labour had proved that it was a social rather than a compulsive spender, Brown was declaring that it could spend again. This was a political program much closer to the social democratic instincts of continental Europe than to the laissez-faire approach on the American side of the Atlantic.

If Old Labour traditionalists anticipated a return to the past, however, they were disappointed. Brown's spending announcements had seemed to indicate that having endured prudence, the government could now flirt with profligacy. The time had come for Labour to reward its own. Once again, Blair was misunderstood by his own party. Because he saw himself as a national rather than a partisan leader, investment in public services was to be a one-nation and not exclusively a Labour project. He insisted that the extra money for public services be spent wisely, which meant, in effect, a decisive weakening of trade union control over those services. In a speech to the party conference in the autumn of 2002, Blair called for the breakup of "monolithic" delivery of health care and education in favor of a new, diversified mix of public- and private-sector provision in schools and hospitals. "Out goes the big state, in comes the enabling state," he declared in a challenge to the prevailing assumption in his party of uniformity and centralized management of public services. In his sights was the stranglehold of the trade unions on the health and education services and the lingering assumption among his own members of Parliament that producers rather than consumers should set the terms of public provision. Only China's Red Army could boast a bigger roll call than Britain's National Health Service (NHS), the prime minister's aides would quip—and the Red Army was more efficient. Blair's plans to create a new breed of so-called foundation hospitals, cut free from the bureaucracy of the NHS, and to foster greater independence for state-financed schools marked a direct challenge to the left's ideological preference for uniformity over excellence. Nine years after Blair had scrapped Clause IV of the party's

constitution, there were still those who preferred standardized medi-
ocrity to the inequalities that would follow from decentralized services.
The push for choice and diversity, the critics said, would inevitably cre-
ate "two-tier" services. Blair's response was that reform alongside invest-
ment was a last chance to preserve the welfare settlement established
by the postwar Labour government. "This is the historic mission of this
government," he said in December 2002. "It is to take the welfare
state . . . and completely revolutionize it for today's world. If we don't
do that we will end up in a situation where large numbers of people,
under the banner of greater equality, actually just get a poor service."

The disquiet of the egalitarians in his party—manifested in more fre-
quent rebellions against government policy by groups of Labour MPs
in Parliament—was not Blair's only problem. As the international stage
beckoned in the wake of September 11, 2001, there were other discon-
tents. The government had been true to its pledge to take a tough line
on crime, the evidence for which came in the form of a rise in the
prison population to record levels. But draconian antiterrorism legisla-
tion in the wake of the attacks on New York and Washington and leg-
islative efforts to weaken the rights of defendants in criminal trials lost
the government its more socially liberal friends. Blair's emphasis on the
responsibilities of citizens chimed with the instincts of David Blunkett,
appointed after the 2001 election as home secretary responsible for law
and order. But it took the prime minister further away from the strong
libertarian tradition in his own party. None of this would matter so
long as he was seen to be in tune with the mood of the nation. But he
was making enemies for the day that fortune turned against him.

The Conservative prime minister Harold Macmillan had been
asked four decades earlier what most troubled the occupant of 10
Downing Street. He had no doubt: "Events, dear boy, events." Blair had
discovered on his own during his first term how these unexpected
storms could blow the government off course, and it was a lesson he
continued to learn. One such storm had begun to gather at the very
moment when Blair was rushing back to London after the attack on
America on September 11, 2001. As the prime minister scripted his

statement of staunch support for the United States in its hour of tragedy, one of his government's political advisers was composing an e-mail. Jo Moore, an aide to Stephen Byers, the cabinet minister responsible for transport, had not grasped the extent of the horror when she pressed the send button on a message that advised the communications staff in the department that this might be "a good day to bury bad news." She could scarcely have imagined that this grotesque suggestion would ever reach the public domain, but it did. Moore's subsequent apology was not sufficient to still the uproar in the interconnecting worlds of politics and the media, for in the minds of many of the government's friends as well as its enemies, the e-mail was a symptom of a deeper malaise. The government's efforts to control the news agenda had too often stepped over the line separating good politics from cynical manipulation. Moore's immediate resignation might have cauterized this particular wound, but instead it was allowed to fester. She clung on for several months before bowing to the inevitable. By then the episode had all but ruined the political career of her political master, Stephen Byers, and tarnished badly the image of the government.

The Moore incident was yet another indication that Blair's administration had not yet learned the value of admitting its mistakes. Haunted by the history of its long political exile before 1997, it found it impossible to show the slightest chink in its armor. A party more confident of its place in government would be more attuned to the advantages of occasionally owning up to an error or conceding that it had had to compromise. The prime minister seemed to acknowledge this in an interview in the summer of 2003, when asked whether one of the government's problems hadn't been an unwillingness to be frank about the constraints placed upon it. "Yes, there is something in that," he said. "Though the difficulty is . . . when you come through a period when your party has been very, very reluctant to do the difficult things and move forward, sometimes that can mean you think any compromise is weakness. . . . And yes, there is a risk that you take that too far. One of the things that I think is necessary for us to do in government is just to relax a bit more about how we have a dialogue with people."

The squalls about spin took place against the background of a big-

ger struggle within Tony Blair's cabinet. The relationship between the prime minister and Gordon Brown, the chancellor, was likened by those around them to an extraordinary political marriage, as tempestuous as it was intense. No two people at the top of British politics had ever worked quite so closely to shape the policy of a government. Their mutual dependency, the passions and the arguments all spoke to a unique partnership. For all its occasional flashes of anger and jealousy, the assumption was that this was the rock on which the government was built.

That was true, but it told only half the story. The marriage had also begun to bear the strains of time, familiarity, and jealousy. Brown, impatient to inherit Blair's crown, often half-joked that history offered one of two fates to chancellors: "Those clever enough to get out in time, and those whose careers ended in failure." He might have added that history had been equally unkind to those who secured the keys of 10 Downing Street after their parties had already had a long spell in government. Brown did not relish the fate of cricket's nightwatchman, sent in to bat as his team's innings drew to their natural close. He carried heavily his frustration with his role as the junior partner. His sense of grievance at the events of 1994, when he had stood down from the leadership contest, had never left him. Now, with New Labour in government, wasn't it obvious that he was its intellectual heavyweight, the substance to the prime minister's superficial style? Such were the thoughts often floated by the coterie of loyal political aides and allies gathered around the chancellor.

Part of the bargain struck with Blair in 1994 had been that Brown's supporters in Parliament would be given powerful ministerial positions within the government. Alongside these ministers who acknowledged their first allegiance to the chancellor was a clutch of close aides to match the influence of Alistair Campbell and the rest in the prime minister's office. Most prominent among them was Ed Balls, a young Oxford- and Harvard-educated economist who acted as Brown's de facto chief of staff. As Blair sought to centralize power in the prime minister's office, Brown was ever more determined to defend the polit-

ical territory that had been ceded to him when the two men had dined that evening in 1994 at Granita.

Senior officials in Downing Street became accustomed to working to the background noise of shouting matches during the chancellor's regular visits to the prime minister's study. These arguments behind closed doors were projected onto a larger screen via the poisonous briefings and counterbriefings from the rival camps. Brown was badly wounded when one of Blair's most senior aides, widely thought to be Alistair Campbell, offered a description of the chancellor as "psychologically flawed." For his part Blair found himself described from the Treasury camp as the government's nonexecutive chairman to Brown's chief executive. On one level, such bickering reflected the typical rivalries of power. But, while all British governments are afflicted by jealousies and jostling for position–Labour administrations more deeply than most–the regular seepage of the Blair-Brown disputes into the public domain painted a picture of a government increasingly disfigured by its personal animosities. Those close to Brown claimed that Blair had given his solemn word in 1994 that he would stand down after ten years as party leader, an idea Blair dismissed as nonsense. Either way, he showed no inclination to take early retirement.

There was a third party to this volatile marriage. Even after he had twice been appointed and had twice been obliged to resign from the government, Peter Mandelson kept his role as Blair's consigliere. Serving as both a foil to Brown and a source of vital strategic advice for the prime minister, he was a New Labour soul mate. But his relationship with Brown was as distant and difficult as that with Blair was warm. And, once again, the tensions between the men dated back to the succession to John Smith in 1994. In the early, pioneering days of New Labour, Mandelson had served both men, but on the assumption that Brown would be first to take the throne. The chancellor considered that Mandelson had betrayed him by defecting to Blair in 1994, a charge Mandelson had always denied. Wherever the precise truth lay, the events of that year had poisoned the relationship, and Brown, never a forgiving politician, continued to treat Mandelson as the en-

emy. Thus the disclosure of the undeclared loan that led to Mandel-son's first resignation came from the Brown camp. The money had been advanced by Geoffrey Robinson, the wealthy industrialist-turned-MP who was close to Brown. The irony was that when details were leaked to the media, the affair cost Robinson as well as Mandelson his ministerial career.

Blair had for years been frustrated by the feuding between his two most able lieutenants. A glimpse of this had come during the opposition years when he had written privately to Mandelson. His letter, subsequently published by Donald Macintyre, Mandelson's biographer, shone a powerful light on the extraordinary intensity of the relationships in this eternal political triangle. "Have you any conception of how despairing it is for me," Blair wrote, "when the two people who have been closest to me for more than a decade, and who in their different ways are the most brilliant political minds of their generation will not lay aside personal animosity and help me to win?" The pleas fell on deaf ears.

As for his own relationship with the chancellor, Blair's attitude mixed admiration, exasperation, and irritation in varying measures. In the early years he went out of his way to pour oil on troubled waters. "He has more intellectual weight than anyone in the cabinet—including me," Blair once remarked after one of the frequent outbursts of acrimony between their respective camp followers. "Don't listen to what anyone else says—our relationship is a strong as it has ever been." On another occasion, he stressed that he was entirely comfortable with Brown's ambitions to succeed him: "Why shouldn't he be ambitious?" These, though, were remarks made during the early years of government. The passing of time saw Blair's patience wear thinner. Other cabinet colleagues—politicians who owed their loyalty to the prime minister—complained of Brown's imperious manner as he rode roughshod over their political territory. Blair's admiration gave way to disappointment, exasperation, and, sometimes, worse.

More than once it seemed the couple was heading for the divorce courts. For all their shared determination to prove that New Labour could manage a modern economy, they differed on how to spend the

fruits of economic growth. Blair sought public services fit for the middle classes of Middle Britain to bind an electoral majority to his vision of a modern welfare state. Brown was more concerned with equity than excellence, preferring to spend any spare billions on direct help to the poorest in society. But the most contentious issue between them, and one that often seemed to threaten a ruinous breach, was the question of whether to join the new European single currency, the euro. In the autumn of 1997 Blair and Brown had agreed that a decision on the matter should be deferred during his first term of government, on the assumption that a second election victory would be the platform for a successful referendum to join. This, Blair believed, involved far more than merely a judgment about economics, about interest rates and exchange rates. Of course, the British and European economies would have to be in sync before sterling was replaced by the euro. But his perspective was the geopolitical one. If Britain was to exercise measurable influence in Europe–and sustain its role as bridge across the Atlantic– it could not stand aside indefinitely from the European Union's most ambitious economic enterprise. By 2001, twelve of the then fifteen members of the Union had joined the Eurozone, leaving only Britain, Sweden, and Denmark outside. Blair was far from content with this place on the margins of influence. The second term, he said just weeks before the 2001 election, would provide the "window of opportunity." "We'll do it, you'll see." First, however, he had to win the referendum on the issue that he had promised to the electorate. What better moment to secure such consent than in the wake of a second election victory? The prime minister was unequivocal. This was about his political legacy, his place in history. His ambition was to put an end once and for all to the ambiguities and hesitations that had dogged Britain's relationship with its European neighbors. Joining the euro would mark a decisive break with the past. It was, Blair told his party conference in the autumn of 2001, Britain's "destiny."

Yet he both underestimated Gordon Brown's hostility to the euro and overestimated his own capacity to persuade him otherwise. The chancellor's doubts were well known and were conveyed to the press by the constant and dour restatement of the mantra that Britain would

join only when he judged the economic conditions were right. Blair seemed to think this public obduracy actually masked a more flexible private position. "I'll handle Gordon," he would tell visitors to 10 Downing Street who pointed out the obvious gulf between their two positions. But the chancellor did not want to be handled. Each time Blair voiced his enthusiasm, Brown arranged for the Treasury to pour cold water on the prospects—and to point out that the arrangements that had been agreed to by the prime minister in 1997 meant that, as arbiter of the five economic tests for participation, the chancellor had the final say.

Brown did in fact share the view that the grand sweep of history would see Britain eventually join the single currency. But to his mind, politics, economics, and personal ambition all militated against a precipitate decision. Brown's stubbornness was partly a matter of pride. The chancellor had remade Britain's economic policy and, unsurprisingly, thought the arrangements he had put in place for interest rate policy and budgetary decisions superior to those in the Eurozone. Mingling with the pride was fear, for if the government fought and lost a referendum on such a major issue it would sustain serious damage. It might withstand the shock, but at the undoubted cost of a much lower majority in the following general election. And Brown himself would be tarnished by the failure, boding ill for his own hopes of a long spell in 10 Downing Street once Blair stood down.

What made the dispute potentially so explosive was its emotional intensity. Brown believed that once again the prime minister was breaking the terms of their bargain. Whatever the truth of what had been said in 1994 about Blair's passing on the leadership, there could be no dispute about his having willingly ceded control of economic policy. Now, by seeking to preempt the Treasury's economic judgment on the euro, he was breaking even that part of the accord. Those who watched this argument from within the corridors of power were at once amazed and dismayed. "It's a train crash waiting to happen," one very senior official observed toward the end of 2002. Others speculated that Blair would have to sack his chancellor—or that Brown himself would file divorce papers by walking out of the government.

As things turned out, the couple stayed together, but only just. Blair had set the summer of 2003 for a decision on whether to call a euro referendum. In the spring of the same year, as all his attention was focused on the war in Iraq, Brown told him the answer must be no. After an exhaustive examination of the economic circumstances–the Treasury's famous five economic tests–he had decided that it was too soon to surrender the pound sterling. Brown carried more than 2,000 pages of dry economic analysis into 10 Downing Street to prove his case. But, in truth, he had made up his mind before a single page had been printed. Brown wanted any decision to be postponed again until a third Labour term. Blair was furious, but, with his mind on foreign policy, he had been outplayed by his chancellor. Brown's insistence that a decision to join was essentially an economic one in the hands of the Treasury had effectively forestalled any concerted campaigning during the previous two years to prepare the voters for a referendum. In the meantime, public opinion had drifted further away from joining, and the pollsters pointed to a big majority against giving up the pound. Brown was able to argue that politics as well as economics made the case for delay. After a stream of tense and sometimes angry meetings in the prime minister's study over several weeks, the best Blair could secure was a pledge from his chancellor that the Treasury would review the position again in 2004. Privately, he continued to insist that joining then was a realistic option. That the two men appeared side by side at a press conference to insist they were in full agreement served only to emphasize the gulf between them.

The marriage now was being held together only by mutual dependency. The affection had long gone, and so, too, had the respect. These were two politicians who needed each other. For all his self-sufficiency, Blair could see no alternative figure in his cabinet with the weight and intellectual authority to command the government's economic program. And Brown, who had built and nurtured a considerable following among Labour parliamentarians, would be more dangerous outside government than within it. The chancellor was an obvious leader for those in the party opposed to Blair's plans for radical reform of public services. Brown's calculation, meanwhile, was that

his own hopes of the succession were better served by remaining inside the New Labour tent. To seek to bring down the prime minister from outside would be too risky. Those with the leader's blood on their hands rarely take the prize in politics. In spite of the frustrations, he would do better waiting for Blair to stand down. Such it seemed were the cynical, sour judgments of two politicians who had once been inseparable.

The government's troubles, of course, were relative. If Blair had learned that the modernization of public services would take longer than he had ever bargained for, it was already evident that the huge investment in education and health was having an effect. So, too, was the co-optation of the private sector into the building of new schools and hospitals. What mattered was that, by the time of the next election in 2005 or 2006, he could say that things were getting better. Even though the economic clouds had darkened after the falls on world stock markets, and Gordon Brown's budget surpluses were soon turning into hefty deficits, the voters seemed to accept the prospect of a tax increase with relative equanimity. There was no obvious alternative. Despite that much of the media had fallen out of love with Blair's presidential style, the Conservatives scarcely seemed a government-in-waiting. Iain Duncan Smith, replaced in the autumn of 2003 by the more experienced Michael Howard, failed to make an impact as a leader. His party attacked the government's public spending spree but was unsure how warmly it could embrace again the politics of tax cutting. Much of the media's hostility toward the government seemed to reflect its frustration with the Conservatives for not providing a robust opposition. The BBC, the nation's public service broadcaster, seemed at times to think that it was its democratic duty to fill the vacuum. So while the headlines insisted that Blair was in trouble, the pollsters confirmed that he was still well ahead.

11. <u>MAKING A FRIEND</u>

BILL CLINTON HAD some parting advice for Tony Blair during his last presidential visit to Chequers in December 2000. How, asked the British prime minister as his friend prepared to pack his bags at the White House, should I play it with George W. Bush? "Be his friend," Clinton replied without hesitation. "Be his best friend. Be the guy he turns to." This was the message Blair had wanted to hear. Such was their closeness, he would never have to apologize to Clinton for cozying up to a Republican in the White House. The mood in the prime ministerial entourage was nonetheless apprehensive when Blair arrived in Washington in February 2001 for his first meeting with the new president. During their telephone conversation in December, Bush had said he himself was comfortable with Blair's friendship with Clinton. On his part, Blair intended to deploy to the full his optimistic charm to win over the new president. For good measure he carried with him the offer of a strategic bargain designed to persuade Bush that he was a reliable and useful ally. But no one could be sure whether the two men would hit it off, and the stakes were much higher for Blair. America's unique power in the world was always at the front of the prime minister's mind. A British prime minister had to stay close to whoever was in the White House. Blair's task was to convince Bush that they could make the transatlantic relationship work to mutual advantage whatever their political differences. Nothing suggested that that would be easy.

The personal chemistry between Blair and Clinton was extraordinary: the two men spoke the same political language, and Clinton, a Rhodes Scholar at Oxford, was an American at ease in Europe. Bush and Blair, however, were from different worlds. A central goal of the

Clinton-Blair relationship had been to find ways to lock conservatives out of power on both sides of the Atlantic. The irony was that George W. Bush was proof they had failed. In addition, the prime minister could hardly expect a meeting of minds on foreign policy. In the Balkans and beyond, he had been the principal cheerleader for Western intervention in the world's trouble spots. While Clinton had been mostly convinced, Bush had run for office as a domestic policy president. Condoleezza Rice, his national security adviser, had signaled that the new administration's foreign policy would be hard-edged, taking a narrow view of America's national interest. It was not interested in do-gooding in far-flung lands and was scornful of the multilateralism at the heart of Blair's outlook. Rice had explained the party's position before the election in an article in *Foreign Affairs* that was closely read in London: "American foreign policy in a Republican administration should refocus the U.S. on the national interest and the pursuit of key priorities." British officials also noted that in 1999 Rice had criticized the prime minister's calls for a stronger Western commitment to Kosovo. Blair's anxieties, then, were understandable, his dilemma summed up by an aide: "The president was committed to expunging the legacy of the Clinton years. The prime minister was part of that legacy."

Christopher Meyer, the British ambassador in Washington, had prepared the ground for the transition. An astute and experienced diplomat, he had been assiduous in cultivating contacts with Bush even before he became the Republican candidate for the presidency. Meyer, who had none of the inhibitions of the political aides in 10 Downing Street, had traveled to Texas to meet Bush at his ranch in Crawford in early 1998. He found the putative candidate friendly and self-deprecating. Bush confessed that the only two places outside the United States that he knew much about were Mexico and Scotland. When Meyer returned to the ranch a year later, he discovered that Bush had been doing his homework. He had appointed Condoleezza Rice and Paul Wolfowitz (later assistant secretary of defense) to his foreign policy team, and the strategy of hard-edged national interest was already taking shape. Meyer began to build a relationship with Bush's advisers and

started sending diplomatic notes advising 10 Downing Street to pay attention to this rising Republican star. Little interest was taken by Blair's aides, however, until the late summer of 2000, when the senior George Bush paid a courtesy call at No. 10 during a private visit to London. Blair saw an opportunity to open contacts with the son and wrote a note to George W. wishing him well during the rigors of the election campaign ahead. It was anodyne stuff, strictly neutral apropos the outcome of the presidential race. The message, as one aide put it, was rather in the very fact that he had *sent* the message. Even so, the episode caused controversy in Blair's political entourage. Their hopes and money were on Al Gore.

Even as their plane crossed the Atlantic, not everyone was as anxious as the prime minister to curry favor with the president. Cherie Blair still believed that Bush had stolen the White House from Gore. Why, she asked more than once during the journey, did they have to be so nice to "these people"? Her disdain was especially obvious when the conversation turned to the gift Blair had brought for the president. Blair's staff had chosen a bust of Winston Churchill, the president's avowed political hero, to adorn Bush's office. But now some voiced concern that the particular sculpture they had chosen was not of sufficient quality for the Oval Office. The aides suggested that they should keep the bust, and Jonathan Powell, the chief of staff, would find a better one on their return to London. In the meantime, the prime minister could tell the president that it was on its way. Cherie scarcely disguised her annoyance at all the fuss, but she was overruled. Indeed, a few months later a fine Churchill bust was delivered to the White House by Christopher Meyer. Sculpted by Sir Jacob Epstein in 1946 and part of the British government's art collection, it now sits in the Oval Office, on loan to Bush for the duration of his presidency.

Blair met with Vice President Richard Cheney in Washington before traveling to Camp David. This first encounter did little to allay the British side's misgivings. As the discussion ranged across foreign policy issues—National Missile Defense, Russia, the Balkans, the Middle East—Cheney was sparing with his words. The atmosphere was courteous

but cool. Blair rehearsed one of the pitches he was to make to the president—that Vladimir Putin was a man the West could do business with. Cheney, one of the administration's foremost cold warriors, seemed unimpressed. He questioned Blair on Europe's plans to build its own defense force following the deal the prime minister had struck with France at Saint-Malo. Wasn't Britain in effect proposing to weaken the North Atlantic Treaty Organization? Blair reassured his host that that was not the case. Overall, Blair thought the meeting had gone quite well, though one or two members of the British contingent took away the impression that here was an intensely partisan conservative with a view of America's place in the world that had little room for the opinions of a left-leaning leader from a small country on the other side of the Atlantic. Such first impressions are sometimes misleading; this one would endure. Even as he established a strong bond with Bush after the terrible events of September 11, 2001, the prime minister would find Cheney the constant grit in the relationship.

At this point, though, the prime minister was more concerned about getting to first base with the president. His foreign policy still rested on the presumption that Britain was to serve as the bridge in the transatlantic alliance. His friendship with Clinton and the new alliances he had cultivated in Europe had been mutually reinforcing. He had been astute in establishing contact with Putin while others were still weighing the Russian leader's intentions. He had then leveraged these relationships to give Britain a voice in world affairs disproportionate to any simple reckoning of its power. But now, if the prime minister was seen to have lost sway in Washington, he would also lose ground in Europe.

The agenda for the Camp David talks had been outlined during a visit to Washington a few weeks earlier by Jonathan Powell, Blair's chief of staff, and John Sawers, his foreign policy adviser. That in turn had been set up by Christopher Meyer. Meyer had endured criticism the previous year from those around Blair who were cheerleading for Al Gore. But the connections the ambassador had established with Condoleezza Rice and others in the incoming administration were now paying off. He had secured from Rice a promise that Blair would be the

first European leader granted an audience with the president–a vital sign to Britain's neighbors that Blair had not been frozen out by the new administration. Powell, Sawers, and Meyer were received by just about everyone but the president. They found Bush's foreign policy advisers hospitable and their meetings productive. The only tricky one, again, was with Cheney. The vice president found it hard to stifle a yawn when Jonathan Powell set out at length Blair's agenda. He seemed much more interested in news of Powell's older brother, Charles, who had become a personal friend while serving as Margaret Thatcher's foreign policy adviser. Blair's aides, though, had also opened another line of contact–this time personal–to the president. Bill Gammell, a Scottish oil industry executive, had been a contemporary at Fettes. By chance, the Gammell and Bush families were old friends– George W. had visited the family home in Scotland several times. Discreetly, Bill Gammell was now enlisted to "put in a good word" with the president.

Blair had prepared carefully for his first meeting with the president. He was confident, as ever, of his own powers of persuasion. But, lest there be any doubt of his intentions, he had brought with him a proposal. The foreign policy set out by George W. Bush on the presidential stump had had ambiguities, but one commitment seemed rock solid: he intended to build a National Missile Defense against potential threats from the nuclear ambitions of the world's rogue states. Testing of missile defense systems had started during the Clinton years, but the outgoing administration had delayed a firm commitment on their development. Most European governments vehemently opposed the idea, fearful that abrogating the Anti-Ballistic Missile (ABM) Treaty between Washington and Moscow would bring down the entire complex of international agreements on arms control that had kept the peace between the superpowers during the cold war. Many in Europe also doubted whether a missile shield could ever be made to work. The notion seemed redolent of the costly failure of Ronald Reagan's "Star Wars" program, a Maginot Line in space. Other allies feared that if, against the odds, the project did turn out to be technically feasible, America's increased security would be at the expense of a more vul-

nerable Europe. As for Russia, Putin was indeed threatening to pull out of other arms limitation agreements if the United States went ahead unilaterally.

Tony Blair put aside all such objections and assured Bush at their first meeting that he could rely on British support for the missile defense program. The prime minister would approve the necessary upgrade of U.S. radar facilities on British territory and would seek to smooth the ruffled feathers of other European leaders. What he asked of the president in return was that the United States try to negotiate a deal with Russia rather than act unilaterally. Bush was impressed; Blair's approach set him aside from most European leaders and from leading figures in his own cabinet. But the truth was, he had made up his mind on the subject several months earlier during a heated internal debate within his government. The Foreign Office under Robin Cook had pressed the case for Britain to stick with the rest of Europe in opposing the American plans. The Ministry of Defence had worried that, if the system worked, Britain would have to buy it. That in turn could swallow up most of the nation's defense budget. Blair, though, had come to a different conclusion. Though Britain would have to be sensitive in handling its European allies, its vital interest lay in staying on side with Washington. Partly this was a question of realpolitik: if an American administration, of whatever political color, was determined to press ahead with a defensive shield regardless, what purpose was there in attracting opprobrium for opposing it? Britain's military relationship with the United States was unique, involving heavy dependence on American defense technology. Shutting the door on missile defense might well imperil that cooperation. Blair, though, was also more alert than many in Europe to the changing strategic geography of the world. Even before the attacks on New York and Washington, he had the sense that the proliferation of weapons of mass destruction–particularly of nuclear programs and missile technology–was the most serious emerging threat to Western security. Whatever the arguments for and against this particular project for missile defense, it was inevitable that the world's sole superpower would seek some means to guard against the threat.

George W. Bush, of course, was unaware of the internal debate that had taken place within the British government. Blair's offer was taken, as he had intended, as testimony to the good intent of a reliable ally. The president told his guest privately what he would later say of Blair in public: he was impressed by the British leader's willingness to think anew about the security challenges facing the West. The prime minister also secured an important concession. Assuring Bush that the project would not undermine the U.S.-led North Atlantic Treaty Organization, he asked for the president's blessing of the Anglo-French plan to create a European military force. Bush tentatively agreed. Blair could now take this assent to Paris and other European capitals as evidence that the British magic still worked in Washington. As their officials put the finishing touches to a joint statement for the waiting press, Bush and Blair left the president's cabin for a walk in the woods of Camp David. This one-to-one conversation was to be the first of many during the next few years. The prime minister always valued such intimate contact with foreign leaders, which allowed discussion to break out of the constraints imposed by the bureaucrats. As Bush discovered, they also gave him a chance to turn on the charm.

At the Camp David press conference that followed their talks, the media caught only a glimpse of the private meeting of minds between the two leaders. The bargain on missile defense and on Europe's military plans could be read between the lines of their joint communiqué— but only just. Blair had work to do at home in persuading his own party to accept the inevitability of the U.S. program, and Bush's acquiescence in the creation of a separate European military force was still conditional. Not surprisingly, many of the next day's headlines missed the story, suggesting that the issues remained a point of tension. Blair also seemed uncharacteristically nervous facing the press. (Before the press conference there had been a curious wrangle with his aides about his choice of casual dress, and in the event, his blue pullover looked odd against Bush's leather bomber jacket.) The body language between the two men was awkward. When a journalist asked the president whether they had anything in common, Bush replied rather lamely that they shared the same brand of toothpaste, Colgate. Nevertheless, Blair had

secured the endorsement of the Anglo-American alliance that he
needed to take back to Europe. Bush declared that his guest had "put
the charm offensive on me, and it worked." More important, he added
that "this is a special relationship between America and Britain, and we
are going to keep it that way. I can assure you that when either of us
gets in a bind, there will be a friend at the end of the phone."

The prime minister had made an important judgment about his host.
Europe's—and for that matter, Britain's—perception of George W. Bush
was of the bumbling backwoodsman from Texas, a leader who knew
little of the world beyond his desert ranch and probably cared less. The
prime minister felt he had met a different president altogether, who,
despite his occasional struggles with the English language, had firm
personal convictions and a much clearer grasp of the strategic issues
than most imagined. The two men had disagreed on the Kyoto climate
change protocol—Blair failed to persuade the president to soften his
implacable opposition—but had done so in a friendly manner. And if
Bush remained skeptical of Blair's insistence that Vladimir Putin had
made the strategic decision to integrate Russia into the West, he lis-
tened attentively to the arguments. One of the prime minister's most
trusted political aides was later asked how Blair had managed to get on
so well with this staunchly Republican president. "The starting point is
he had to," this aide said in acknowledgment of Britain's strategic in-
terest. "But he also found that Bush was straightforward. Both decided
at the beginning to make a real effort. Bush is organized. He breaks up
meetings into segments—an hour on this, an hour on that. And he says
what he thinks. There is no hidden side to him, no hidden meanings.
That worked for Blair." The prime minister took away another impres-
sion from this first meeting. Bush, who had asked for his guest's
thoughts on France's Jacques Chirac and Germany's Gerhard
Schröder, seemed unconcerned with the ideology of other political
leaders. What really counted for the president was that they be as
straight with him as he would be with them—that they said what they
thought and stood by their words. This was a vital insight, one central
to their future relationship. Blair played it straight.

By the time the two men met again for talks at the prime minister's country residence at Chequers in July 2001, Blair had won a second sweeping election victory over the Conservatives. Bush was talking to someone who would be Britain's prime minister for at least the next four or five years, and the president seemed to have decided he could get on with him. A few weeks earlier at a European-American summit in the Swedish city of Göteborg, Bush had been ambushed by European leaders over his repudiation of the Kyoto climate change treaty, an experience he had hated. Condoleezza Rice later remarked to a British official, "You really should know, the president doesn't feel comfortable with Europeans. He much prefers Latin Americans." Although the prime minister was on the same side as his European allies in the Kyoto dispute, he had played a subtler hand, seeing little gain in publicly berating Bush. He had also begun to act, entirely in secret, as an informal go-between for the president and Vladimir Putin. In March 2001 the new U.S. administration announced the expulsion from Washington of fifty Russian diplomats who were allegedly KGB spies. Putin, already alarmed by Bush's plans to abrogate the ABM Treaty, had viewed the move as a hostile political act rather than one of the periodic spats between the two countries over intelligence-gathering. He considered massive retaliation. But during a conversation on the margins of a European Union–Russia summit in Stockholm, Blair reassured the Russian leader that the U.S. had not intended a broader political message. Putin ultimately decided on a measured response, ordering the quid pro quo departure of only a handful of American diplomats from Moscow. The tension subsided.

When Bush arrived at Chequers, his administration's attitude to Putin had shifted. The Russian leader was still suspect–he was, after all, a former leader of the KGB–but Rice had modified her earlier cold war views, and the president was now willing to give Putin a chance to demonstrate whether he was serious about aligning Russia with the West. Blair continued to impress Bush with his openness to the idea of different security responses in the post–cold war world. "The thing I appreciate about the prime minister is that he is willing to think anew

as we head into the future," the president said after their talks. "It is hard for any country to commit to vague notions. But there are some leaders who just out of hand reject any willingness to think differently about security. And Prime Minister Blair is not that way. He has been very forthcoming. He had great questions. He has been more than willing to listen to the philosophy behind moving beyond a treaty [the ABM Treaty] that has codified a relationship that no longer exists."

If there was one false note at the meeting it came late at night when the two leaders and their wives dined alone, their officials banished to the competing splendor of a nearby castle for the evening. For all her outspoken resentment on the flight to Camp David, Cherie had behaved impeccably at that first meeting with the president. To the great relief of her husband and aides, she had been at pains to make friends with Laura Bush. But as the two couples sat down to dinner at Chequers, Cherie could not resist an argument. As her legal career had prospered, she had become a founding partner in a practice specializing in human rights cases. The subject she turned to at the dinner was the death penalty, a subject on which her views were blunt: judicial executions were an immoral violation of human rights, an affront, under the U.S. Constitution as much as under European laws, to the fundamental principles of justice. This opinion was delivered to a politician who had signed the warrants for more than 150 executions during his tenure as governor of Texas. Cherie's later account of the dinner suggested that her husband had squirmed, even though he shared her opposition to the death penalty. An official later added an amusing codicil to the story. Cherie, it seemed, was not the only one who sometimes disagreed with her husband. Dinner conversations between the two couples had ranged over other moral issues. Laura Bush had made it perfectly clear that her views on abortion were a great deal more liberal than those of her Bible-thumping husband. The president, too, had been embarrassed.

Tony Blair was working on a speech in a hotel suite in Brighton on England's south coast on the day the world changed. As he made final adjustments to his text, the television in the adjoining room began to

broadcast pictures from New York. The images of the first passenger jet ramming into the twin towers brought horror and puzzlement. When the second hit, everything stopped. The speech prepared for the annual conference of Britain's trade unions was discarded without ceremony, and the prime minister returned to London for an emergency meeting with senior colleagues and security staff. The gathering of the so-called Cobra committee—named after "Cabinet Office Briefing Room A," a windowless, white-walled bunker deep beneath Whitehall—saw Blair craft an immediate statement of unconditional support. Even as George W. Bush continued to circle the skies in Air Force One, the prime minister appeared in Downing Street to announce that he would stand "shoulder to shoulder" with America. "This is not a battle between the U.S. and terrorism, but between the free and democratic world and terrorism. We therefore, here in Britain, stand shoulder to shoulder with our American friends in this hour of tragedy, and we, like them, will not rest until this evil is driven from our world."

An intuitive politician, Blair grasped sooner than most the extent of the shift in the geopolitical tectonic plates wrought by the destruction of the twin towers. As a big-picture leader, he is never more adept than when plotting and analyzing the changes in the contours of the political landscape. This was one of the biggest. The last time America's mainland had been invaded was when the British sacked Washington in 1812. For nearly two centuries since, it had seemed invulnerable. September 11, Blair knew, had shattered that assumption and, with it, the global order that had prevailed since the fall of the Berlin Wall more than a decade earlier. Nothing could be the same again in the relationship between the single superpower and the rest of the world. As Blair observed, in retrospect, the new millennium had marked merely a moment in time. It was September 11 that represented the true turning point in history. The question he—and for that matter, every world leader beyond America's shores—asked himself was how the United States would respond to this terrible demonstration of its vulnerability. His own shock at the scale and the indiscriminate nature of the killing caught the mood of Britain. Muslims and Jews had died alongside Christians and those of others faiths as the twin towers collapsed. The

first calculations of the casualties also suggested that hundreds of British citizens had died. The public expressions of sympathy in Britain—the crowds pouring into London's Grosvenor Square to lay carpets of flowers outside the U.S. embassy, the Queen's Coldstream Guards playing "The Star-Spangled Banner" outside Buckingham Palace—reflected heartfelt solidarity. But just as this act of terror changed the world, so it seemed to energize the prime minister. Privately, he was fearful about how America would react.

The international system on which the West's, and Britain's, security depended was imperiled. The threat from international terrorism, from the chaos of the world's failed states, and, looming on the horizon, from the proliferation of weapons of mass destruction had been made real. There was a second danger, though, which in the long term was altogether as significant. America might choose to respond to the attack on its homeland with ferocious and unilateral force. At once uniquely powerful and uniquely vulnerable, the United States, Blair said privately in the days after September 11, could simply decide to "jump out of the international system" in pursuit of its enemies. The Bush administration had already shown itself impatient with the perceived constraints placed on its national interest by international treaty commitments. There would now be intense pressure in Washington to ignore the United Nations, the North Atlantic Treaty Organization, and the panoply of other international institutions in favor of unbridled revenge. That, to Blair's mind, would be a disaster—for the security of the West and for Britain's own role as the mediator between the United States and Europe, as well as, ultimately, for America itself. The specter he saw on the near horizon was a "clash of civilizations" between Christendom and the Islamic world, a fractured transatlantic alliance, and the development of a Russia-China axis against the United States.

The prime minister decided to strain every fiber to persuade Bush of the merits of a multilateral response. Bill Clinton's advice came to mind: he had to get "close up" to the president, to make himself, in Clinton's words, "the guy he turns to." And even as he sought to persuade Washington to build an international coalition to defeat the terrorists and their supporters, he would seek to convince other world

leaders to be staunch in their support of the United States. Blair, in other words, proposed to cast himself in the role of pivotal player in the unfolding drama. There was more to this decision than realpolitik. Blair saw an opportunity as well as a threat. His own politics had always been informed and infused by the concepts of interdependence and community—the idea that self- and mutual interest operate in harmony rather than conflict as long as rights are matched to responsibilities. This was the moment to take such values onto the world stage.

In the days after September 11 George W. Bush was receptive to advice. The impression in Downing Street was that he was taking time to recover his balance. Bush's advisers seemed to think that the decision to keep the president out of Washington in the immediate aftermath of the attack had been a mistake. Blair spoke to the American leader by telephone on the day after the attacks, following up the conversation with the first of what would become a series of lengthy personal notes. More telephone calls followed. Then came an invitation to visit Washington to hear Bush's planned address to a joint session of Congress. For a moment, the staffers in Downing Street hesitated. If he said yes, his critics would cast him as the president's "poodle." Bush's dead-or-alive rhetoric and his unfortunate characterization of the war on terrorism as a "crusade" were already stirring popular unease in the UK. To the prime minister's irritation, Clare Short, the senior minister responsible for overseas development issues and the self-appointed conscience of the liberal left in the cabinet, publicly voiced doubts about American policy. Other Labour members of Parliament warned against precipitate military action. Although the domestic politics of the relationship with Bush had to be played carefully, Blair brushed aside any hesitations. This was his chance to "get up close" to the president, to make himself the indispensable ally. So on September 20, after attending a memorial service in New York, Blair found himself seated next to Laura Bush in the visitors' gallery of Congress. The honored guest received a standing ovation as the president declared that America "has no truer friend than Great Britain."

During their talks in the White House that evening Blair offered

unequivocal support alongside candid advice. Britain's military forces, he told the president, were ready to fight on the ground alongside the United States in the coming war against the Taliban and Osama bin Laden's Al Qaeda. He had already issued mobilization orders. The campaign, though, should be not be rushed–there was no purpose in bombing sand. America should gather together the widest possible international coalition. That meant military action should be limited to Afghanistan–there was no evidence as yet to link Saddam Hussein's Iraq to the terrorist attacks. And, finally, the military defeat of those responsible for September 11 should be linked to a wider political commitment–nation-building in Afghanistan and peacemaking in the Middle East. On most of these points the prime minister found that he was pushing at an open door. In spite of the muscular militarism of conservatives and neoconservatives inside and outside the administration, the president seemed in no mood to lash out indiscriminately. On the fate of Saddam Hussein one British official noted the president's reply as follows: "I agree with you, Tony. Afghanistan is the priority. We will come back to Iraq in due course." For now, at least, Blair's team had the impression that they were reinforcing the advice Bush was already receiving from his father and from the less hawkish members of the administration, particularly Secretary of State Colin Powell. Only on the issue of the Middle East was Blair disappointed. Because the president was preparing to wage war he had no time for peacemaking between Israel and the Palestinians.

Blair pulled all these threads together in a speech to his party's annual conference in Brighton at the beginning of October. It was a bravura performance, an address lauded around the world for its force and passion. On a personal level it demonstrated the fusion of Blair's politics and his religious faith. On a political level it underlined the melding of strategic calculation and moral fervor in the prime minister's world vision. Here as never before, the politician and the prelate, the thespian and the statesman were unified in a single persona. Blair staked his claim at once as the most articulate spokesman for military action against those responsible for September 11 and the evangelist for a new international order to confront the chaos and poverty in

which terrorism flourished. In Britain the speech drew almost universal acclaim, with even the Conservative-supporting *Daily Telegraph* declaring, in Churchillian terms, that it marked the prime minister's "finest hour."

Blair's starting point was that Britain's support for military action against Al Qaeda and the Taliban would be uncompromising. British forces would stand shoulder to shoulder with American GIs in Afghanistan. He faced head-on the arguments already being heard from some in his own party: "Don't overreact, some say. We aren't. We haven't lashed out. No missiles on the first night just for effect. Don't kill innocent people. We are not the ones who waged war on the innocent. We seek the guilty. Look for a diplomatic solution. There is no diplomacy with bin Laden or the Taliban regime." Facing such indiscriminate terror, the civilized world had a simple choice: "Defeat it or be defeated by it. And defeat it we must." As for those who somehow seemed to believe that America had itself to blame for the murderous attack on its homeland, Blair was contemptuous: "Some of the reaction to September 11 betrays a hatred of America that shames those that feel it."

The defeat of Al Qaeda, though, was only the start. Blair took up the themes of global interdependence and international community he had begun to develop two years earlier at the time of the Kosovo war. The hardheaded realist ready to send British troops to war in Afghanistan was also the apostle for a new global system rooted in moral values. There was an opportunity to be seized even as the civilized world sought out the perpetrators of the crime. The memorial to those who had lost their lives, he said, "can and should be greater than simply the punishment of the guilty. It is that out of the shadow of this evil should emerge lasting good; destruction of the machinery of terrorism wherever it is found; hope amongst all nations of a new beginning where we seek to resolve differences in a calm and ordered way; greater understanding between nations and between faiths; and above all justice and prosperity for the poor and dispossessed, so that people everywhere can see a chance of a better future through the hard work and creative power of the free citizen, not the violence and savagery of the fanatic." Around the world, he continued, September 11 had

brought a realization of the fragility of national frontiers in the face of the world's new challenges. "Today conflicts rarely stay within national boundaries . . . I have long believed this interdependence defines the new world we live in." As in domestic politics, so in the international arena, self-interest could no longer be separated from shared security. This vision of a new world order extended well beyond the immediate battles ahead: "The starving, the wretched, the dispossessed, the ignorant, those living in want and squalor from the deserts of northern Africa to the slums of Gaza, to the mountain ranges of Afghanistan: they too are our cause. . . . The kaleidoscope has been shaken," he concluded. "The pieces are in flux. Soon they will settle again. Before they do, let us reorder this world around us."

Some who listened to the speech in the conference hall in Brighton that day—the same hall where he had been due to speak to trade unionists on September 11—thought Blair had at times been carried away. Others felt uncomfortable with the Manichaean certainty of the prime minister's worldview. For those uncomfortable with Blair's Christianity, the podium had become a pulpit, the politician a preacher. The words heard in the White House during the dark days after September 11 had been redolent of the Old Testament's "eye for an eye" ethos of revenge; Blair's sermon, in contrast, carried the New Testament's message of redemption. George W. Bush would cast out evil. Tony Blair would do good in the world. Yet for all the hyperbole of his speech, the prime minister had found language that united the security imperative with the moral case. This conviction that the West must act to confront the chaos of failed and failing states was no sudden flash. He had seen in the Balkans how crime, violence, and human misery could spill over national borders. Well before September 11, 2001, one of the prime minister's foreign policy advisers had warned how this dismal picture might yet be painted on a bigger canvas. Robert Cooper, a freethinker in the Downing Street foreign policy establishment, had warned of the threat to the West of "zones of chaos" in the world beyond its borders. Criminals, drug syndicates, and terrorists thrived in states that had

failed, he had said in a paper he prepared for the prime minister. Governments might have to take on new "imperial" responsibilities in these regions to counter the threat. With what turned out to be grim prescience, Cooper had singled out Afghanistan as a case in point.

That autumn the prime minister traveled the globe. During the months following the assault on America he clocked up 50,000 miles touring foreign capitals in the effort to broaden the coalition to fight terrorism. Trips to Berlin, Paris, and Moscow were interspersed with dashes to Amman, Riyadh, Muscat, and Cairo. There were visits to Jerusalem and the Gaza Strip, and to Islamabad and Delhi—and of course shuttles across the Atlantic to see George W. Bush. Jack Straw, the foreign secretary, covered the cities Blair missed, casting the net as widely as Tehran in an effort to persuade nations previously hostile to the United States that they could make a clean break. British officials calculated that Blair had talked with more than fifty world leaders in this self-chosen role as the coalition's chief cheerleader. When Blair was not traveling, or talking to Bush on the telephone, he was giving interviews to Arab television stations. His familiarity with the Koran stood him in good stead as he made the case that Al Qaeda's terrorism was a corruption of the Islamic faith. The sermon was the same in every city: in the rubble of the twin towers lay the opportunity for the international community to build something new; this was not a conflict between the West and Islam but between the forces of civilization and terror; war would be followed by nation-building in Afghanistan and peace-making in the Middle East. There were awkward moments. The prime minister's famous grin froze into a rictus when he was given a public dressing down by Syria's young leader Bashar Assad during a stopover in Damascus. The visit to Riyadh was tense—the prime minister's hosts refused him permission to fly directly from Saudi territory to his planned next stop in Jerusalem. Elsewhere, he took away the message from Muslim leaders that nothing would really change until there was a just resolution of the Israeli-Palestinian conflict, and from European ones that loose talk in Washington about extending the war on terror

to Iraq risked fracturing the alliance. Everything was relayed back to the White House. Blair's bargain with Bush was that public support would be accompanied by private candor.

Blair thrived on the tireless diplomacy. At times he looked gaunt and exhausted. He lost weight–the consequence as much of an increasingly vigorous exercise regime as an irregular diet. But this was the sort of politics–high-stakes deal-making, face-to-face with other world leaders–that pumped his adrenaline. "He loves it," said one of his aides in November 2001 when asked if Blair had started to tire of the if-it's-Monday-it-must-be-Moscow routine. Yet quite apart from the physical toll, the prime minister seemed to be ignoring two of politics' cardinal rules: never take risks when someone else determines the outcome, and avoid responsibility when power resides elsewhere. For all his influence at the White House–and it was real–Blair was the junior partner in the coalition. The British Special Forces operating in Afghanistan were fighting an American-led war. The prime minister's pledge to the people of Afghanistan that they would not be forgotten once the conflict was over depended on converting the president to the virtues of nation-building.

Bush was duly appreciative of Blair's efforts. When American intelligence agencies bridled at the idea of showing their hand by producing hard evidence of Al Qaeda's responsibility for September 11, Blair published his own intelligence-based dossier. During a meeting at the White House in early November Bush said of the prime minister, "I've got no better person I would like to talk to about our mutual concerns." Downing Street officials, meanwhile, claimed credit for a decision by the administration to include more European states in its military coalition. Yet the rhetoric in most of Washington was not that of an administration about to embrace the internationalism of Roosevelt and Truman. The president, one senior Downing Street aide observed about this time, was "unilateralist in principle but multilateralist in practice." The problem was that much of the world heard the unilaterism, but missed the multilateralism. Elsewhere in the administration,

Richard Cheney and Donald Rumsfeld made little secret of their disdain for Blair's vision of a new global order—or of their resentment of his influence in the White House. British officials began to hear that the prime minister's influence was being criticized—presumably on Cheney's behalf—by Lewis "Scooter" Libby, the vice president's chief of staff. Blair had unwittingly become a participant in the bitter interagency struggles in Washington that pitted Colin Powell against the hawks in the office of the vice president and the Pentagon. He had no assurance which side would win.

An early harbinger of the intentions of the Washington hawks had come at a meeting of the North Atlantic Treaty Organization soon after September 11. In solidarity with the United States, NATO had taken the unprecedented step of invoking Article 5 of its constitution, signifying that the attacks on New York and Washington had in effect been carried out against the whole alliance. NATO's military assets were accordingly now at Washington's disposal. But when Paul Wolfowitz visited the alliance's headquarters in Brussels, he had seemed at best cool toward the offer, or, as one senior European diplomat characterized his response, "Don't call us and we probably won't call you." America had no intention of fighting a war encumbered by the joint decision-making processes of NATO. The same message was conveyed by Wolfowitz's superior, Donald Rumsfeld, when he declared that the mission to defeat terrorism should determine the coalition rather than the coalition the mission. Many of Blair's fellow European leaders took this as a decisive rejection of the multilateralism at the heart of the Atlantic alliance. The image that conservatives such as Rumsfeld and neoconservatives such as Wolfowitz liked to conjure up was that of the sheriff and the posse: America was the sheriff; if others wanted to join the posse that was fine, but there could be no doubt who was in charge. This was a metaphor that caused much disquiet in Downing Street, for it did not rest easily alongside the prime minister's own vision of a new international community based on partnership. Rumsfeld had also made it clear to the British that the war in Afghanistan was being run by the Pentagon rather than the White

House, more than once embarrassing Blair by delaying the deployment of British forces in the combat theater. "If only he would shut up," one senior British minister said of Rumsfeld as 2001 drew to a close. It was a sentiment that would be heard many times in Downing Street.

Blair had to content himself with Bush's reassurances. The prime minister weighed the perils of staking his own reputation on decisions taken in Washington against what he saw as the bigger danger of the United State's slipping the reins of the international system. Closer to the White House than any other world leader, he was more aware of just how significantly September 11 had transformed the psychology of America. The world's only superpower was in an unpredictable mood. Blair's decision to act as America's envoy was thus as much a matter of geopolitical calculation—of a cool assessment of Britain's national interest—as of moral zeal. For nearly half a century Britain's security had been anchored in the transatlantic system. If the alliance splintered, British power and influence would be severely compromised. While Blair's response to September 11 was true to his personal conviction, in this case the right thing to do happened also to be the astute thing to do.

During those last months of 2001, the transatlantic bridge held. Blair's stature in Europe rose in tandem with the warmth of his welcome in the White House. When in early November the prime minister invited Jacques Chirac of France and Gerhard Schröder of Germany to a Downing Street dinner, other European leaders clamored to join the party. Italy's Silvio Berlusconi invited himself. José María Aznar of Spain also appeared on the guest list. By the time the group sat down for dinner, the table also had placements for Belgium's Guy Verhofstadt and the Dutch leader Wim Kok. There were some afterwards who thought the event had been a diplomatic blunder, for those European leaders who had been left out took personal offense. But that in itself was a measure of Blair's influence. No one could recall a previous occasion when Europe's elite had been so eager to sit at the table of a British prime minister.

Yet even as the fall of Kabul confounded the gloomy predictions of

those who thought the war in Afghanistan would draw coalition forces into a costly quagmire, tensions had begun to emerge at home and abroad. In certain segments of the British media Blair was lampooned as the president's lackey, all too eager to please the "cowboy" in the White House. Within his own cabinet Blair faced the sniping of Clare Short, who complained that the American-led campaign against the Taliban was inattentive to the country's humanitarian needs. Labour members of Parliament were already lodging preemptive protests against any war with Iraq. Blair's personal ratings remained high, but he was well aware that the voters could be notoriously unappreciative of warrior prime ministers. While admirers drew comparisons with Winston Churchill, critics recalled that Churchill had been turned out of office by an ungrateful electorate at the moment of victory in 1945. There were also whispered criticisms in other European capitals, notably Paris and Brussels. The prime minister's famous bridge, one senior French diplomat observed acidly, often seemed to carry traffic in only one direction. Europe heard constantly from Blair of Washington's demands. But Europe's preoccupations never seemed to travel much further than Downing Street.

Beneath these petty jealousies of politics real differences were emerging. On one level Blair shared most of the concerns of his European allies—he was pushing Bush at every opportunity to unlock the Middle East process, he was anxious to keep the United States in the multilateral fold, and he worried that Washington wanted to fight and move on rather than to engage in the arduous business of nation-building. "What we were telling Chirac and Schröder was that these things were best said privately," one of the prime minister's principal aides remarked. Yet on another level—the need to respond aggressively to threats from terrorists and rogue states—Blair was temperamentally closer to Bush than to his European allies. He had never understood why France had seemed indifferent to Saddam Hussein's violations of United Nations resolutions. Gerhard Schröder's commitment of German troops to Afghanistan had marked a major break with that country's post–World War II prohibition on the deployment of its military overseas, a gesture that Blair applauded. But the leader who had sent

British forces into action in Kosovo and Sierra Leone and in the skies over Baghdad voiced private frustration with those European leaders who seemed to argue simultaneously that Europe should build its own military force but should eschew armed intervention. Blair was by instinct a multilateralist, but his commitment to international institutions was conditional–the United Nations, he would often say, could not be an excuse for inaction.

Such tensions and stresses would later shatter Europe's unity. But even among his critics, Blair won plaudits for courage and conviction in these early months after September 11. He had seen a chance to combine principle with pragmatism, to draw the connection between national self-interest and the interests of the wider international community. That was what had happened after World War II, when Roosevelt and Truman had designed the architecture of a new multilateral system. The opportunity to recast these structures to fit the new age had been lost after the end of the cold war, when countries such as Afghanistan had been left to rot. Blair was determined that the chance should not be left to slip away a second time.

12. THE RIGHT THING TO DO

SADDAM HUSSEIN. The name ricocheted around 10 Downing Street in the opening weeks of 2002. Tony Blair was as strong as he had ever been, a politician who had shown rare leadership at a time of international crisis. The success of the military campaign in Afghanistan had confounded critics. Dire warnings of a new Vietnam, of conflagration in Pakistan, of an Islamic uprising across the Arab world had proved ill founded. To be sure, Osama bin Laden was still at large, but Al Qaeda's most important base had been destroyed. Afghanistan, a country left to fall into the cruel chaos of Taliban rule after the end of the cold war, was a better place. Blair's role in the war had been at once America's reliable ally and the agent of international solidarity. The coalition assembled against the Taliban had survived the doubts of many European allies and the disdain of the hawks in Washington. Much of the credit was due to the British prime minister. As they contemplated the coming year, though, the aides and advisers in Downing Street knew that Afghanistan was first base, the opening salvo of George W. Bush's war on America's enemies. Now, on the near horizon, lay a still bigger challenge to the strategic calculations and moral convictions of the prime minister. Even before the president spoke in his State of the Union address of the "axis of evil" threatening American security, Tony Blair was thinking about the decision he would have to confront. Was he ready to take Britain to war against Saddam Hussein? The prime minister knew in his heart that his answer would be yes. It was the right thing to do.

If Bush's defining and incautious phrase caused almost as much anguish among diplomats in London as in the rest of Europe, the president's intent was no surprise to the British prime minister. When the

two had met in Washington the previous September Bush had readily agreed to put the issue of Saddam Hussein off to the future. But he had added a caveat–the administration would come back to Iraq once it had dealt with Al Qaeda and its Taliban protectors in Afghanistan. Anyone with half an ear to the rising chorus of hawkish voices in Washington knew that Saddam was fast rising to the top of America's target list. In his September speech to a joint session of Congress Bush had declared war on international terrorism and on those countries that harbored terrorists. The State of the Union speech added the third enemy–the "rogue" states developing weapons of mass destruction, a roll call that included Iran and North Korea as well as Iraq. But the immediate target was Iraq. For Tony Blair, the question, in the words of a senior adviser, was a simple one: "Would we be with the Americans?" Blair, who had spoken many times about the lethal nexus of tyrannical regimes and weapons proliferation, had few doubts that the answer would be yes. The prime minister was convinced that Saddam Hussein had to be confronted, that the cat-and-mouse game of the previous decade could not continue. Indeed, he would later say that had the Bush administration not taken that course, he would have urged it on the president. From this flowed a realization that given Saddam's track record–he was a leader, as diplomats would say, who had never missed an opportunity to miss an opportunity–war was more likely than not. Blair made no secret of his belief that the world would be a better as well as a safer place once it was rid of the Baghdad regime. Here, in the strategic calculations of the British leader, was one of those classic cases where idealism and pragmatism, the ethical impulse and realpolitik, sat side by side. The moral justification for removing Saddam was as strong as the strategic one. "I can't understand why people on the [political] left oppose it," he would tell visitors to his Downing Street study. "I know why the isolationists on the right are against it . . . but hasn't the left always been committed to fighting injustice in the world?" Saddam, a leader who murdered his own people, had used chemical weapons against Iran and the Kurds in northern Iraq, and had twice invaded his neighbors, was surely as bad, as well as dangerous, as they got. Yet Blair did not make, as some opponents of the Iraq war

later claimed, an irrevocable decision at the outset to go to war in each and every circumstance. In the prime minister's mind, the Iraqi leader's fate still lay in his own hands.

The post-Afghanistan rhetoric in Washington had set alarm bells ringing through the British government, as had the implication in the State of the Union speech that Bush might consider preemptive military strikes against Iran and North Korea. But Saddam, Blair considered, was a "unique" threat. The steady flow of reports from British intelligence indicated that, since the departure of United Nations inspectors at the end of 1998, he had begun to reconstitute his weapons programs. The UN sanctions regime was also breaking down—it was thought that Saddam was receiving up to $3 billion a year from sanctions-busting. If Blair were honest with himself, he knew that Saddam was not about to start another war. It was looking ahead to the next two, five, ten years that concerned him. If the international community ducked the challenge now, the policy of containing Iraq would gradually crumble.

There was another, critical point, more important in its way than the direct threat from the Iraqi dictator. Blair's gaze was fixed on the wider picture of the post–September 11 world. The evils of terrorism and weapons proliferation, he had said many times in the months since the destruction of the twin towers, defined the threat to strategic security in the twenty-first century. The international community could deal with such threats only if it stood united. Yet by the same token, multilateralism could not become an excuse for inaction. If Saddam was allowed to defy the United Nations, what prospect was there that other rogue states would respond to international pressure? How long before weapons of mass destruction found their way into the hands of terrorists? Iraq was a test case, a choice, between a new world order and global chaos. Blair's question was simple. Would the West be united and resolute or divided and weak?

Confronting Iraq thus became a necessary condition for the world to take the path of order. Yet, of itself, the looming showdown with Saddam was not sufficient to meet the new global threats. In this respect Blair's commitment to go to war was conditional. The installa-

tion of a new regime in Baghdad of itself was not enough. In the prime minister's design for the new global architecture, the "how" of dealing with Saddam mattered as much the "whether." The international community had come together to confront Al Qaeda. It had to be held together. Iraq had to be fitted into a wider framework, to be part of what Blair called "an integrated approach to the new insecurities of the twenty-first century." Central to that context was a determined attempt to broker a just peace in the Middle East and a broader commitment to rebuild the failed states in which terrorism flourished.

This was the message that Tony Blair took to the president's ranch in Crawford, Texas, in early April. The media characterized his visit as "a council of war." The momentum for war was certainly building; as one British official would observe, that the "whiff of inevitability" mingled with the smell of barbecue at the Bush ranch. The removal of the Iraqi dictator, this aide judged, had by now been "hardwired" into the administration's thinking. Privately, and in the press conference after their talks, Bush made clear that his policy was regime change. But the debate over the "how" and the "when" was far from over. Here Blair could deploy his influence. He considered that there were two ways the world might view the defeat of Saddam. The first was as a demonstration of raw American power, an act of lethal retribution for the events of September 11, 2001, and a warning to those who might contemplate any further challenge to American hegemony. The second was as a decision by the international community to build a new security system based on a commitment to peacemaking and nation-building as well as military might. The Washington hawks were in the first camp; Blair in the second. The president, his guest hoped, was to play for. Implicit in this calculation, however, was that Britain would stand alongside the United States if, and more probably when, it came to war.

An invitation to deliver a speech at the nearby George Bush Presidential Library and Museum in College Station gave Blair the chance to distill his thoughts. The speech reprised the philosophy of international interventionism that he had espoused during the Kosovo war. The old tension in international affairs between utilitarian self-interest and utopian idealism, he said, was fast dissipating. "I advocate an en-

lightened self-interest that puts fighting for our values right at the heart of the policies necessary to protect our nations." The hard-edged side of this approach meant, "We must be prepared to act where terrorism or weapons of mass destruction threaten us . . . if necessary the action should be military and again, if necessary and justified, it should involve regime change." As for Saddam, "To allow WMD to be developed by a state like Iraq without let or hindrance would be grossly to ignore the lessons of September 11 and we will not do it." But there was another vital dimension to the effort to rebuild security–a willingness to seek an end to the conflicts and injustices that provided the fertile soil in which terrorism flourished. The most obvious of these was the confrontation between Israel and the Palestinians: "The Middle East requires continuous focus and engagement. The role of peacemaker, where hatreds are entrenched, is never easy. But it is massively in our interests to try." This preoccupation with the Israeli-Palestinian conflict was nothing new. As early as 1998 Blair had appointed a personal envoy to the Middle East in the shape of Lord Levy. Labour's chief fund-raiser had strong connections with Israeli, Palestinian, and Arab leaders and frequently traveled to the region carrying personal messages from the prime minister. September 11 had only reinforced the prime minister's belief that a settlement in the region was the vital condition of the West's security.

A broader backcloth was his emerging view that the world of the early twenty-first century should be run by something resembling a virtuous cartel of its leading powers. He never put it in quite those terms, but it was there as an assumption. The balance of power politics that characterized the cold war was at an end. "'Spheres of influence' is an outdated concept," he said at College Station. "A series of interlocking alliances with a common agenda on issues of security, trade, and stability should replace old rivalries." The linchpin was the transatlantic partnership, but this global entente should also embrace Vladimir Putin's Russia and, eventually, China and India. "[Blair's] view is of a world run by the big nations–a benign ascendancy based on values as well as power," one close friend explained. This concept of a directorate of the great powers was in its way a reworked version of the

Concert of Europe, the arrangements to keep the peace put in place at the Congress of Vienna in 1815. William Gladstone, of course, had tried, and failed, to rebuild the accord.

By the time Tony Blair traveled to Camp David in early September the drumbeat of war had become a discordant din. His summer vacation had been regularly punctuated by calls from his officials to keep him in touch with the public debate raging on the other side of the Atlantic. Former secretary of state James Baker and other luminaries from the administration of George H. W. Bush were urging the president to take the case against Iraq to the United Nations. Ranged against them, Richard Cheney and Donald Rumsfeld pressed for a unilateral decision to depose Saddam. In Europe, meanwhile, Blair could sense popular opinion hardening fast against war. The prime minister was told that while the president had still to choose between the opposing factions, war looked inevitable. The reports sent back to London by Sir Christopher Meyer, the British ambassador in Washington, reflected the bellicose mood in the administration. David Manning, Blair's chief foreign policy adviser, caught the same intonations in his frequent telephone conversations with Condoleezza Rice. During a visit to Washington, Manning warned Rice that Blair could win political backing for war only on the basis of a United Nations resolution.

Bush had upped the stakes in June when he visited West Point. His speech there unveiled a new doctrine of preemptive military action against America's enemies. Tearing up the strategic rules that had guided policy through the cold war, Bush had declared, "Deterrence, the promise of massive retaliation against nations, means nothing against shadowy terrorist networks with no nation or citizens to defend. Containment is not possible when unbalanced dictators with weapons of mass destruction can deliver those weapons on missiles or secretly provide them to terrorist allies. We cannot defend America and our friends by hoping for the best. We cannot put our faith in the word of tyrants who solemnly sign nonproliferation treaties and then systematically break them. If we wait for threats to fully materialize then we will have waited too long." America, in other words, would decide for itself what constituted a threat to its security—and act preemptively to remove it.

Blair had been traveling in a similar direction when he declared at College Station that the West had to be ready to respond to the twin dangers of terrorism and weapons of mass destruction. But there was a vital difference: the prime minister's presumption was that the international community would act as one; Washington was declaring that in the future, it would make its own decisions.

Arriving at the presidential retreat in the Catoctin Mountains, Blair sought assurance that Bush would go to the United Nations. If there had to be war, he told his host, Britain would be there, but America and its allies had at least to make the argument. During the previous few months the debate had been conducted from the extremes. On one side were those in Europe who dismissed military action in any circumstances; on the other were the hard-line American conservatives determined to bring about a regime change whatever the cost. The voices that tended to be heard outside America were those of hawks like Donald Rumsfeld, Paul Wolfowitz, and Richard Perle, chairman of the Pentagon's Defense Policy Board. As a result, political and public opinion in Europe, and in Britain, was turning against war. The central case for confronting Saddam—that his defiance of the international community posed a significant threat to all civilized nations—was going by default. It could be made effectively, Blair argued, only if the president was ready to seek the support of the United Nations.

Later, this meeting in the quiet of Maryland would be at the center of the intense postwar controversy in Britain over whether the prime minister had deceived his countrymen on the path to war. He would be accused of treating the United Nations process as a charade—a cover for a war that he had in fact agreed to with Bush as they talked in the presidential cabin. He denied the charge forcefully when he gave evidence before a parliamentary committee in July 2003 and described the Camp David talks as follows: "What I said to him [the president] was . . . 'Look; if we can resolve this through the UN route let us resolve it through the UN route,' and he accepted that was so. . . . The idea that we had some prearranged agreement that there was to be conflict, that the UN process was a charade, is completely and totally untrue."

Blair might have added, though, that any expectation of Iraq's com-

plying with a new United Nations resolution was slight. A senior British official put it thus: "For us the September meeting with Bush was about nailing down the U.S. strategy. Yes, we did think it would probably come to war, and we agreed that, if that proved the case, the first quarter of 2003 was the time to do it–but that was not in itself a decision to go to war." This official thought that the president, after the public infighting within the administration during August, had probably already decided to go to the UN. The prime minister reinforced him in that view. "What Bush deduced from his meeting with Blair is that Britain is with me on this one–but he needs me to go through the UN," the official said. In any event, February 15 was now a date penciled in political calendars for the start of military action to depose Saddam. Blair, though, attached another condition for his support. Returning to the theme of his speech at College Station, he said that any action against Iraq had to be put in the wider context of achieving peace in the region as a whole. In June Bush had stated unequivocally that resolution of the Middle East conflict required a "two-state solution"–an Israel secure within its boundaries alongside a viable Palestinian state. But after an earlier abortive tour of the region by Colin Powell, U.S. engagement to revive the peace process had fallen into abeyance. Blair wanted a new Middle East conference to present Israel and the Palestinians with a road map for peace.

One person close to the president, though, remained implacably opposed to the British strategy. Although Blair had met Vice President Richard Cheney two or three times before, he was surprised to find him sitting alongside Bush at Camp David. Cheney was known to be aggressively hostile to the very process Blair was now proposing. The initial thought among the senior officials accompanying the prime minister was that Bush wanted Cheney present to test his visitors. But as the talks progressed it seemed that, on the contrary, the president had wanted his taciturn but powerful deputy to listen to Blair's case and to lock him into the subsequent decisions. Cheney did not give up that easily, however. He had never disguised his impatience for war and his scorn for the suggestion that the U.S. needed the blessing of the UN to remove Saddam. As George H. W. Bush's defense secretary dur-

ing the Gulf War, Cheney had been among those who counseled halting the advance of American troops on the road to Baghdad, and later had spoken eloquently of the chaos that would have ensued if the U.S. had sought to occupy Iraq. Now, however, he was determined to rewrite that particular passage of history. "Once we have victory in Baghdad, all the critics will look like fools," Cheney told one high-ranking British official during the summer of 2002. If Tony Blair had grand designs for a new international order based on alliances and partnerships, the vice president's vision was of a world in which America asserted its primacy through the muscular use of military force. In occasional contacts with British officials, his chief of staff, Scooter Libby, made little secret of their scorn for multilaterism. Blair, to them, was an unwelcome irritant. "Oh, dear, we'd better not do that," Libby would jibe, "or we might upset the prime minister."

At the end of August, Cheney had abruptly dismissed calls for the return of UN inspectors to Iraq. In a speech seen as greatly accelerating the momentum toward war he had declared that "there is no doubt that Saddam Hussein now has weapons of mass destruction; there is no doubt that he is amassing them to use against our friends, against our allies, and against us." Speaking to veterans in Nashville, Tennessee, Cheney said that if UN inspectors were allowed back into Iraq, their presence would "provide no assurance whatsoever of his compliance with UN resolutions. On the contrary, there is a great danger that it would provide false comfort that Saddam was somehow back in his box. Meanwhile, he would continue to plot." This speech, more than any other utterance from Washington, stoked the fires of political opposition to war in Berlin, Paris, and elsewhere in Europe. Bush implicitly rejected that analysis in his talks at Camp David with Blair in early September, but even as the prime minister returned to London, Cheney set about undermining the Anglo-American understanding.

The vice president's occasional, acid interventions during the Camp David meeting—which included a rebuke for Alistair Campbell, Blair's director of communications—were evidence he had not changed his mind. During the following days and months he would be the constant disrupting force in the Anglo-American relationship. If Donald Rums-

feld discomfited Blair with his public disdain for multilateralism, Cheney sought to undermine the prime minister privately. In the days before the president's scheduled speech to the United Nations General Assembly on September 12, the vice president sought to dilute the commitment to the UN process. While Blair had emphasized the need for a new UN resolution to put Saddam on the spot, Cheney argued that the president should simply call on the UN Security Council to "meet its responsibilities" under existing resolutions against Iraq. Anything more would "trap" the United States in the UN process. British officials, in close touch with the White House, watched from a distance as the president's speech went through its many drafts: "As we heard it, the call for a new resolution kept falling in and out," one British official said. "At one stage we were up to drafts 23 and 24. It wasn't until Bush actually spoke that we knew that Cheney had not prevailed." Later the president told Jack Straw, the British foreign secretary, that the passage in his speech calling for a second resolution had actually fallen off his teleprompter. In the end he had ad-libbed. On the British side, officials suggested that Cheney had taken charge of the teleprompter—they were only half-joking. In any event, the vice president did not give up. As the effort to secure a new UN resolution got under way, British officials saw Cheney's influence in repeated efforts to undermine the search for consensus on the Security Council. "He waged a guerrilla war against the process. . . . He's a visceral unilateralist," one Blair aide remarked. "Cheney fought it all the way—at every twist and turn, even after Bush's speech to the UN," agreed another. The first text for a resolution suggested by the administration included the extraordinary provision that U.S. troops would accompany UN weapons inspectors in Iraq. Seeing Cheney's hand in the draft, Downing Street told the White House it was destined to fail. Failure, they assumed, was Cheney's purpose.

Now Blair had to make the case at home. The decisions that would put Britain on the path to war were the prime minister's alone to make, although he would discuss and consult with a handful of his senior ministers. Gordon Brown would eventually throw his formidable weight behind the war, but most of the time he preferred a studied si-

lence. Jack Straw was central to the diplomatic process, his influence enhanced by the strong rapport he had established with Colin Powell, the secretary of state. The two men took to speaking to each other daily, and a secure telephone line was established between their homes so they could continue the dialogue on weekends. But it was Blair who set the course, and he seemed alone in his certainty. Others in the British cabinet were at best lukewarm about the prospect of hitching the government's fortunes to decisions about peace and war made by a Republican administration in Washington. "What do you think?" was the frequent response of senior ministers when asked for their opinion. Some were sanguine about the political fallout. "As long as we win without too many casualties it should be fine," one offered in the autumn of 2002. Others hoped that a conflict could yet be avoided. One or two–the former foreign secretary Robin Cook among them–were already thinking in terms of resigning from the government. What united them all, though, was curiosity at just how Blair could be so sure. They would leave his study in 10 Downing Street shaking their heads in slightly nervous wonderment at his certainty. "He just didn't have any doubts . . . none at all," one senior minister would later remark. This, then, would be Tony Blair's war. "Had anyone else been leader we would not have fought alongside Bush without a United Nations mandate" is how one cabinet minister put it. Blair's aides did not disagree.

Yet, curiously enough, Blair saw the paradox that the opponents of military action seemed to ignore. Even if the most likely outcome was war, it was just possible that Saddam would retreat. But this possibility, albeit slight, would only be feasible if the Iraqi leader understood that regime change was not an empty threat. In the psychology of this confrontation, the dispatch of troops to the Gulf seemed to create an unstoppable momentum for war. Yet the military buildup was also the only way to keep alive the slim hope of a peaceful outcome. The same paradox threaded itself through international diplomacy. If the United Nations held firm, the Iraqi leader might just disarm to save himself. If the Security Council split between war and peace, then war was inevitable.

A year earlier Blair had abruptly abandoned his planned speech to the annual conference of Britain's trade unions in the wake of the attack on the World Trade Center. Now, returning from Camp David, he kept the appointment to address the unions. It was clear to all that his mind was set. Anticipating Bush's speech to the UN General Assembly, Blair said it was "right to deal with Saddam through the United Nations." But the multilateral route could not be a pretext for refusing to take action: "The challenge to all in the UN is this: the UN must be the way to resolve the threat from Saddam, not avoid it." His audience, however, was unconvinced. So, too, was the nation beyond. Two weeks later the prime minister recalled Parliament from its summer recess to put forth the case again. To coincide with the debate, the government took the unprecedented step of publishing a dossier of the intelligence it had gathered on Saddam's weapons programs. Two startling claims grabbed the headlines–that Iraq had weapons of mass destruction that could be readied for use within forty-five minutes, and that Baghdad had sought supplies of uranium from Africa for its nuclear weapons program. In truth, the so-called dossier added little to the sum of knowledge about Saddam's intentions. Most of it was historical in nature, focusing on the chemical agents and the biological toxins unaccounted for when the United Nations inspectors had left in 1998. Much else, typical of intelligence material, was speculative. Blair's claim that it provided evidence that the threat was "serious and current" was barely sustained by the hard facts.

As events unfolded, however, the dossier and Blair's accompanying speech to the House of Commons struck at the heart of the dilemma that would haunt the prime minister in the approach to war and beyond. To his mind, the reasons for confronting Saddam were manifold. The strategic reality was that if the international community walked away from Iraq it would have proved itself powerless in the face of the proliferation of weapons of mass destruction. Rogue states and international terrorists alike would capitalize on that fatal weakness, and sooner or later terrorists would come into possession of weapons of mass destruction. The humanitarian case for a confrontation was similarly powerful; merely to state Saddam's atrocities and brutal repres-

sion of his own people was to make the case. But the realities of British domestic politics and the stern advice of the government's senior lawyers both said these were not judgments that could be turned into a justification for war. Noncompliance with United Nations resolutions was the only possible casus belli. Blair acknowledged as much during the parliamentary debate: "The ending of his regime would be cause for regret for no one other than Saddam. But our purpose is disarmament.... Disarmament of all WMD is the demand. One way or another it must be acceded to." George W. Bush faced no such constraints when he requested and won congressional support for war later in the autumn. The result was that while Washington could be candid about its goal of regime change, the British government found itself putting too much weight on the immediate threat posed by Iraq's WMD programs, which would later provide powerful ammunition for Blair's critics.

Even as Blair sought to bind the U.S. president into the United Nations process, the European end of the transatlantic bridge was beginning to buckle. The emotional solidarity evoked by the tragedy of September 11 had given way in Europe to growing hostility toward what was seen by many as the arrogance of American power. Bush's "axis of evil" speech at the beginning of the year had had a profound effect on the political mood of the Continent. The suggestion that Washington might deploy its military might against countries like Iran and North Korea as well as against Iraq triggered alarm and anger in equal measure. Chris Patten, the European Union's external affairs commissioner, was far from alone when he described the president's analysis as "simplistic and absolutist." The obvious disdain of senior figures in the Bush administration for what Donald Rumsfeld would later call the "Old Europe" of France and Germany held up a mirror to the reciprocal resentment in Paris and Berlin. For Washington, the preemption doctrine at the heart of its new National Security Strategy was vital to the defense of America. In Europe it was seen as an assertion of U.S. hegemony, the determination of what the French politician Hubert Vedrine called the "hyperpuissance" to impose its will on the rest of the world.

Iraq came to symbolize a fundamental clash of strategic cultures be-
tween continental Europe and the United States. Europe's concept of
security was anchored in the multilateral institutions that had kept the
peace in the post–cold war era. Washington, seeking invulnerability as
well as invincibility, treated the same institutions as an irrelevant relic
of the past.

Blair found himself constantly seeking to reassure his European col-
leagues that Bush was more committed to the international system
than his rhetoric implied. The prime minister's aides would often de-
scribe the president as far more pragmatic than it sometimes seemed.
The word from 10 Downing Street was that Bush spoke the language
of American primacy but understood the importance of alliances:
"Don't listen to the words. Watch what he does," Blair would tell other
European leaders. Most were unconvinced and recoiled from a favorite
metaphor in Washington, which saw the international peace enforced
by an American sheriff followed by a posse of willing but powerless al-
lies. Some of their irritation was directed toward Blair. The prime min-
ister's bridge across the Atlantic, it was said more frequently in Paris
and Berlin, seemed to be a one-way highway. It was all very well, the
British prime minister carrying America's demands back to Europe;
but what about making Europe's case in Washington?

The passage of United Nations resolution 1441 on November 8,
2002, seemed for a time to square the circle. It had taken weeks of in-
tense and occasionally bad-tempered diplomacy to persuade the Secu-
rity Council to confront Saddam Hussein. Every phrase and sentence
had been fought over. But in the end the resolution had secured the
unanimous backing of the Security Council. And it seemed, on the sur-
face, to be uncompromising. The Iraqi leader, it stated, was in material
breach of his responsibilities under previous UN decisions. The inter-
national community was giving him a "final opportunity" to comply.
Behind the apparent solidarity, of course, there were deliberate ambi-
guities. Washington had wanted an automatic "trigger" in the text that
would authorize war in the event that Saddam rejected the demand to
disarm; France had demanded an explicit commitment to a second res-
olution before any military action could be contemplated. The very

British compromise was that the Security Council would consider again how to respond if United Nations weapons inspectors were frustrated in their task.

For all the ambiguities, Blair seemed to have cause to be content: Bush had honored the rules, the Security Council seemed to have delivered, and Britain had become a significant player in the interagency debate in Washington. Although it was impossible to say whether it had been Blair's influence or the president's own judgment that kept the U.S. in the multilateral game, the prime minister was careful to downplay his role. To boast about his influence would be to erode it. Bush, he continued to insist even in private conversations, was a clear-thinking, deliberate politician. The western gunslinger image that kept the cartoonists in business bore no resemblance to the leader he knew. The two leaders spoke frequently by telephone, and Blair felt confident enough in the relationship to write lengthy private notes to the president on their evolving strategy. A recurring theme was of the benefits that would accrue from seeking United Nations authorization if war proved unavoidable. An international community that had legitimized the removal of Saddam Hussein would be obliged to share the burden of rebuilding Iraq. Later, after the war was over, Blair told a parliamentary committee that he had conveyed another message to the White House in the autumn of 2002. "I recall the exact conversation with him [Bush] . . . when we went through the United Nations and we got the UN resolution. I said to him, 'You have to realize that if Saddam Hussein cooperates in full with the inspectors we have to take yes for an answer. If that happens there is no conflict,' and he agreed with that fully." Others may doubt whether the president would have been prepared to pull out the American troops already pouring into the Gulf. British influence was reinforced by the strong relationship between Jack Straw and Colin Powell. Although both men in the end supported the war, it was no secret that, in their different ways, they were more reluctant warriors than their political masters. Powell cautioned Bush on the need to bring along the international community, just as Straw tempered Blair's moral fervor by constantly emphasizing that Britain could go to war only if and when such a course bore the stamp of in-

ternational legitimacy. The prime minister, a lawyer himself, some-
times seemed impatient of the fine legal print. Straw read every line.

Yet if the autumn of 2002 seemed briefly to see the multilateralists
in the ascendant, the cracks were already beginning to appear in the
foundations of Tony Blair's European alliances. A few months earlier
Jacques Chirac had won reelection for a second term as French presi-
dent, and his right-of-center supporters had secured a majority in the
French National Assembly. After years of "cohabitation," when his am-
bitions had been thwarted by the Socialist-led government of Lionel
Jospin, Chirac had regained full command of the French political
scene. He was conscious that cohabitation had badly weakened France
in the councils of the European Union. The country's vital alliance
with Germany had fallen into disrepair, as Gerhard Schröder, the left-
of-center German chancellor, seemed to spend more and more time
with Tony Blair. The European Union had been built on Franco-German
understanding. The partnership, central to French power and prestige,
was now being questioned.

Chirac's first diplomatic move, though, was to get closer to Tony
Blair himself. Seen from the British side, the prime minister's relation-
ship with Chirac was not as solid as that with Schröder, but it was
warm enough for Blair to display in his Downing Street apartment a
photograph of the French president holding his baby son, Leo. Both
leaders also knew that any ambition of developing a European defense
capability depended on agreement between the only two countries in
Europe capable of projecting significant military force. So when they
met for a private dinner at the Elysée Palace within days of the French
elections, the atmosphere was convivial. France and Britain must seize
the opportunity, Chirac told his guest. Their interests coincided on a
range of issues, not least the creation of a viable European defense
force. France wanted its relationship with Britain to be as strong as its
historic ties with Germany. For an instant, it seemed that this was the
start of another beautiful friendship—but only for an instant. By Octo-
ber everything had changed. Against the run of the opinion polls, Ger-
hard Schröder was reelected as German chancellor in September on
a platform of staunch opposition to war in Iraq, to George W. Bush's

fury. That mirrored France's own position, but Chirac had leaned toward the center-right candidate, Edmund Stoiber. By contrast, in spite of their differences over Iraq, Blair had been supportive of Schröder. It was unsurprising, then, that Schröder chose to break with tradition and travel to London rather than Paris on his first postelection trip. The slight was not missed by Chirac.

Even before the election the mercurial French president had decided it was essential to repair the relationship with Germany. Now, with Schröder irritated by Chirac's support for his rival, the task took on an added urgency. The new alliance with Blair could wait. As one French diplomat put it, "The Franco-German relationship is the foundation of France's position in Europe. We had to rebuild it." The chemistry between Chirac and Schröder had never been good, but their joint opposition to war with Iraq now provided a platform from which the two leaders could begin anew. Inadvertently George W. Bush had played the role of matchmaker. In a meeting with Schröder in Berlin earlier in the summer Bush had assured the German leader that any military action against Iraq would take place after the German election. In return, Bush believed he had received a personal assurance that Schröder would not seek to capitalize on the rising tide of antiwar sentiment to win reelection. That version of the conversation was disputed in Berlin, but in any event, Schröder put the antiwar message at the front of his campaign and found himself shunned by a president who considered he had broken his word. Its effect was to push Schröder into the welcoming embrace of Chirac and to end Germany's decades-long commitment to its relationship with Washington.

This important shift in the geopolitical constellation caught Blair unawares, testimony perhaps to his tendency to see the world as he wanted it to appear rather as it was. In late October the prime minister arrived at a summit of European leaders in Brussels to find that Chirac and Schröder had precooked a deal on reform of Europe's costly farm policy. The accord was presented to Blair—and to other European Union leaders—as a fait accompli, with Chirac informing him that it was nonnegotiable. Paris and Berlin, the deal said, were once again in Europe's driver's seat. The actual details of the accord were not that far

from Blair's own position, but he was irritated by the way the agreement had been prepared and by Chirac's imperious manner. So as the fifteen leaders sat around the summit table Blair launched a vigorous attack on France's defense of the heavily protected European farm market. It sat ill, he concluded, with France's grand rhetoric about helping the poorest countries in Africa. Chirac was enraged, and British officials reported him as saying that no one had ever before dared to speak to him in such terms. To show his displeasure Chirac declared that a scheduled December Anglo-French summit would be postponed indefinitely. Such was the mood of the mutual antagonism between the leaders of Europe's only two significant military powers as the world confronted the possibility of war.

With the passage of UN resolution 1441, it seemed for a time that the fences could be mended. When one of Chirac's senior ministers visited London in early December, Blair invited him to 10 Downing Street for a private conversation. The "good cop, bad cop" routine between the U.S. and Europe at the UN had worked, the prime minister told his guest. The hawks in Washington had been obliged to compromise, and Bush had been kept in the multilateral game. But it would have worked even better had Britain and France more closely coordinated their positions. Blair intended his comments as a lesson for the future, but it was one both sides would choose to ignore. During the next few months Blair came to believe–partly on the basis of reports from British intelligence–that the dispute over Iraq was in fact a proxy for a much more serious contest. Chirac, these reports said, had decided that Blair had usurped his own position as the natural leader of Europe. It was time for the French president to reassert himself and to clip the wings of perfidious Albion. In other words, this feud was personal as well as political.

Unsurprisingly, French officials dismissed this analysis. But Blair came to believe it, telling close aides that Chirac was "out to get him." Whatever the truth, behind the clash of personalities lay a more fundamental difference on ideology. Chirac had decided, in the tradition of General Charles de Gaulle, that America could not go unchallenged. What was seen in London as U.S. leadership was translated in Paris as

U.S. hegemony. Blair's concept of a partnership between Europe and the U.S. as the basis for what he called a "unipolar world" was viewed by Chirac as mere submission to American power. The Blair perspective had Europe influencing U.S. policy from within; the French view saw an imperative to challenge it from without. The prime minister regarded transatlantic rivalry as fatal to the security of the West. Chirac called for a "multipolar" world in which Europe defined its positions independently of those in Washington. Blair was slow to recognize that the bridge across the Atlantic was becoming a bridge too far.

His troubles in Europe were accompanied by increasing unrest at home. The outpouring of sympathy for America that had followed September 11 gave way to a national mood of suspicion. Bush was lampooned in much of the British media as the Texan cowboy, Blair as his lapdog. For all Blair's efforts to persuade people otherwise, the U.S. administration defined itself by the rhetoric of its hawks rather than by the more deliberate decisions of the president. Donald Rumsfeld's frequent infelicities earned him a weekly slot–the "Donald Rumsfeld sound bite of the week"–on Britain's national public radio. The prime minister was nonetheless careful not to turn his conversations with Bush into constant grumbles about the careless words of the Washington hawks.

It was left to David Manning to tell Condoleezza Rice how difficult the administration was making things for its most reliable ally. During a September parliamentary debate some fifty of Blair's own Labour MPs had defied the government on a technical motion to show their opposition to war. Even bigger protests were registered at the Labour Party conference in Blackpool two weeks later, muted only by Bill Clinton's support for the prime minister. Unease in Blair's own party was reflected in the opinion polls, which showed large majorities against any conflict not specifically authorized by the United Nations. Part of the prime minister's strength had always been the fact that he was invariably more closely attuned than his party to the political pulse of the nation. Iraq was an exception. "It's the first time I can recall when the party has been entirely in tune with the country," one of Blair's close aides joked in a moment of dark humor.

By December 2002 war had hardened from probability to certainty. On December 8 Saddam Hussein responded to the demand in resolution 1441 that he make full disclosure of his weapons programs by delivering a 12,000-page document that essentially said nothing new. From this Tony Blair and George W. Bush drew the same conclusion: Saddam, as they had expected, had defiantly refused to take the final opportunity to comply. It was "an absolutely clear sign that he had no intention of shutting this stuff down," Blair said in the summer of 2003. The declaration marked the start of "an agonizing period when I could see exactly what needed to happen but I couldn't get people to do it." What needed to happen, in short, was the presentation of a "clear ultimatum." The focus in Washington turned immediately from the diplomacy of the United Nations to that of war, to securing agreements with Iraq's neighbors to move troops and equipment through their territories. British officials caught the change of mood in the White House; the president, they judged, had made an irreversible decision. Military planning in Britain also accelerated, and within another three months some 40,000 British troops would be stationed in the Gulf. Still, Blair could not give up on the United Nations, for without a second resolution authorizing the use of force he could not be sure of carrying his party or his country on the path to war. British officials recognized, but could never admit, a stark divide between Washington and London. Bush already had the support of Congress for war. The endorsement of the Security Council would be nice to have but was far from essential. For Blair, however, it was vital to secure his political base.

Yet the countdown to the collapse of the diplomacy at the United Nations had already started. Even as Hans Blix and his inspection teams began their searches in Iraq, the semblance of transatlantic unity embodied in resolution 1441 was fracturing. The effort to sustain unanimity at the United Nations was soon colliding with the military buildup in the Gulf. At a Franco-German summit in Paris during the third week of January, Jacques Chirac and Gerhard Schröder bluntly rejected the logic of war. "War is always an admission of defeat," Chirac declared with Schröder at his side. From the other side of the Atlantic, Donald Rumsfeld responded with his soon-to-be-famous retort about

the shortcomings of "Old Europe." The gulf between France and the U.S. was also played out at the United Nations, where Dominique de Villepin, the French foreign minister, enraged Colin Powell with a passionate assault on America's preparations for war. Blair himself added fuel to the fires by attaching his signature along with those of seven other European leaders–including the prime ministers of Spain and Italy–to an article in the *Wall Street Journal* backing the U.S. stance. The purpose of the article, and an associated statement published by ten governments of the former Communist countries of eastern Europe, was to demonstrate that France and Germany could not claim to speak for Europe. But for Blair this gesture was also an inadvertent admission of defeat. He had set as his mission maintaining the integrity of the transatlantic alliance. But Europe had now broken into two. The assumption in Downing Street had been that France would not ultimately use its veto on the Security Council against a second resolution. Chirac, the old diplomatic hands said, was bluffing to gain the maximum possible leverage. Blair thought that Russia, too, could be brought round, albeit at the price of a large American check to buy out its financial interests in Iraq. Surely Vladimir Putin had invested too much in integrating Russia into the Western community to risk a breach now. All these were reasonable suppositions, buttressed by the judgments of seasoned officials. They were also wrong. The prime minister preferred to think otherwise. He had never lost his faith in his own powers of persuasion. Here the self-belief that was so often a political strength showed itself as a weakness. Blair had overreached himself but was unwilling to admit it.

At the end of January Tony Blair made the now-familiar trip across the Atlantic to see George W. Bush. The two leaders had planned to travel from the White House to Camp David. But in an ominous harbinger of the diplomatic storms ahead, the helicopters due to transport them to the president's cabin in the Maryland mountains were grounded by high winds and snow. The British prime minister had two requests of the president. He wanted Bush's support for a second United Nations resolution, and he wanted more time: time for

Hans Blix to set out a case against Saddam that would carry a majority in the Security Council, and time for his own government to rally support for war at home. The British prime minister knew the argument had to be reframed. Britain and the United States had allowed the search by the weapons inspectors for a "smoking gun" to define the public debate: as long as nothing was found, Saddam could be considered innocent. The burden of proof had to be shifted back to the Iraqi leader–either he cooperated, or the UN would declare he was once again in breach. Recasting the case, Blair told Bush, would take time; they should be ready to wait until the end of March. Blair found his host sympathetic, yet also perceived the distance between them. The February 15 target date had already fallen victim to a slower-than-expected buildup of forces in the region, but Rumsfeld wanted no further constraints on the military planning. Bush had made his decision; in Washington military logic had taken over from diplomacy. American soldiers could not fight in the scorching heat of the Iraqi summer, which meant the war had to start sooner rather than later. The president was giving no guarantees to his British friend. The tension between them was evident in their awkward body language at the press conference held after their White House talks. Blair was clear that he wanted a second UN resolution to ensure the conflict had international legitimacy. "What is important is that the international community comes together again and makes it absolutely clear that this [Saddam's noncooperation] is unacceptable," he told the media. For Bush, though, another decision in the Security Council was optional. "Should the United Nations pass a second resolution, it would be welcomed if it is yet another signal that we are intent on disarming Saddam Hussein. But 1441 gives us the authority to move without any second resolution." Blair's aides said later that Bush had actually given the prime minister firmer assurances in private. They blamed Ari Fleischer, the White House press secretary, for ruining the choreography of the press conference by insisting on last-minute changes to the president's script. But that, in a real sense, was irrelevant. What mattered now was the yawning gap between the U.S. and Britain on one side and the other

three permanent members of the Security Council—France, Russia, and China—on the other.

Hans Blix did not offer succor. In his first report to the Security Council the Swedish lawyer turned chief weapons inspector had been tough on Saddam's failure to comply fully with 1441. But those who knew Blix understood that he had no intention of handing a gun to the American president. Like everyone else he was aware of the deep hostility toward him within the U.S. administration. He resented the pressure and was dubious of many of the claims made by American and British intelligence agencies. When Colin Powell presented intelligence evidence to the Security Council, Blix did little to hide his skepticism. And in mid-February his second report on the progress of inspections put a positive gloss on Iraqi cooperation. Blair had sensed Blix's equivocation when he had invited him to Chequers. Now he realized that he needed a second resolution that did not rely on the weapon's inspector's judgment.

The Anglo-French summit postponed by Jacques Chirac in October had eventually been rescheduled for the first week of February. Even though that was only a few days away, Blair was anxious to travel immediately to Paris after his return from Camp David. As soon as the prime ministerial entourage touched down in London after the flight from Washington, David Manning telephoned French officials. Blair, Manning said, was keen to debrief Chirac on the talks with Bush. His French counterpart, he was informed, preferred to wait. When the two leaders did meet a few days later in the French coastal resort of Le Touquet, they seemed, almost unconsciously, to acknowledge that the die had already been cast. Instead of engaging in serious debate about a way forward, exploring the prospects for compromise, or even clearing the air by shouting at each other, the two leaders chose to put Iraq to one side and talked instead about everything they could agree on. The fate of Saddam Hussein received just ten minutes of their time—and that in a discussion of how best to minimize their differences in front of the waiting media.

February into early March was a diplomatic blur in Downing Street. The prime minister remembered it as a constant stream of telephone

calls and lobbying, cajoling, or struggling to build a majority at the United Nations and shore up support at home. It was also a rude awakening. Blair was a politician who had never really experienced failure. His capacity to frame an argument, his charm, his formidable powers of persuasion had always carried him through. This time they would fail him. The arithmetic seemed to say it was still possible to secure the necessary nine votes in the Security Council for a second resolution. Spain and Bulgaria could be counted alongside Britain and the United States; France, Russia, China, Germany, and Syria were ranged against. Technically, that left the outcome with six states—Mexico, Chile, Pakistan, Cameroon, Angola, and Guinea. Blair set about winning them over to a new resolution that would set precise benchmarks for Saddam's cooperation and authorize military action if he failed to meet them. With this "Blix-proof" formulation, Blair hoped, he would dare an isolated Chirac to use France's veto. Whitehall had rarely seen a diplomatic exercise of such intensity. In New York, Britain's experienced and accomplished ambassador to the United Nations, Sir Jeremy Greenstock, barely slept. David Manning was dispatched to Santiago to see Ricardo Lagos, the president of Chile. A Foreign Office minister toured the capitals of the African states. Blair was never off the phone. But the notional arithmetic could not overturn the geopolitical reality: most of the nations represented on the Security Council did not want war. The weapons inspectors, they judged, should be given more time before disarmament gave way to regime change.

As it happened, the military timetable did get pushed back, mainly because of the ineptness of the Pentagon in seeking, and failing, to persuade Turkey to allow the passage of U.S. land forces. But Bush was not ready to give Blair the extra weeks that might, just might, have allowed a coalition to be reassembled. And only reluctantly did the president accede to the requests from 10 Downing Street to signal that the United Nations would have a significant role in the reconstruction of Iraq.

There were moments during these weeks when Tony Blair, exhausted, demoralized and unable to shake off a persistent chest cold, fell into depression. On February 15 an estimated one million people

took to the streets of Britain's major cities to protest against the loom-
ing conflict. Blair, addressing a Labour Party conference in Scotland on
the same day, was publicly resolute: "I do not seek unpopularity as a
badge of honor. But sometimes it is the price of leadership and the cost
of conviction." The private Blair, however, was sometimes bleak, and a
visitor to his Downing Street study a few days later was shaken by the
prime minister's gaunt appearance. Yet, for all these moments of de-
spair, he was the last to give up hope that the international community
would come together at the eleventh hour. Sir Jeremy Greenstock at
the United Nations could see that the votes simply were not there for
a second resolution, but Blair refused to accept defeat, returning to the
telephone again and again to try to convince the swing nations. A
friend later explained this as follows: "Partly it was the self-belief. He
couldn't accept that he couldn't bring people round. But it was also his
utter conviction that it was the right thing to do. If he could see that,
why couldn't others?" An aide had a slightly different perspective: "He
was doing what he does best: making his case, making the argument."

At home Blair's personal ratings had fallen sharply in opinion polls,
which showed strong majorities opposed to any war without the au-
thorization of the United Nations. Yet even among his domestic critics
there was admiration for the prime minister's eloquence and courage.
Aides were instructed to seek out the most difficult audiences for his
television appearances—on one show he was confronted with a group
of women chosen specifically for their implacable antagonism. His
quiet, sober demeanor in the face of televised personal insults and the
slow handclapping that is a sign of disapproval revealed to the nation
a different prime minister. How could this be the same politician who
only a few years ago had been obsessed with focus groups, hooked on
headlines? The explanation was there in the speech he had delivered
nearly a year earlier at College Station. "The only purpose of being in
politics," he had said then, "is to strive for the values and ideals we be-
lieve in: freedom, justice, what we Europeans call solidarity but you
[Americans] might call respect for and help for others. These are the
decent democratic values that we all avow. But, alongside the values,

we know we need a hardheaded pragmatism—a realpolitik—required to give us any chance of translating those values into the practical world we live in." Dealing with Saddam united values with realpolitik.

There was also, of course, the question of political survival. Blair had promised the second United Nations resolution to his party. Without it he could not be sure of carrying his own MPs in the House of Commons, let alone the country. A debate in the Commons on February 26 saw 121 Labour MPs vote against war. Their protest had been on a technical motion, and it was clear that a substantive vote on war would trigger an even larger rebellion. As February became March, Labour's party managers in the Commons warned the prime minister that 200 or more of his own MPs—perhaps more than half the total—could vote against war. Assured of the support of the Conservative opposition and thus of an overall majority, Blair could still take Britain to war. But his own position as Labour leader and prime minister could scarcely survive such a vote of no confidence from his own MPs. Among his aides there was talk that the vote should be postponed until the conflict had actually started—there was no constitutional requirement for a vote before hostilities, and once British troops were engaged in combat the mood would swiftly change. Jack Straw, the foreign secretary, dismissed the idea. Whatever the formal position, he argued, no modern British government could go to war without a vote in Parliament. The prime minister agreed. Though publicly loyal to Blair, Straw privately expressed deep unease about going to war without United Nations approval. If he was going to support him, Straw told the prime minister, then it had to be on the basis that he was free to speak his mind in private. He had been appalled during the previous year by the bellicose rhetoric of the hawks in the U.S. administration and their obvious determination to sideline Colin Powell. As one senior minister put it after the conflict, "If Colin Powell had been U.S. president and Jack Straw the prime minister you can be pretty sure that there would not have been war."

In any event, by the end of the first week of March Straw had concluded that it was highly unlikely that the United States and Britain would secure the necessary majority at the United Nations for a sec-

ond resolution. Returning to London from a meeting of the Security Council in New York, he began to draft a lengthy memorandum for Blair on the narrowing options facing the government. The confidential document concluded that rather than seek to force a vote on the Security Council that probably would be lost—and thus leave on the table a decision against war as the UN's last word—the government should prepare to abandon the quest for a second resolution. In such circumstances, though, Blair would have to prepare for the possibility that a majority of Labour MPs would vote against war. Were that the case, Straw concluded, the government would not be able to send British forces into action with the Americans, and accordingly should plan for the possibility that the most it could offer Washington was military support in stabilizing Iraq after Saddam had been deposed. Geoff Hoon, the British defense secretary, made the same point about the government's need to win over a majority of Labour MPs in a private telephone conversation with Donald Rumsfeld. Much to his and Blair's discomfort, Rumsfeld then publicly cast doubt on British participation in the impending conflict by asserting that the United States was ready to go it alone.

It was an exquisite irony that it was Jacques Chirac who did more than anyone to rescue the British prime minister. By now Blair had been persuaded by intelligence reports that Chirac was indeed intent on ruining him politically in Europe. The snippets of the French president's private conversations reported to the prime minister suggested that he would like to see him fall. The attitude toward the French in Downing Street was as belligerent as it had ever been during the long history of rivalry between the two nations. But when Chirac declared on March 10 that France would veto any attempt to pass a second resolution at the United Nations, he unwittingly gave Blair the excuse he needed to go to war without further United Nations authorization. Blair's promise that Britain would go to war only after a second vote in the Security Council had been cleverly hedged. If such a vote was impossible because of an "unreasonable" veto, military action would be legitimate under existing resolutions. Chirac's comments that France could block authorization for war "in all circumstances" was Blair's es-

cape clause. The Entente Cordiale was torn up. The prime minister and other ministers exploited Chirac's statement relentlessly over the following days, rekindling the national tradition of hostility toward France. With Blair himself, Gordon Brown, John Prescott, and a clutch of other ministers pressing each and every potential rebel to fall into line, the number of dissidents began to fall. The Paris government protested in vain that the low politics of all this hardly suited the high principle that Blair claimed for his stance. "It would be so much easier if the vote was about war with France," one Blair loyalist only half-joked as the prime minister scrambled for votes. George W. Bush, meanwhile, provided sympathy without much concrete assistance. The waverers in Blair's party wanted assurances that the United Nations would have the central role in the reconstruction of Iraq and that war would be followed by a concerted push for peace in the Middle East. At a brief summit held in the Azores on March 16 the two leaders were joined by José María Aznar, the Spanish prime minister. The leaders' statement provided some support for Blair, but the president seemed unconvinced.

On March 18 Tony Blair delivered two speeches in Parliament. Those who heard both say the more powerful was the one made to a private meeting of Labour MPs. The prime minister spoke to his own party with eloquence and passion in equal measure and, even those who later voted against him would concede, with courage. "Don't vote for me out of loyalty," he told the MPs at one point. "Vote for me because it's the right thing to do." The world heard his speech to the House of Commons a few hours later. It was a more structured, formal address, which had been worked and reworked, honed and tuned. The choices it posed were between an Iraq free of tyranny and misery and a dangerous regime in Baghdad that had shown the international community to be weak and irresolute; between a world determined to confront the existential threat from rogue states and weapons of mass destruction and one preferring the appeasement of the 1930s; and between a Britain ready to fight for its values and one that at the moment of truth would pull back its troops. What was conveyed most strongly to those listening in the small, wood-paneled debating chamber and

beyond, was the conviction. "To retreat now, I believe, would put at hazard all we hold dearest, turn the United Nations into a talking shop, stifle the first steps of progress in the Middle East; leave the Iraqi people to the mercy of events on which we would have relinquished all power to influence for the better. Tell our allies that at the very moment of action that Britain faltered. I will not be party to such a course. This is not the time to falter. This is the time . . . to show that we will confront the tyrannies and dictatorships and terrorists who put our way of life at risk, to show at the moment of decision that we have the courage to do the right thing." Three ministers resigned rather than back the war, and Robin Cook, the former foreign secretary, was in his way as eloquent in framing the countercase. At the end of the debate on March 18 some 139 Labour MPs could still not be swayed. But Blair could live with that. The vote had been won. Twenty-four hours later Britain went to war.

EPILOGUE

ON JULY 17, 2003, Tony Blair traveled again to Washington. The invitation to address a joint session of Congress was a privilege bestowed on few foreign leaders. Margaret Thatcher had been the last British prime minister to stand at the rostrum on Capitol Hill. As another token of American gratitude for his support during the war, the Senate and House of Representatives had voted to award Blair the Congressional Medal of Honor. Yet even as America's staunchest ally crossed the Atlantic, events at home were taking an unpredictable and ugly turn. A personal tragedy would soon engulf the prime minister in a political maelstrom. Dr. David Kelly, a respected British scientist and expert in weapons of mass destruction, left his home that same hot July afternoon for a walk in the English countryside. By the time Blair received the rapturous applause of American legislators, Kelly was lying dead, having slashed his wrist in a small wooded area near his home in Oxfordshire.

The war that they had watched in the command bunkers below Whitehall was not the one seen by the outside world. As in any conflict, there were many moments of confusion, deep concern, and high anxiety. With news of the loss of British soldiers, painful human reality intruded into decisions that had hitherto inhabited the abstract realm of politics. Blair had taken Britain to war twice before, yet those around him sensed that his personal moral compass had never before so clearly mapped the line connecting the policy choices he made in Downing Street to the deaths of particular brave young men on the battlefield. Yet from a strictly military standpoint the war went better

than the prime minister could have dared hope. This was the first high-intensity conflict fought against a particular regime rather than a nation—a war designed to minimize rather than maximize death and destruction. If the pictures and commentary relayed from the front lines by the "embedded" media were often of military setbacks and stalled advances, the reports the politicians received from the military commanders were almost universally positive. Afterward it was asked how Blair and others could have made the mistake of believing that Saddam Hussein and his sons had been killed in their first air strike on Baghdad. The answer was quite simple. Throughout the war the coalition commanders were baffled by the complete absence of strategic direction from Saddam's military headquarters to Iraqi forces in the field. The easiest explanation was that the Iraqi leader had perished. Overall the American military plan had said it could take up to 125 days to take full control of Iraq, what Blair called the "outside limit." But in the event it was only three weeks before the people of Baghdad marked the end of the regime by tearing down the infamous towering statue of Saddam. Three weeks after that, on May 1, President Bush declared an end to major hostilities.

For a time Blair basked in the afterglow. Public opinion had swung behind the conflict once British forces went into action. The British troops, given a bigger role than many had expected, had shown their customary skill and professionalism. Confidence in the prime minister rose. While the war had divided the British media as sharply as it had the nation, even among his opponents there was grudging respect for a prime minister who had been ready to stake his career on his conviction. When Blair celebrated his fiftieth birthday on May 3, most of the newspaper and television features covering the event portrayed a leader who had come of age, one who had demonstrated beyond doubt the conviction and courage among the palette of his political skills.

Politics, though, is a fickle business; public opinion even more so. Later, in the summer of 2003, the controversy that had preceded the war with Iraq was soon rekindled. One of the first priorities of the coalition troops had been to locate Saddam's weapons of mass de-

struction. But the initial searches yielded nothing. Clare Short, the left-leaning British cabinet minister responsible for international development issues who had many times threatened to resign before the war, decided to do so after the conflict was over. Short had lost much of her political credibility by the public parading of her conscience while still in office. But her departure brought to the surface an important tension between London and Washington. Having watched the international community fracture before the war, Blair wanted it to reassemble for the postwar reconstruction of Iraq. In early April, George W. Bush had repaid in part the prime minister's many trips to Washington by himself crossing the Atlantic to meet Blair in Belfast. There the president had agreed to a statement saying the United Nations would have a "vital" role in postwar Iraq. Once again, however, Blair's strategy bumped up against the implacable unilateralism of Richard Cheney and Donald Rumsfeld. The U.S. defense secretary, one senior British minister remarked during this period, had made it absolutely plain that, having opposed the war, "Old Europe" would be shut out of the running of the new Iraq. So, too, to a large degree were America's allies. The U.S. defense secretary had locked out Britain—not to mention the State Department—from the strategic planning for postwar Iraq. "It's to the victor the spoils," one senior British minister said of Rumsfeld. "And in this case the victor is defined as the Pentagon." British as well as American soldiers in Iraq were soon paying the price "with their lives" of what was widely seen in London as the Pentagon's ideological ineptitude and for the early hubris of Richard Cheney's prediction "We will be greeted as liberators."

It was into the tinderbox of emerging chaos in Iraq and a resurgence of disquiet at home that the British Broadcasting Corporation threw a match. The trail that led to the discovery of Dr. Kelly's corpse in the southern English countryside on July 18 had in fact started more than a month earlier, when the BBC carried a report charging that the prime minister's office had embellished the intelligence report it had published the previous September on Saddam Hussein's weapons of mass destruction. Citing senior intelligence sources, BBC defense cor-

respondent Andrew Gilligan suggested that parts of the dossier–notably a passage claiming that Iraq could strike with weapons of mass destruction within forty-five minutes of Saddam's issuing the order–had been inserted at the direction of 10 Downing Street for political effect, even though the government probably knew it to be false. While the finger of blame, Gilligan said, pointed at Alistair Campbell, this grave charge also struck at the prime minister. It said, in effect, that Blair had tricked the nation into war.

By now the government was already under renewed pressure because of the failure of coalition forces in Iraq to discover any evidence of WMD. Blair had been further embarrassed by the disclosure that another Downing Street document outlining the threat from Iraq and published in February had included, without acknowledgment, work produced many years earlier by an American doctoral student. All this took place against a backdrop of rumbling popular discontent at the early failure of the coalition forces to quickly reestablish order and security in occupied Iraq. Critics of the war felt vindicated as a speedy military victory had been followed by a distinctly messy peace. Saddam was still at large, and coalition soldiers were being killed every day. In the continuing absence of any weapons of mass destruction, Blair was vulnerable to allegations that he had exaggerated the threat from Saddam. The charge of those such as Robin Cook, the former cabinet minister, was that Blair had gone to war not in response to a real threat but in order to preserve Britain's special relationship with the United States by staying close to George W. Bush.

The evidence for the BBC's allegation was always scant–there had indeed been grumbling among some senior analysts in the Ministry of Defence about the dossier, but the final document had been approved by the heads of the intelligence services. The denials of Campbell and Blair of any political interference were endorsed by two separate parliamentary investigations. But for a time the dispute spiraled out of control, with the BBC unwilling to retreat and Campbell publicly accusing the broadcaster of lies and bias. David Kelly, a scientist and weapons inspector employed by the government, had spoken to Gilli-

gan about the September document. Now he found himself caught up in the firestorm of controversy about what precisely had been said during their short conversation in a London hotel. Unaccustomed to public controversy and pressured by superiors at the Ministry of Defence, he cracked. As Tony Blair traveled from Washington on a scheduled trip to Tokyo, Kelly's body was discovered.

Blair, personally shaken and politically threatened by the tragedy, appointed an eminent judge, Lord Hutton, to conduct an inquiry into the circumstances of Kelly's death. The investigation fixed a searchlight on the deepest recesses of the British government. Blair and a stream of his senior ministers and officials were called to give public evidence. Minutes of meetings in 10 Downing Street, private e-mails between ministers and officials, and secret intelligence assessments were all laid open to the nation's gaze. While the public hearings lent no support to the charge that the prime minister had embellished the dossier against the advice of the intelligence services, what did emerge was a sense of the inevitable weaknesses and gaps in the available intelligence on Iraq.

The inquiry also exposed to public gaze the enduring tension between what Blair had seen from the outset as the broad strategic case for war (preserving the authority of the UN in the face of the threat from rogue states and the proliferation of weapons of mass destruction) and the much narrower grounds (the threat from Saddam's weapons programs) on which he had justified the cause to the British parliament and public. The tension was caught in a private e-mail—published by the Hutton inquiry—that Blair's chief of staff, Jonathan Powell, had sent to John Scarlett, the head of Downing Street's Joint Intelligence Committee, in advance of publication of the September dossier. Powell cautioned that the intelligence in the dossier was "convincing for those who are prepared to be convinced," before adding: "The document does nothing to demonstrate a threat, let alone an imminent threat from Saddam. In other words it shows he has the means but does not demonstrate that he has the motive to attack his neighbors, let alone the west. We will need to make it clear in launching the document that we do not claim we have evidence that he is an immi-

nent threat. The case we are making is that he has continued to develop WMD since 1998, and is in breach of UN resolutions. The international community has to enforce those resolutions if the UN is to be taken seriously." Personally, Powell never doubted the case for war, but as an experienced diplomat he foresaw the risk that the government could drift into exaggerating the immediate threat. Unfortunately for Blair, Powell's cautionary words were often forgotten over the following months as the government sought to win support for military action. The undue emphasis on the immediacy of the threat from Iraq was the center of Robin Cook's critique after he resigned from the government.

The government's treatment of Kelly–he was thrust into the limelight as a pawn in Downing Street's battle with the BBC–also gave an insight into the administration's ruthless determination to win. It was a strain the weapons inspector, unfamiliar with the ways of politics and subjected to the full glare of the media and Parliament, simply could not endure.

Blair himself was among the dozens of witnesses who appeared before Lord Hutton's inquiry during the summer of 2003. It was only the second time in the nation's history that a prime minister had been questioned in such circumstances. The first occasion had seen the Conservative prime minister John Major quizzed by a similar tribunal, headed by Lord Scott, a decade earlier. Ironically, the subject of that investigation had been the sale of British arms to Saddam Hussein's Iraq during the 1980s. Blair, his senior officials, and the heads of the relevant intelligence agencies all testified that there had not been overt political interference from 10 Downing Street to deliberately exaggerate the threat from Saddam presented in the September intelligence dossier. The volumes of written evidence showed that some intelligence officials had indeed voiced doubts about the robustness of the dossier but essentially supported the Downing Street denials of any deliberate duplicity. Blair–in his evidence to the inquiry and in other public statements and private conversations–seemed genuinely surprised that the coalition forces in Iraq had failed to find concrete evidence of

Saddam's weapons. While some Downing Street aides began to speculate that the intelligence provided by the agencies might eventually turn out to have been badly flawed, the prime minister insisted that the proof of the weapons would eventually be found. For all that, the inquiry gave force to Robin Cook's argument that the UN inspectors should have been given more time to carry out their task and that the decision to go to war had reflected Washington's determination to depose Saddam rather than a clear and present danger to Western security. And while the BBC's reporting of the alleged manipulation of intelligence was shown during the inquiry to have been flawed, there were embarrassing revelations, too, about the way the government had treated Dr. Kelly once he was revealed as the source. For his part, Blair never shifted from the conviction that the war had been the right course. As he told the joint session of Congress in July, "Can we be sure that terrorism and weapons of mass destruction will join together? Let us say one thing. If we are wrong, we will have destroyed a threat [Saddam] that at least is responsible for inhuman carnage and suffering. That is something history will forgive. But if our critics are wrong, if we are right, as I believe with every fiber of instinct and conviction I have that we are, and we do not act, then we will have hesitated in the face of this menace, when we should have given leadership. That is something history will not forgive."

In one sense all this was a tragic distraction. In his own mind, Blair had always cast the threat from Iraq in broad strategic terms rather than suggest that Saddam was an immediate danger. Yet the furor at once crystallized popular unease about the war and its aftermath and highlighted the gulf that Jonathan Powell had identified between Blair's rationale for war and the narrower case made to the country. The government's opinion poll ratings fell—and so, still more sharply, did public trust in the prime minister. His conviction carried another price. Blair's geostrategic ambition in the aftermath of September 11 had been to help construct a grand coalition against the new security threats of the age by binding together America and Europe. The conflict over Iraq, though, had left the transatlantic alliance badly damaged. While the governments of Spain and Italy had supported the

war, as had those of Poland and several other of the former Communist states of central and eastern Europe, France and Germany had remained implacable in their opposition. Blair would argue that it would have been more dangerous still had Europe united in the cause of appeasement. But international relations were in serious disrepair. Even though George W. Bush did keep his promise to Blair to reengage in the Middle East peace process, neither Israel nor the Palestinians seemed willing to exchange violence for the road map to peace.

These, of course, were snapshots of troubled times. Enemies as well as friends of the prime minister agreed that much now rested on whether an Iraq liberated from Saddam could find a peaceful, more democratic future. And for all the drama in the Westminster village–Britain's equivalent of Washington's Beltway–the fall in the prime minister's ratings was relative. The polls showed that even at the moments of most heated controversy, the government was running neck and neck with the Conservatives in the polls. For a British administration that is a comfortable place to be at midterm. For his part, Blair said many times he was content to await the judgment of history on the war. That, his aides were convinced, would depend ultimately on the success of efforts to rebuild Iraq as a stable, peaceful nation. As the summer of 2003 turned to autumn, though, there was a realization in Downing Street that it was time for a different style of government, one more in tune with Adlai Stevenson's dictum that the best politics is good government. After nine exhausting years with Blair, Alistair Campbell decided to step down. His departure marked the end of an era. Anji Hunter, another member of the original administration closest to Blair, had left sometime earlier for a career in business. Alexander Irvine, Blair's mentor in the law, was asked to move on by his former pupil. The magic circle around Blair was vanishing.

The Tony Blair I spoke to in his small Downing Street study at the end of July 2003 was scarcely recognizable as the fresh-faced man who had become his party's youngest leader less than a decade earlier. The burdens of office were etched deep into the lines under his eyes. His hair had thinned. His skin had the grayish hue that tells of stress and ex-

haustion. A decade earlier his mission had been to remake his party; more recently he had been trying to remake the world. This was a tougher, self-sufficient politician, one who had surrendered a craving for affection to the necessity of making his own choices. Some would say he had become too self-sufficient. "He's much more impressive now," one close political friend told me. "The trouble is he is too impressed with himself." But, as another countered, "Leaders have to make decisions, the rest of us only have to commentate."

For all the difference in scale between these two endeavors—reinventing his party and redrawing the geopolitical map—you could still trace the path along which Blair had traveled. The most frequent misjudgment of him was to confuse a disdain for traditional ideology with an absence of belief; and to mistake an eagerness to be liked for an unwillingness to make hard decisions.

What puzzled many people, even close cabinet colleagues, was his certainty that he was right about Iraq. I asked him whether this moral sureness was rooted in his Christian faith.

"I don't know that this is referable necessarily to my Christianity, but I do think it is important that you follow through on the values you have. When you are faced with a situation like Kosovo, or Afghanistan, or Iraq . . . you have got to work out what is the right thing to do and try to work that out in a clear way so you don't shelter behind an unreal view. The thing I always used to say about the hardest of those three—which is Iraq—is, 'Don't think if we don't get rid of Saddam, nobody in Iraq dies.' Actually thousands of people were dying there every single year, probably tens of thousands of young kids dying in a country that has been run in an appalling way. What happens often in our world is that if something is not on our television screens it is not happening. . . . But you shouldn't take that view. If it is happening, it is happening, and you should be prepared to act on it. One of the things I have always said to people is, 'Look, people from our perspective—leave aside the Christian perspective—we are interventionists.' I can imagine some Republican or some Conservative coming to me and

saying what had it got to do with us that people in Sierra Leone are dying. But actually if we are progressive politicians we should be saying, 'Well, it does have something to do with us.' Now, how you then act is another matter, but I have never understood the reluctance of the left to take these things on. I don't see why people on the left are not putting us under more pressure to intervene in Zimbabwe or Burma. . . . Of course, there is going to be a limit to what you can do . . . but our value system has got to be hard-edged, it can't just be soft. The soft thing to do is to leave Saddam there and then it is not in the news–and then the fact that he is still killing thousands of people every year, it doesn't matter?"

So, had he been eager to go to war all along? Was the United Nations, as his critics said, simply a feint? He insisted not.

"I was always very clear on this issue [the need to confront Saddam], even before September 11, 2001, and after September 11 particularly clear. But I was going to work very hard to deal with it peacefully, and I thought it was possible that we might be able to do that. If that proved impossible I was prepared to take action. I still believe actually that if we had come back together and given a proper ultimatum at an international level, we probably could have got Saddam out."

What of the postwar controversy about the intelligence and the failure thus far to find weapons of mass destruction? Iraq, Blair replied, had to be set in the wider framework of the post–September 11 world.

"Containment [of Iraq] wasn't working, is the truth. But you need to set this thing in an overall context in order to see the threat. That is why it was difficult, but I have no doubt it was the right thing to do, because I think the security threat to all of us is absolutely clear. There is no doubt at all to my mind that the combination of rogue states with weapons of mass destruction and terrorism is the thing we have got to fear. And the truth is it will only take one time for it to happen and then

everyone will say, 'My God, why weren't they doing something about that?' And I don't think you can do this unless you start . . . you had to start with Iraq because of the United Nations history and all the rest of it."

So war was justified as much by the need to set an example to others as by any direct threat from Iraq?

"It was justified in either case. It [the Iraqi regime] was something in its own terms that had to be dealt with, but also we were never going to be able to deal with this [the broader threat] at a serious level unless we were going to make it absolutely clear that the international community, having taken this position, was going to enforce it."

Among Blair's critics on the left of British politics, it sometimes seemed that the prime minister's crime was not going to war per se but doing so with George W. Bush. How was it that an avowed friend of Bill Clinton seemed so close to a Republican in the White House?

"Look, the difficulty for me is, if people say to me do I get on with George Bush, the simple answer is, 'I do.' I can't really be bothered saying to people, 'I don't' just because, you know, because it offends people's sensibilities. . . . Where this relationship really does work is that we both believe very much that you have to carry things through . . . that, for example, we started this thing in Iraq and we have got to finish it and see it through. We certainly share the same perspective on what the threat to the world at the moment is. I think part of the trouble is that people don't believe that I believe this threat really exists–and I do really believe it. Part of what I have to do constantly is to persuade people that, even though he [Bush] is a Republican and comes from a completely different political position, September 11 really has changed things and we have come to a common view of this threat."

Even then the political divide between this Labour prime minister and a Republican president was not quite as wide as some would say:

"Look, we come from a different perspective altogether in terms of our politics. Though if people really want me to be honest, I think the honest truth is that these value systems aren't so totally divorced in this century as they were in the last century. Sometimes it just makes everyone feel more comfortable if everyone says, 'No, these differences are absolutely fundamental and never the two shall meet.' But I am not sure how much in the twenty-first century that it really is true. Yes, of course, we all come from different political traditions, and that is fine, but we are engaged in a battle at an international level, in which we do share the same perspective and analysis, and the same determination to get the job done. And you know, to be blunt, so do other Democrats inside the United States, so do certain Conservatives here."

As we spoke, Blair was within a few days of a much-needed summer vacation, but with the storm raging around him, I wondered whether he ever thought that he had had enough, that at some point before the next election he might choose to pass the baton—perhaps even to Gordon Brown?

"No, no. It is a privilege to do the job. And even if it . . . Look, you have to become very resilient in this because you have to believe in what you are doing, and, in the end, it is for the British people to decide. And I suppose what my strength is that my life doesn't end if it ends. But on the other hand I believe passionately in what I am doing and want the chance to carry on doing it. But in the end they [the people] are the boss, they decide."

In truth, the Iraq war had united Tony Blair in all his different characters. The nineteenth-century leader of conscience determined to do good in the world stood alongside the ruthless pragmatist; the private man of deep Christian faith next to the leader practiced in the art of low politics; the politician-as-warrior hand in hand with the husband and father with a rare devotion to his family; the thespian born for a bigger stage, and the preacher who set his moral compass according to the writings of an obscure Scottish philosopher. Blair transformed his

party, and in so doing rewrote the rules of British politics. But as far as the world beyond was concerned, the kaleidoscope he had spoken about in the aftermath of September 11, 2001, was still turning, the pieces still in flux. The world had found in him a politician convinced that he had been true to his conscience in doing the right thing, and a leader of no little courage. The question that concerned him was which of the many characters would be history's choice.

SELECT BIBLIOGRAPHY

Ashdown, Paddy. *The Ashdown Diaries, Vols. I and II*. London: Allen Lane, 2000.

Blair, Tony. *New Britain*. London: Fourth Estate, 1996.

Blair, Tony. Prime ministerial speeches and press conferences. http://www.number-10.gov.uk.

Blumenthal, Sidney. *The Clinton Wars*. London: Viking, 2003.

Bryant, Christopher. *Reclaiming the Ground*. London: Hodder & Stoughton, 1993.

Butler, David, and Dennis Kavanagh. *The British General Election of 1997*. London: Macmillan, 1997.

Clinton, Hillary Rodham. *Living History*. London: Headline, 2003.

Cooper, Robert. *The Breaking of Nations*. London: Atlantic Books, 2003.

Cradock, Percy. *Know Your Enemy*. London: John Murray, 2002.

Gould, Philip. *The Unfinished Revolution*. London: Little, Brown, 1998.

Hennessy, Peter. *The Prime Minister: The Office and Its Holders Since 1945*. London: Allen Lane, 2000.

Kampfner, John. *Blair's Wars*. London: Simon & Schuster, 2003.

Macintyre, Donald. *Mandelson, the Biography*. London: HarperCollins, 1999.

Mandelson, Peter, and Roger Liddle. *The Blair Revolution*. London: Faber & Faber, 1996.

Mitchell, George. *Making Peace*. London: William Heinemann, 1999.

Naughtie, James. *The Rivals*. London: Fourth Estate, 2001.

Rawnsley, Andrew. *Servants of the People*. London: Hamish Hamilton, 2000.

Rentoul, John. *Tony Blair, Prime Minister*. London: Little, Brown, 2001.

Riddell, Peter. *Hug Them Close*. London: Politico's, 2003.

Seldon, Anthony. *The Blair Effect*. London: Little, Brown, 2001.

Sopel, Jon. *Tony Blair, the Moderniser*. London: Michael Joseph, 1995.

Stothard, Peter. *30 Days*. London: HarperCollins, 2003.

Woodward, Bob. *Bush at War*. London: Simon & Schuster, 2002.

Young, Hugo. *This Blessed Plot: Britain and Europe from Churchill to Blair*. London: Macmillan, 1998.

INDEX